OECD
Economic Surveys

AF182270

...UNIVERSITY ...OLITAN ...RAWN

Sweden

For REFERENCE only
not to be taken
from the Library.

2008

OECD

ORGANISATION FOR ECONOMIC CO-OPERATION AND DEVELOPMENT

The OECD is a unique forum where the governments of 30 democracies work together to address the economic, social and environmental challenges of globalisation. The OECD is also at the forefront of efforts to understand and to help governments respond to new developments and concerns, such as corporate governance, the information economy and the challenges of an ageing population. The Organisation provides a setting where governments can compare policy experiences, seek answers to common problems, identify good practice and work to co-ordinate domestic and international policies.

The OECD member countries are: Australia, Austria, Belgium, Canada, the Czech Republic, Denmark, Finland, France, Germany, Greece, Hungary, Iceland, Ireland, Italy, Japan, Korea, Luxembourg, Mexico, the Netherlands, New Zealand, Norway, Poland, Portugal, the Slovak Republic, Spain, Sweden, Switzerland, Turkey, the United Kingdom and the United States. The Commission of the European Communities takes part in the work of the OECD.

OECD Publishing disseminates widely the results of the Organisation's statistics gathering and research on economic, social and environmental issues, as well as the conventions, guidelines and standards agreed by its members.

Also available in French

Corrigenda to OECD publications may be found on line at: *www.oecd.org/publishing/corrigenda*.

© OECD 2008

OECD freely authorises the use, including the photocopy, of this material for private, non-commercial purposes. Permission to photocopy portions of this material for any public use or commercial purpose may be obtained from the Copyright Clearance Center (CCC) at *info@copyright.com* or the Centre français d'exploitation du droit de copie (CFC) *contact@cfcopies.com*. All copies must retain the copyright and other proprietary notices in their original forms. All requests for other public or commercial uses of this material or for translation rights should be submitted to *rights@oecd.org*.

CREF 330.9485059 SWE

Table of contents

Boxes

Tables

Figures

This book has...

StatLinks

A service that delivers Excel® files from the printed page!

Look for the *StatLinks* at the bottom right-hand corner of the tables or graphs in this book. To download the matching Excel® spreadsheet, just type the link into your Internet browser, starting with the ***http://dx.doi.org*** prefix.
If you're reading the PDF e-book edition, and your PC is connected to the Internet, simply click on the link. You'll find *StatLinks* appearing in more OECD books.

This Survey *is published on the responsibility of the Economic and Development Review Committee (EDRC) of the OECD, which is charged with the examination of the economic situation of member countries.*

The economic situation and policies of Sweden were reviewed by the Committee on 9 October 2008. The draft report was then revised in the light of the discussions and given approval as the agreed report of the whole Committee on Thursday 23 October 2008. It was further updated to reflect the projections of the Economic Outlook published on 25 November 2008 and financial market developments through 12 November 2008.

The Secretariat's draft report was prepared for the Committee by Jens Lundsgaard and David Turvey under the supervision of Vincent Koen. Research assistance was provided by Roselyne Jamin.

The previous Survey of Sweden *was issued in February 2007.*

Information about the latest as well as previous Surveys and more information about how Surveys *are prepared is available at* www.oecd.org/eco/surveys.

BASIC STATISTICS OF SWEDEN

THE LAND

Land area, 1 000 sq. km	410	Inhabitants in major cities	
Lakes, 1 000 sq. km	39	31 December 2007, thousands	
Arable area, 1 000 sq. km	27	Stockholm	795
Woodland, 1 000 sq. km	227	Göteborg	494
		Malmö	281

THE PEOPLE

Population 31 December 2007, thousands	9 183	Civilian labour force 2007, thousands	4 838
Number of inhabitants per sq. km	22	Civilian employment 2007, thousands	4 541
Net natural increase 2001-07, thousands	7.6	As a percentage of total	
Net natural increase per 1 000 inhabitants, 2001-07	0.8	Agriculture, forestry, fishing	11.7
Net inward-migration 2001-07, thousands	35.1	Industry (including construction)	30.7
		Services	57.6

THE PRODUCTION

Gross domestic product 2007, Kr billion	3 071	Gross domestic product at factor cost	
Gross domestic product per capita 2007, USD	49 670	by origin 2007, per cent of total	
Gross fixed capital formation, 2007		Agriculture	2.7
Per cent of GDP	18.9	Industry (including construction)	24.5
Per capita, USD	9 408	Services	72.8

THE GOVERNMENT

Public consumption, 2007, per cent of GDP	25.9	Composition of Parliament	
Public investment, 2007		Social democrats	130
Per cent of GDP	3.0	Moderates	97
Per cent of total investment	15.6	Liberals	28
Total general government current spending 2007		Christian democrats	24
Per cent of GDP	51.4	Left	22
Total general government current revenue 2007		Centre	29
Per cent of GDP	54.9	Greens	19
		Total	349
		Last general election : September 2006	
		Next general election : September 2010	

THE FOREIGN TRADE

Exports of goods and services		Imports of goods and services	
2007, per cent of GDP	49.5	2007, per cent of GDP	40.3
Main merchandise exports, per cent of total		Main merchandise imports, per cent of total	
January-July 2008		January-July 2008	
Wood and paper products	10.8	Wood and paper products	2.9
Mineral products	11.4	Mineral products	10.0
Chemical products	11.4	Chemical products	12.5
Energy products	8.2	Energy products	15.0
Engineering products	47.5	Engineering products	41.7
Other products	10.7	Other products	17.9

THE CURRENCY

Monetary unit : Krona		October 2008, monthly average of spot rate	
		SEK per USD	7.43
		SEK per euro	9.87

Executive summary

Thanks to strong economic institutions and fundamentals, Sweden is well prepared to cope with fall-out from the global financial crisis. The cycle has turned and, clearly, the key near-term challenge is to steer through the slowdown without jeopardising longer-run macroeconomic stability.

With sound structural reforms, material living standards have risen strongly in Sweden over the past 10 to 15 years. Market opening has boosted productivity growth, and recent reforms have curbed labour market exclusion and benefit dependency. The relative decline of previous decades is gradually being reversed. This Survey focuses on how to further promote economic growth while preserving social cohesion and examines the following policy challenges:

Keeping fiscal policy on a sustainable track and continuing tax reforms to promote growth. *The ample fiscal surplus and relatively low public debt allow for some policy easing, but the fiscal framework should be strengthened by linking targets more clearly to long-term considerations. Sweden used to have the highest tax-to-GDP ratio in the OECD but has started to move down the list. The challenge now is to continue with tax cuts, focusing on the worst impediments to growth resulting from corporate and personal income taxation – with due regard to equity concerns.*

Improving education and employment outcomes for youth. *Despite a high overall employment-to-population ratio, youth unemployment is widespread. One reason is that with a high wage floor and stringent employment protection rules, strong skills are required to get a regular job. The quality of compulsory school can be improved, especially regarding mathematics and science. Upper secondary education could make youth more "job ready", notably via more work-place contact. Students should complete higher education and enter the labour market earlier. Universities could benefit from more freedom to develop, possibly based on tuition charging. But in the end, disproportionate youth unemployment can probably only be overcome if also addressing the core labour market rigidities.*

Taking privatisation further. *Starting with a large portfolio of government-owned enterprises, it was easy to identify a list of first candidates for sale. Going forward, privatisation will have to be taken further in those numerous areas where societal objectives are better served by open but regulated markets rather than by public ownership.*

ISBN 978-92-64-05423-3
OECD Economic Surveys: Sweden
© OECD 2008

Assessment and recommendations

Regaining higher relative living standards is a key challenge

With an active, forward-looking approach to economic reform, Sweden has enjoyed considerable international attention in recent years. Around 1970, Swedish GDP per capita was less than 10% below that of the United States, but following the deep crisis in the early 1990s the gap had widened to nearly 25%. Sweden has since started to catch up as market-oriented reforms boosted productivity growth and, most recently, reforms to promote the attractiveness of work have reduced the share of adults living on income benefits. This *Survey* focuses on how Sweden can continue to catch up *via* better policies to promote economic growth. Pursuing a growth-oriented reform agenda can help with social cohesion: a growing tax base would ease pressures on public finances and measures in education and labour markets could promote more equal employment outcomes and equality of opportunity.

Specifically, the following key challenges are reviewed in this *Survey*:

- *Long-term fiscal sustainability and a growth-oriented tax system.* A sound fiscal position has been achieved through consistent consolidation efforts since the crisis of the early 1990s. Now it must be sustained: the fiscal framework should be strengthened with targets more clearly derived from long-term considerations. Building on the recent tax cuts, further reforms could boost growth. In this process, exemptions serving special interests must be avoided.
- *Education policies and employment outcomes for youth.* Despite a high overall employment-to-population ratio, youth continue to face problems on the Swedish labour market. Both the education system and labour market institutions need attention.
- *Privatisation and competition.* Reducing the scope of public ownership, which currently reaches into a wide range of business sectors, will benefit the Swedish economy. Going forward, it will be important to combine privatisation with reforms to ensure effective competition which should enhance welfare.

GDP growth will be weak in the near term…

The key near-term economic challenge will be to cope with the fall-out from the financial crisis. Growth has stalled since the start of 2008 due to weak consumption and exports, with consumers facing higher interest rates and food and energy prices, slowing house prices and a weakening labour market. Export growth is likely to remain subdued, given the slowdown in key trading partners. Businesses are likely to cut back investment. As a result of weaker demand, considerable margins of slack are set to emerge. Ultimately, the slowdown could be even stronger if large write-downs of Swedish banks' Baltic assets were to undermine balance sheets, restricting credit in Sweden.

... and macroeconomic policy has started to ease

On the fiscal side, strong automatic stabilisers will provide a substantial cyclical cushion. In addition, the government has announced a number of measures to be included in the 2009 Budget, implying a reduction of the cyclically-adjusted surplus by almost 1% of GDP next year. This has to be seen in the context of the large surpluses recorded in recent years, with government net lending reaching 3½ per cent of GDP in 2007 – far above the targeted 1%. The cyclically-adjusted budget balance is set to remain above 1% of GDP in 2009, even after the planned loosening. Accordingly, the longer-term soundness of public finances would not be undermined. However, suggestions for further discretionary measures should be weighed against the fact that fiscal balances often worsen more during downturns than anticipated using standard cyclical-adjustment techniques.

Over the summer, inflation reached levels last seen in the early 1990s, at over 4%, driven by high fuel and energy prices. In addition, mortgage interest costs for owner-occupied dwellings increased rapidly since mid-2006, directly pushing up CPI inflation. At the same time, inflation expectations rose, including at longer horizons, leading the Riksbank to hike the repo rate to 4¾ per cent by September. With the intensification of the financial crisis, the outlook for growth has weakened and inflation risks have diminished, leading a number of OECD central banks, including the Riksbank, to cut interest rates in early October. The repo rate was cut again to 3¾ per cent in late October, but even further easing may be warranted in the coming quarters.

What fiscal targets and rules should Sweden have in the future?

Sweden's strong fiscal performance has been achieved via a policy framework that has helped contain spending and reduce debt, involving net lending targets, expenditure ceilings and balanced-budget requirements for local governments. The general government net financial position has improved from net debt of over 25% of GDP in the mid-1990s to net assets of 20% of GDP by 2007. Moreover, thanks to the pension reform of the late 1990s, Sweden is better prepared for ageing than most OECD countries.

To ensure that sound public finances are sustained over the longer term, the surplus target should be refined and set on the basis of foreseeable long-term fiscal developments as well as the need to retain scope for fiscal action in the event of serious cyclical downturns. Ensuring sustainability should be emphasised as the central goal, meaning that policies can remain unchanged without the need for higher taxes and without leading to rising debt that could ultimately push up interest rates and cause macroeconomic as well as financial market instability. Sustainable public finances are also a precondition for an equitable distribution of resources between generations. A careful analysis of the government's balance sheet, detailed long-run projections of spending, plus fiscal sustainability and intergenerational equity assessments should be used to underpin the fiscal targets. The targets could be set based on assumptions and methodologies audited by the Fiscal Policy Council. The government has begun work on a review of the fiscal framework in order to strengthen it and safeguard the sustainability of the public finances.

Dealing with long-run fiscal pressures will require a multi-faceted approach. Current policies rely on pre-funding and increased labour supply to boost tax revenues and reduce spending on income benefits. A measure of pre-funding is appropriate, particularly in the income pension system where surpluses reflect an excess of contributors over beneficiaries – a situation that will reverse in the not-too-distant future. But other approaches will also be needed, in particular to meet demands for higher service standards, for which pre-funding would not be appropriate. Moderating spending growth should therefore be a consistent policy focus, including measures to raise efficiency *via* user choice and contestability. Also, some of today's publicly-funded services could be paid for privately.

Tax and growth: what direction should Sweden take?

In recent years, Sweden has implemented ambitious tax cuts aimed at boosting growth: it used to have the highest tax-to-GDP ratio in the OECD, but it is now starting to edge down the list. This process should continue, in parallel with spending restraint. The recent OECD *Tax and Growth* study found corporate income taxes to be the most distortive, followed by personal income taxes and then consumption taxes, with housing taxes being the least inimical to growth. Against this background, the envisaged reduction in the corporate tax rate from 28% to 26.3% in 2009 is sensible. Continued gradual reductions of corporate income taxes and the recent abolition of wealth taxes improve Sweden's attractiveness in the context of growing capital mobility. By contrast, lower employer contributions for small and medium-sized companies, as sometimes discussed, risk impeding their growth and would distort competition.

Further reforms are needed as regards personal income taxation. The total marginal tax wedge (contributions, income and consumption taxes combined) still rises to 70%, beginning not much above average full-time earnings and affecting a third of the full-time employed. Such a high marginal tax wedge is probably part of the reason why average working hours are short, and it is not conducive to entrepreneurship, human capital formation or retaining and attracting highly-skilled staff from abroad. It is therefore encouraging that raising the income threshold for the state income tax, as proposed in the previous *Survey*, is now being considered. Based on detailed models, it has been estimated that the ensuing dynamic effects in terms of labour supply would be larger than from expanding the in-work tax credit. The case for reducing the state income tax would be even more compelling if the effects on human capital formation and international mobility were taken into account.

As these effects are likely to become more important, it is essential to find pragmatic ways to continue to reduce the state income tax. It brings in revenue of just 1.3% of GDP; even large reductions would be relatively cheap when dynamic effects enlarging the tax base are factored in. Such cuts are often contested as the state income tax is one of the few remaining elements creating progression in the Swedish tax system. However, equity is better served by policies to promote learning outcomes for children of all backgrounds and to widen labour market inclusion than by retaining very high marginal taxes for high-income earners or the wealth tax which was recently abolished. Moreover, there would still be ample redistribution in the form of publicly-funded services like child care available to all and relatively generous social security. A socially acceptable – and efficient – approach could be to further move up the threshold from where the state income tax is paid. At some point, consideration should also be given to reinstating Sweden's well-functioning housing tax of 0.7% of each owner-occupied home's market value, which was replaced by a capped municipal fee in 2007. This would boost redistribution in a growth-friendly way.

Some liberalisation of rental housing is under way

Given the absence of market-determined rents, rental housing is allocated through queuing, extensive search processes and, in some instances, black market trading. As a consequence, some households may have to wait up to ten years for their preferred accommodation or have to buy property when they would prefer to rent. It is therefore welcome that recent reform proposals go in the direction recommended in the previous OECD *Survey*. Letting rents rise where there are queues addresses the most important problem of Swedish rent regulation, namely that rents are not allowed to adjust in response to supply and demand. Yet, the system remains administratively complex. The gradual approach of capping rent increases to 5% annually probably helps broaden support for the reform, even though more rapid adjustment would be desirable to bring efficiency gains forward. Measures to spur competition in the construction sector and ease land planning processes are also required.

Clear progress has been made on long-standing problems with labour market exclusion and benefit dependency

The share of working-age adults living from income benefits has fallen considerably in recent years. After hovering around 20-21% in 1997-2005, it fell to 18% in 2007. This is partly thanks to cyclical buoyancy. But, as analysed in the previous *Survey*, recent benefit reforms and other measures addressing labour-market exclusion should have lasting positive effects in the form of higher participation and lower structural unemployment. Much of the improvement reflects falling sickness absence. For a number of years, sickness absence was by far the highest among OECD countries, with 25 working days lost per full-time equivalent employee in 2004. Since then, administration has been tightened and both sickness absence rates and the inflow into disability benefits have fallen by about a third. Even so, sickness absence and the stock of disability benefit recipients remain among the highest internationally. Further reforms, beyond the July 2008 requirements to be ready to change job-function and ultimately workplace, might therefore be needed.

Youth unemployment remains high, revealing weaknesses in education as well as labour markets

By international standards, educational attainment in Sweden is high. Over 90% of the younger cohorts have completed upper secondary education, a share among the highest in the OECD and above the other Nordic countries. However, youth unemployment is widespread, even if it has declined from 22.8% of the labour force in 2005 to 19.2% in 2007 on the back of buoyant economic growth. In Denmark, Iceland, the Netherlands and Norway, where social preferences are similar, youth unemployment is just a third of the Swedish rate. Unemployment is particularly high among youth with poor schooling and among immigrant youth. This indicates problems both in the education system and in the labour market. An education system that helps children and youth from all backgrounds realise their full potential is vital for continued prosperity and for reducing labour market exclusion among youth and the low skilled – notably in the context of relatively generous income benefits and a narrow wage distribution.

Compulsory school must ensure a stronger start for all

Learning outcomes in compulsory education are not as good as they used to be. At age 15, student proficiency measured by PISA is above the OECD average for reading but not for mathematics and science. Moreover, 15-year olds' interest in learning about science, time spent on science-related activities outside school and interest in working with science later in life are well below the OECD average, raising questions about how children's natural curiosity and interest in science can be nurtured. The continued development of tests to better monitor progress during school would help. So would the proposed system for accreditation of teachers, with more weight given to their specific competences when allocating tasks among staff. Once the accreditation scheme is well established, greater wage flexibility could reward the best teachers.

Upper secondary schooling should prepare students better for labour-market entry

Upper secondary vocational education needs to better prepare students for work. The introduction of apprenticeships is a promising route, emphasising more hands-on practical learning and perhaps giving immigrant and second-generation youth a better understanding of relations in a Swedish workplace. However, apprenticeships must avoid being so specific that students miss the more general skills they might need to reorient professionally later in life. Independent private upper secondary schools have expanded remarkably fast, with the share of students enrolled rising from 3% to 17% in just ten years. The competition they generate is welcome, not least because it shows where the public system could improve. Lack of scale, for example, may hold back vocational programmes from developing well in public secondary schools. Given the deficiencies of vocational programmes, it could be of interest to analyse the consequences of moving responsibility of upper secondary education from the municipalities to the State. Such an analysis could also look at other levels of schooling. To support choice, there should be more transparency for potential students about the labour market prospects associated with alternative options, for instance by publishing data for employment outcomes of recent school leavers.

Higher education also faces challenges

Swedish higher education has a number of strengths. However, a particular weakness of the Swedish system is that students complete higher education late. In order to speed up labour market entry, financial support for students' living costs could be altered with loans replacing grants when studies get prolonged, or with explicit rewards for early entry and completion on time. Quality could be enhanced by basing the allocation of funding for core research and higher education on more transparent criteria and by giving universities more freedom to develop their own strengths. Relying solely on tax-financing of higher education might be a hindrance in this context. One approach would be to move gradually towards a system where students pay for tuition, while extending government loans available for students in order to finance tuition costs. This is done in a growing number of OECD countries to meet both efficiency and equity objectives, *inter alia* in the light of growing high-skilled mobility. In Sweden, legislation to introduce fees for non-EU students is currently being considered. Reducing the state income tax, as recommended above, would boost the returns to higher education, which are rather low by international standards.

Labour market institutions are too rigid

Shortcomings in the education system cannot alone account for high youth unemployment: Denmark and Norway have PISA scores similar to Sweden's, but much better youth labour market outcomes. Education reform is needed, but the rigidities in the labour market must also be addressed. High minimum wages and a compressed wage structure make the entrance on the labour market difficult for youth, especially for immigrants and those with incomplete education. Labour demand has been stimulated by a general reduction of the employer contribution for individuals younger than 26. The rebate makes it easier for youth to enter the labour market, but the deadweight costs are presumably large, and its positive effect on youth employment might be offset by demands for higher wages. Active labour market policies are being improved with the Job Guarantee for youth, shifting the focus onto enhancing job-search coaching in the early phase of youth unemployment spells, and reducing the statutory replacement rate after 20 weeks, compared with 40 weeks for others. Still, benefits are effectively more generous for youth than for prime-age adults as, for example, the ceiling on unemployment benefits is less frequently binding for youth. Dualism in employment protection is of particular concern. The recent extension of the maximum duration of temporary contracts may allow employers to better "try out" young job applicants. However, there is a risk of youth being locked into temporary contracts rather than regular employment. One approach would be to clear the pathways to regular employment by easing the definition of a fair dismissal and lengthening the trial period for regular contracts. The complexity of these issues would call for a review of the broader implications, including with respect to collective wage bargaining.

Privatisation should continue

An important recent achievement has been the progress made in privatising government-owned enterprises. This is warranted, given that the Swedish State's portfolio of state-owned enterprises is estimated to be worth the equivalent of around one-quarter of the market capitalisation of the Stockholm stock exchange. The scope of the public enterprise sector is among the broadest in the OECD. State ownership of businesses may hold back innovation and entrepreneurship and deter potential entrants. Privatisation should

OECD ECONOMIC SURVEYS: SWEDEN – ISBN 978-92-64-05423-3 – © OECD 2008

therefore continue – although financial market turmoil may require some transactions to be postponed so as to secure the right price for asset sales. Following on from the current programme (with a bank, a mortgage lender and the incumbent telecom operator yet to be sold under existing parliamentary approval), priority should be given to selling other companies that already operate under market conditions (such as the incumbent airline, other transport companies and forestry companies). Monopoly power should be reduced in some cases, for example in railways and retail, with appropriate regulatory changes to protect consumer welfare. In the case of firms entrusted with special societal interest, there may be other forms of policy intervention that might achieve the same goals without the government needing to own enterprises. As a general rule, asset sale proceeds should not be used to finance new spending or reductions in revenue that would have adverse long-term fiscal implications; rather, they should serve to reduce government debt.

ISBN 978-92-64-05423-3
OECD Economic Surveys: Sweden
© OECD 2008

Chapter 1

Key challenges for the Swedish economy

Sweden has contributed to the fame of the Nordic model, where high per capita income and open markets go hand in hand with social cohesion. The current downturn and the fallout from the global financial crisis pose a key challenge to policymakers seeking the most appropriate mix of financial market measures and monetary and fiscal policy responses. Over the longer term, key challenges for the Swedish economy lie in: finding the right path for fiscal policy, given the current large structural surpluses and future fiscal pressures; tackling the most distortive elements of the tax system; improving education and reducing the high rate of youth unemployment; and improving productivity through privatisation. This chapter lays out these key challenges, and reviews policy progress on those challenges identified in previous Surveys, within the framework of a medium-term growth assessment based on potential labour supply and productivity growth.

The Swedish economy has enjoyed a vigorous expansion in recent years, building on the policy foundations put in place after the financial and economic crisis of the early 1990s. National income is fairly high by international standards and Sweden has benefited more than many other countries from the take-off of information and communications technologies (ICT). Most recently, the Swedish economy has been affected directly and indirectly by the international financial crisis and growth has slowed markedly. Inflation rose above 4% during the summer, but it is likely to recede quickly as slow growth is set to lead to considerable economic slack. Against this background, the Riksbank cut interest rates by 100 basis point in October. The strong fiscal policy framework and recent large surpluses mean that the government is well placed to respond to the downturn, and a fiscal stimulus of close to 1% of GDP will be imparted in 2009. If any further fiscal action is deemed necessary, it should focus on measures to help raise long-term growth (Chapter 2), notably *via* tax reform (Chapter 3).

Beyond the near term, the Swedish economy is expected to grow more slowly than during the past decade, due mainly to weaker growth in potential labour supply. Continued net immigration may not translate into a significant boost to labour supply as immigrants are generally less well attached to the labour market. Policies to integrate immigrants into the labour market will remain important. It has taken more than a decade to reduce the high structural unemployment rate that resulted from the early 1990s crisis and there are still many people outside the labour market living on public welfare. In particular, youth unemployment is high by international standards, reflecting both deficiencies of the education system and features of the labour market. Improving the connection between school and work offers promise (Chapter 4). While economic growth can be boosted by further efforts to increase labour supply, productivity growth remains key to sustaining increases in prosperity. The recent spell of weak productivity growth is mainly cyclical but serves as a reminder to continue to focus on productivity-enhancing measures in education and competition policy, including further reduction of the scope of government involvement in the private sector (Chapter 5).

Despite strong macroeconomic performance in recent years, GDP per capita in Sweden remains around one-fifth lower than in the United States (Figure 1.1). Measured at constant prices and purchasing power parities, it would seem that Swedish GDP per capita is catching up with the leading countries, but with a trend decline in the terms of trade partly resulting from the ICT intensity of Swedish production, the real income gap, measured based on current prices and purchasing power parities has narrowed just marginally since the mid-1990s.[1] Labour utilisation (measured as hours worked per head of population) and labour productivity (GDP per hour worked) are both about 10% below the US level. The crisis of the early 1990s significantly reduced the employment and participation rates in Sweden, widening the gap in GDP per capita. While the employment rate has moved back up since, total hours worked per capita remain below the pre-crisis level.

OECD ECONOMIC SURVEYS: SWEDEN – ISBN 978-92-64-05423-3 – © OECD 2008

Figure 1.1. **GDP per capita evolution and decomposition**[1]

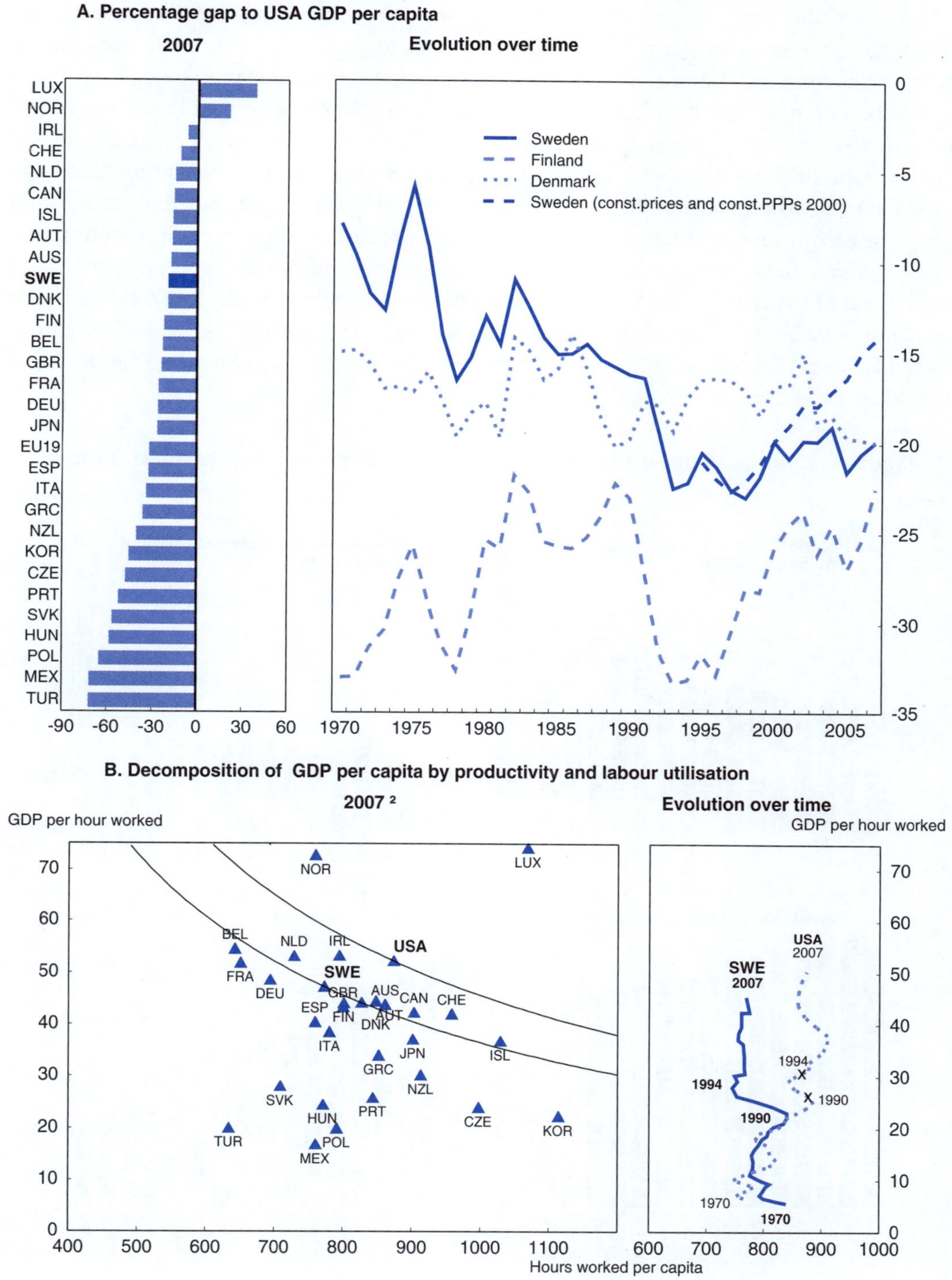

StatLink http://dx.doi.org/10.1787/484746515456

1. GDP is measured at current price purchasing power parities. Productivity is GDP per hour worked. Labour utilisation is hours worked per capita.
2. The lines running through Sweden and the United States show the different combinations of GDP per hour worked and hours worked per capita that produce the same level of GDP per capita.

Source: OECD, *Productivity database* and OECD Secretariat estimates.

The Swedish model

The Swedish economic model has recently received much international attention for its ability to combine growth-oriented policies, openness to globalisation and structural change with social cohesion. Domestic-focused product market regulation is relatively liberal, and would be amongst the most liberal in the OECD with lower state control and fewer legal barriers to competition. Regulations that affect foreign trade and investment are also liberal but are generally so in OECD countries. Comparatively low levels of corruption and high levels of trust also underpin the effective functioning of markets and contribute to a sound business environment (Figure 1.2). With a market-oriented regulatory environment and a skilled labour force, Sweden ranks high in broad surveys of overall "competitiveness" – fourth out of 134 countries in the WEF ranking (World Economic Forum, 2008) and ninth out of 55 in the IMD's (Institute for Management and Development, 2008). These policies can be traced far back and explain why, by 1970, Swedish GDP per capita had reached about 90% of the US level, before a relative decline set in.[2]

Figure 1.2. **Market openness and trust – key features of the Swedish model**

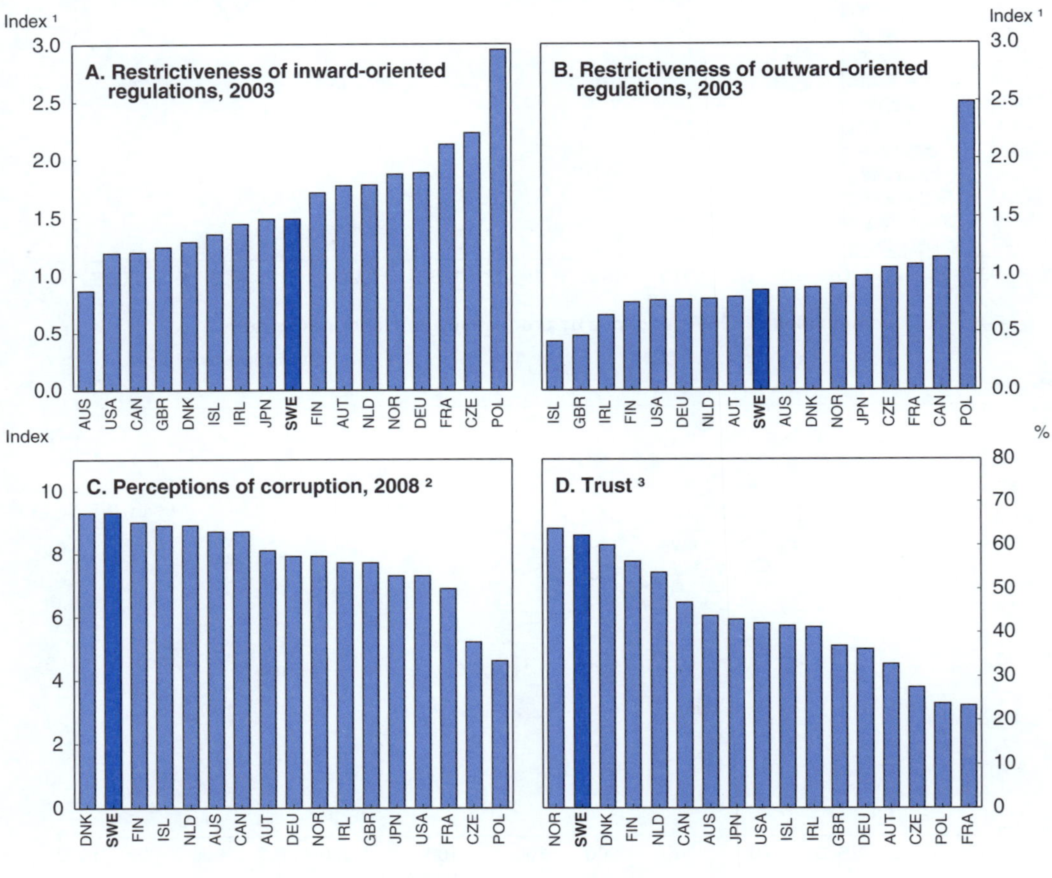

StatLink http://dx.doi.org/10.1787/484788433012

1. A lower index denotes less restrictive regulation.
2. This score relates to perceptions of the degree of corruption as seen by business people and country analysts and ranges between 10 (very clean) and 0 (very corrupt).
3. Proportion of survey respondents answering that most people can be trusted when asked "generally speaking, would you say that most people can be trusted or that you need to be very careful in dealing with people?" as part of the World Values Survey. The data are the averages of all available observations from the World Values Survey so do not relate to a specific year. In the 2005 wave, for which data were released for some countries in October 2008, Sweden's position is similar to the longer-run average shown in the figure.

Source: OECD *Product Market Regulation database*, Transparency International, and Bjørnskov (2008).

An equitable income distribution and strong emphasis on equal opportunities are other central features of the Swedish model – which existed already before generous income benefits were introduced in the 1960s and 1970s. The distribution of disposable income among individuals is the second flattest in the OECD (Figure 1.3). The distribution of individual market income among men (including wages, capital income, earnings of self employed and those income benefits that are liable for taxation) has been remarkably stable over the past fifty years. Developments for women illustrate how essential labour market participation is for achieving income equality: the Gini coefficient halved from 1950 to 1980 as more women joined the formal labour market (Figure 1.4). Since 1990, the income distribution has widened a bit. The change is most pronounced for ages below 30, partly reflecting growing enrolment in education and thereby more people having limited income while studying.

Figure 1.3. **Indicators of equity**

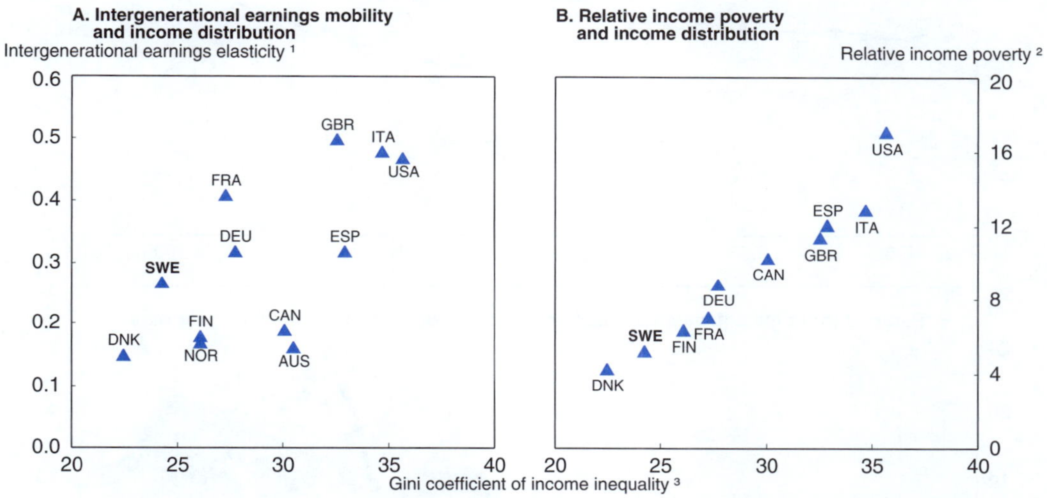

StatLink http://dx.doi.org/10.1787/484807602168

1. Fraction of earnings differences among fathers that, on average, is passed on to their sons (the lower the elasticity, the higher intergenerational mobility). The elasticity is derived by estimating a regression in which the adult income of the child is expressed as a function of the average income of the children's generation, parental income and other influences not associated with parental income. The intergenerational earnings elasticity is the coefficient on parental income in this regression.
2. Share of the population with disposable income equal to less than half of the country's median disposable income.
3. Measures the extent to which the distribution of income among individuals or households within an economy deviates from a perfectly equal distribution. A Gini coefficient of zero represents perfect equality and 100, perfect inequality.

Source: OECD (2006).

In recent decades, Sweden has experienced substantial problems with labour market exclusion and benefit dependency. The compressed earnings distribution of the 1950s and 1960s reflected a well-developed education system which, combined with high union density and coordinated wage formation, generated a narrow dispersion of productivity among workers (Borg, 2008). Meanwhile, government welfare spending in a wider sense was no more generous than in continental Europe. This changed in the late 1960s and 1970s as social insurance schemes became more generous, public consumption grew strongly and, consequently, the tax pressure rose. Labour market regulations were also made more stringent, such as with the introduction of the last-in-first-out rule. In the context of the economic crisis of the 1990s, it became clear that these institutions had weakened the economy's ability to adjust, as the initial strong rise in unemployment was followed by a persistent rise in the share of working-age adults living from income benefits (Figure 1.4). Moreover, while income dispersion is very compressed in Sweden, intergenerational earnings mobility is weaker than in Australia, Canada and the other Nordic countries (Figure 1.3). This might indicate that the extensive redistribution of income has not necessarily increased equality of opportunity.

Figure 1.4. **Income disparities went down, but labour market exclusion went up**

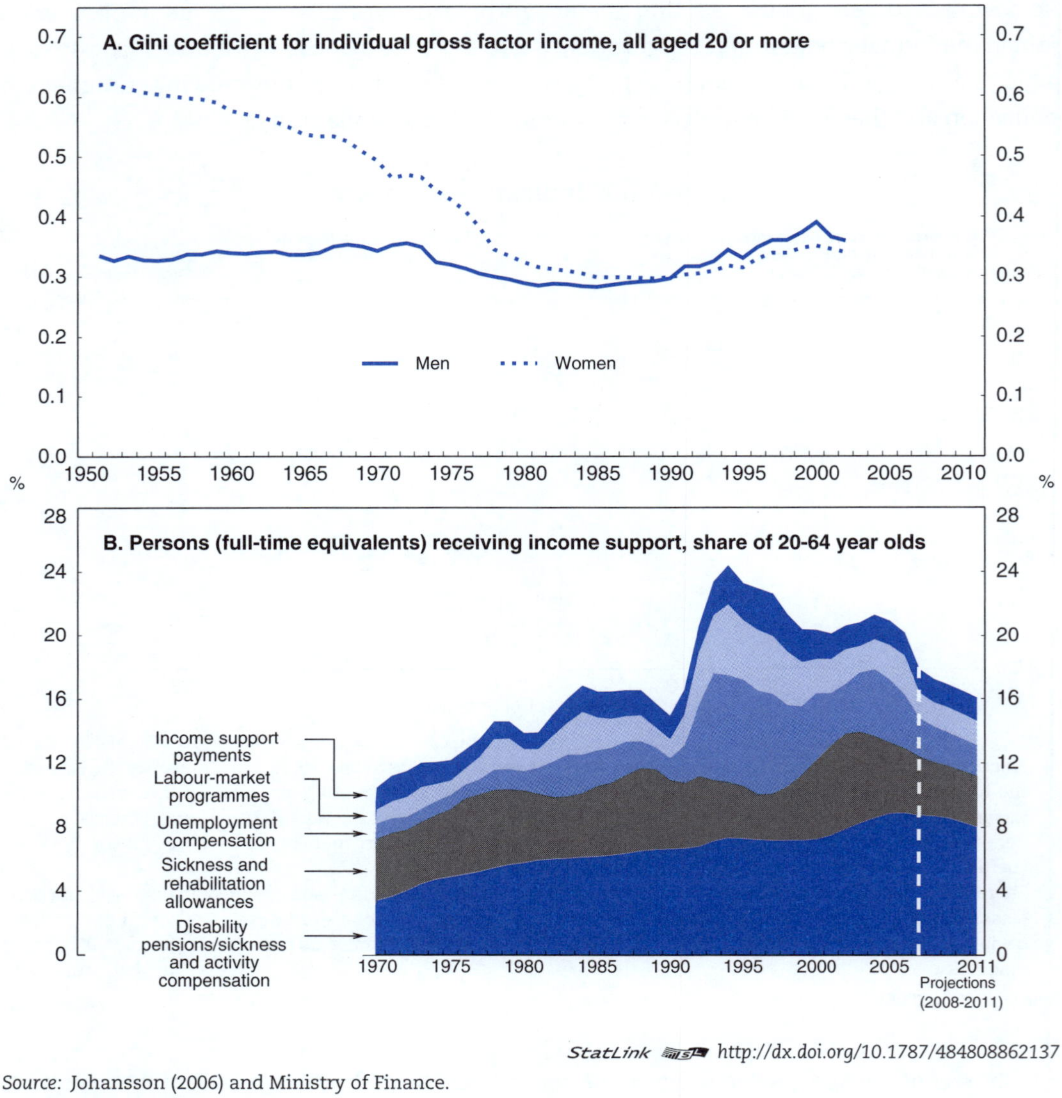

StatLink http://dx.doi.org/10.1787/484808862137

Source: Johansson (2006) and Ministry of Finance.

One of the most important challenges for the Swedish economy is therefore to re-establish the economy's capacity to achieve equity without widespread dependency on income benefits. Striking the right balance in such reforms is important because collective mechanisms for risk sharing, *i.e.* a social safety net, may ease the adjustment costs for individuals affected by structural change – and thereby also help sustain public support for growth-oriented policies, including open markets (Andersen *et al.*, 2008). Important progress has been made in recent years with reforms making benefits and labour market policies more focused on return to work (Annex 1.A1). Better focusing redistribution is another important way forward. Some 80% of all income redistribution arising from government programmes is redistribution over the life cycle rather than between individuals (Pettersson and Pettersson, 2007). Redistributing income over the lifetime of a given individual via government intervention can be warranted in some cases, but it would seem to have grown beyond reasonable proportion in Sweden. Chapter 2 discusses the possibility of greater private funding responsibility for some of today's publicly funded services, so as to ensure that high standards for the most essential public services can be sustained for future generations. Moreover, fostering equity via improvements in the education system to ensure equality of opportunity is likely to be more growth-friendly than redistribution of income *via* benefits and high marginal taxes (Chapters 3 and 4).

The current economic slowdown

While the global slowdown has already affected the Swedish economy, it entered the downturn in a sound position. The macroeconomic policy framework is strong, with fiscal policy producing substantial surpluses and low government debt; monetary policy has focused on maintaining low inflation. Consistent current account surpluses since the mid-1990s have put Sweden's net international investment position on course to turn positive in the near future. In the two years to mid-2007, the Swedish economy expanded rapidly, and faster than the euro area, whilst unemployment fell by almost 2 percentage points (Figure 1.5).

Real GDP essentially stalled in the first half of 2008 and the output gap, which was positive in late 2007, is likely to have been negative already around mid-year. The slowdown was driven by weak growth in exports and, to a lesser extent, investment. Private consumption growth also slowed, though not as much as might have been expected given the fall in consumer confidence. Indeed, one of the earliest signs of the effects of international economic turbulence on the Swedish economy was the deterioration in consumer sentiment from mid-2007. Initially, consumers were concerned mainly about the general state of the economy rather than their own finances, but conditions gradually deteriorated and sentiment is now well below the historic norm and down below the levels seen in the trough of the 2001-03 slowdown (Figure 1.6). The unemployment rate has started to move back up, firms are cutting back hiring and vacancy rates have fallen.

Inflation picked up from less than 2% over the past few years to 4.4% by September 2008. Higher inflation has been driven by only a few categories in the CPI, particularly food, energy and household interest costs (Figure 1.7). However, underlying inflation also slowly trended up, consistent with the economy operating in excess of its capacity. Inflation expectations rose in line with actual inflation and the observed increase in long-term inflation expectations was of particular concern. With inflation well above the 2% target, the Riksbank lifted the policy interest rate (the repo rate) three times over the first three quarters of 2008 – stressing the need to ensure that inflation expectations remain anchored. Recent falls in commodity prices and slower growth should translate into lower consumer price inflation and it is anticipated that inflation expectations will follow. Indeed, some, although not all, measures of inflation expectations have already eased.

Given the crisis in global financial markets, the outlook for economic growth has weakened considerably, and there is a risk of a deep and/or protracted slowdown. The authorities have introduced a number of measures to sustain the functioning of financial markets (Box 1.1). Yet spreads between interbank rates and interest rates on short-term government securities are far above normal levels and equity prices have fallen

Figure 1.5. **Short-term economic indicators**

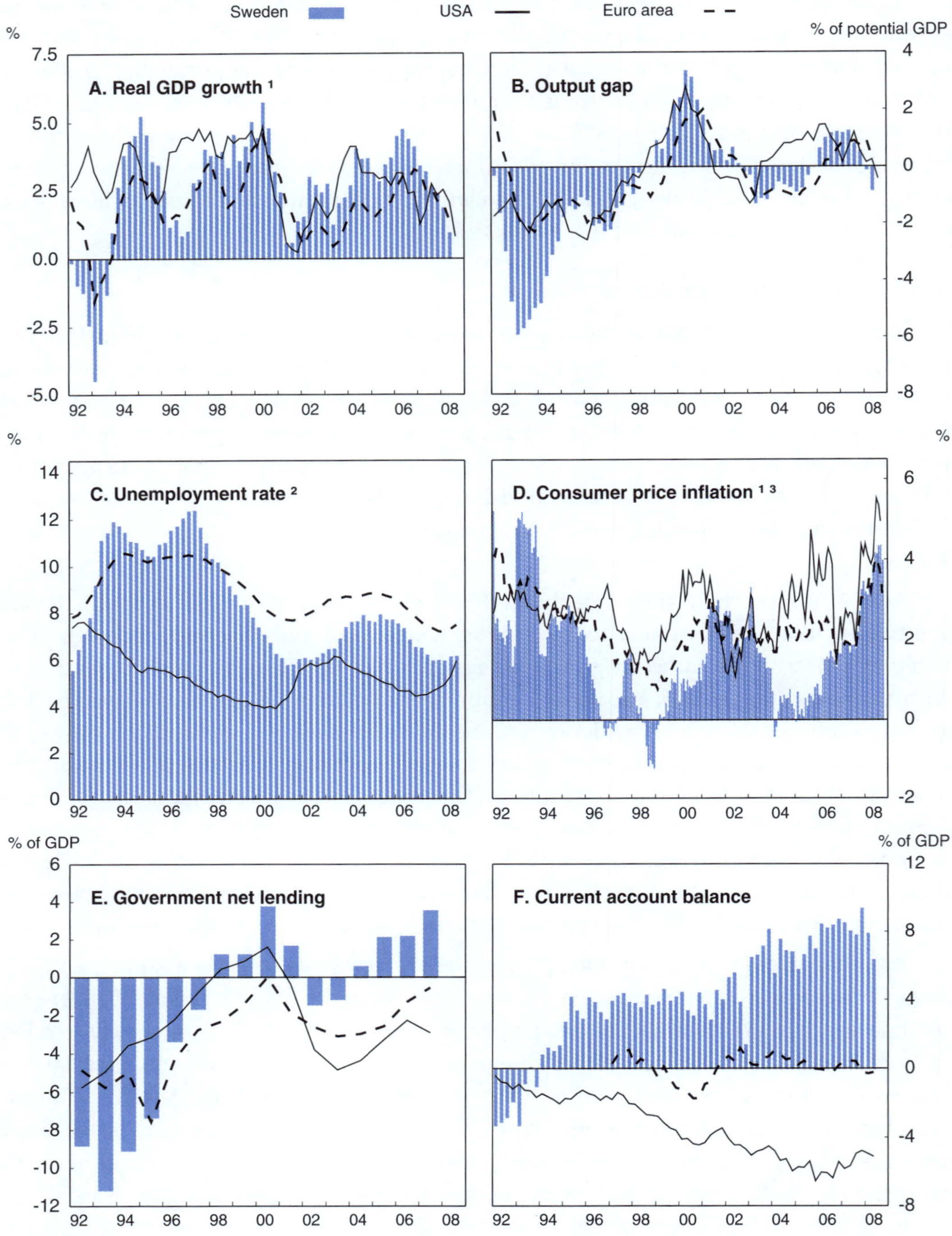

StatLink http://dx.doi.org/10.1787/484854315544

1. From same period of previous year.
2. For the USA, the unemployment rate is from the monthly Current Population Survey of persons aged 16 and over. For the euro area, the unemployment rate is derived from aggregating labour force data for individual euro area countries. For Sweden, the series is described in Annex 1.A2.
3. Harmonised index of consumer prices for the euro area.

Source: OECD, Economic Outlook 84 database and *Analytical database*.

Figure 1.6. **Business and consumer confidence have fallen sharply**[1]

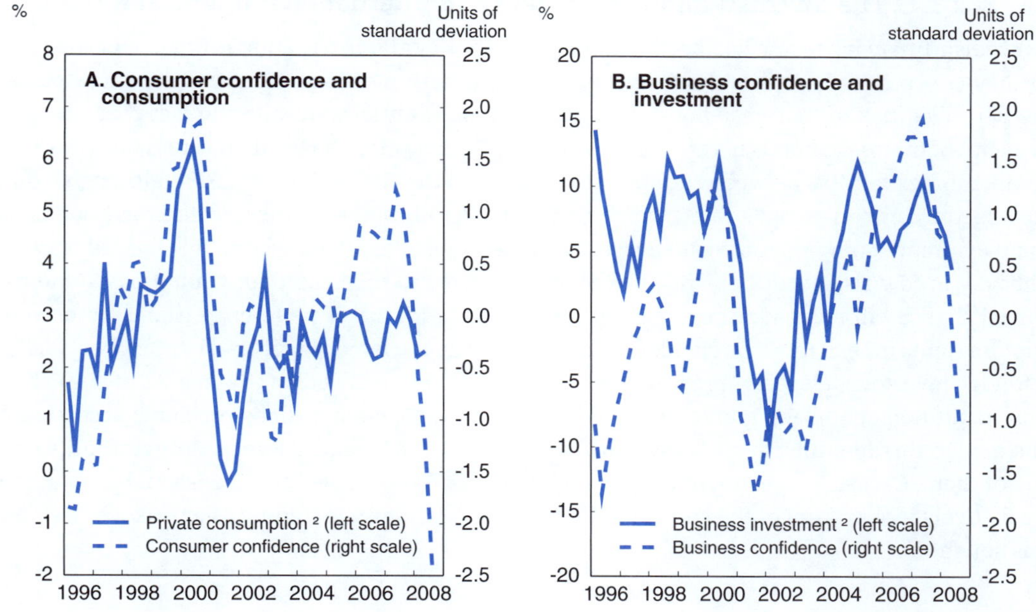

StatLink http://dx.doi.org/10.1787/484875244531

1. Seasonally-adjusted confidence indicator from the quarterly NIER Business Tendency Survey and monthly consumer confidence index from the Consumer Tendency Survey, converted to quarterly frequency by averaging the months. Both series are normalised by subtracting the mean from each observation and dividing the result by the standard deviation.
2. Change from a year earlier.

Source: National Institute for Economic Research Economic Tendency Survey and OECD *Analytical database*.

Figure 1.7. **Inflation and inflation expectations**

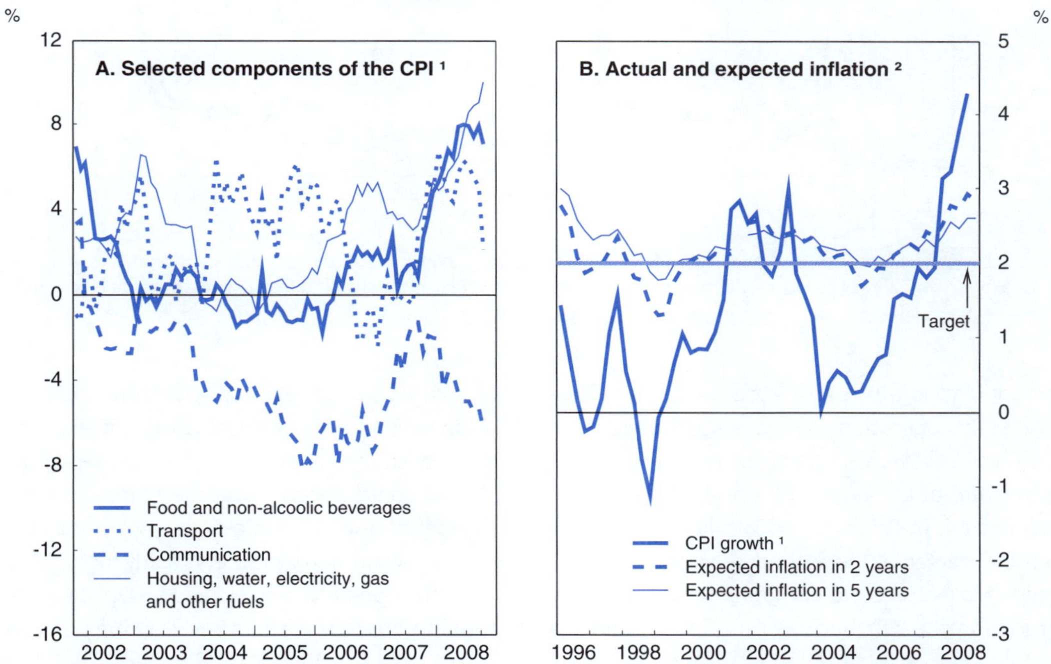

StatLink http://dx.doi.org/10.1787/485027008466

1. Year-on-year percentage change.
2. Expected inflation is the rate of inflation anticipated for the second year from the survey date (12-24 months forward) and the fifth year from the survey date (48-60 months forward).

Source: Statistics Sweden, TNS Prospera.

Box 1.1. **The Swedish financial system and international financial turmoil**

The Swedish financial sector has been seriously affected by the international financial crisis. Interbank spreads have risen sharply, as has the spread between 3-month mortgage rates and the expected repo rate, and the perceived risk of mortgage bonds has increased substantially, despite the fact that the underlying credit quality of mortgage bonds is very high (Figure 1.8). Equity prices have fallen across all sectors – the key stock market index fell 40% between the start of January and the end of October 2008 – although a number of financial-sector companies have fared worse than the overall market. Banks, investment banks, pension funds and insurance companies have taken losses on the value of financial assets. This has led them to invest more heavily in low-risk securities and take other measures to increase their capital base (one bank has announced that it will raise additional capital through a new issue of preference shares with preferential subscription rights for existing shareholders). The currency depreciated, particularly in October 2008, possibly due to foreign investors deleveraging and reducing their portfolios of Swedish equities. As of late October, two financial institutions had been granted special loans from the Riksbank, since problems accessing funding were deemed to threaten the payments system. In November, the Financial Supervisory Authority concluded that one of them, Carnegie Investment Bank, could no longer keep its banking license and the National Debt Office effectively took control of the bank in order to allow it to continue trading as a bank while a new stable owner is sought for.

Figure 1.8. **Developments in market interest rates**

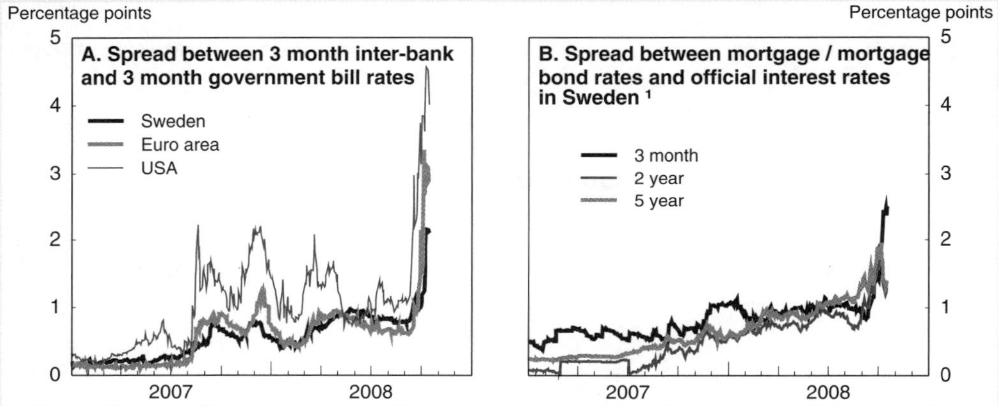

StatLink http://dx.doi.org/10.1787/485070110888

1. Spread between the 3-month mortgage rate offered by mortgage provider SBAB and the expected repo rate, between 2-year mortgage bond and 2-year government bond yields and between 5-year mortgage and 5-year government bond yields.

Source: Riksbank *Monetary Policy Report* 2008:3 and *Riksbank interest rate database*.

A key concern is the risk of significant credit losses, particularly given the sharp growth in recent years in Swedish bank's operations in the Baltic States.* About 5% of Swedish banks' lending in 2007 was in the Baltic States, following several years of strong lending growth in the region, and some Swedish banks recently earned up to one-third of their operating profits in the region. In 2008, economic growth in the Baltics collapsed and inflation soared. In Estonia, and Latvia, real GDP, which was expanding at double-digit rates until just over a year ago, contracted in the second quarter of 2008. Adjustment in the property market is a key factor behind the slowdown. Household and corporate borrowing from credit institutions has also slowed sharply, partly due to stricter loan terms. Further deterioration in Baltic assets could reduce Swedish banks' earnings. The value of collateral held against loans could fall as housing markets deteriorate, and banks' funding terms would worsen if there were a general reassessment of risk in the region, further reducing the share prices of Swedish banks and increasing borrowing costs. This, in turn, would lead to credit restrictions, as banks reduce their balance sheets, and higher lending rates to Swedish consumers and businesses (Riksbank, 2008c).

 OECD ECONOMIC SURVEYS: SWEDEN – ISBN 978-92-64-05423-3 – © OECD 2008

Box 1.1. **The Swedish financial system and international financial turmoil** *(cont.)*

Similar effects could arise from increased credit losses in the domestic economy. Economic conditions have deteriorated sharply. The value of household net financial assets fell by 12% in the first half of 2008 and has plummeted further since as equity prices continued to fall. After a number of years of strong growth, house prices may now fall. The economy is likely to contract in late 2008 and unemployment to rise. In these circumstances, the proportion of impaired domestic loans may rise, further affecting banks' profits and share prices.

However, the banking system is considered to be solvent. Stress testing shows that even if cumulative credit losses were to reach as much as 15% of total lending in the Baltic countries, 3¾ per cent of total lending in Sweden and almost 2% of lending in other countries, Swedish banks would need only moderate adjustments in their business practices to continue complying with capital requirements (Finansinpektionen, 2008a). This scenario is based on a significantly worse economic outlook for Sweden than currently envisaged, but does not take into account the global nature of the current financial crisis. Pension funds were assessed in June 2008 as having significant buffers to meet payment requirements, even in the event of large declines in asset prices. The ongoing turmoil has reduced these buffers so, while funds are still deemed to be solvent, they are more vulnerable to continued price falls (Finansinpektionen, 2008b).

The Government has taken measures to help reduce the systemic risks associated with credit losses. SEK 15 billion are set aside in a fund to handle future solvency problems in the banking sector. Capital from this fund would be available only if the government considers that the institution in question is systemically important. All credit institutions will be charged a fee in connection with this fund and any capital injection would be provided in return for preference shares. In addition, the Government has been allowed by Parliament to proceed with forced nationalisation of financial companies at market prices, should this be needed. Under new rules on state aid to credit institutions, the Government has given the National Debt Office a broad mandate to intervene if institutions get into serious financial difficulties. These new powers were used in the case of Carnegie Investment Bank. The National Debt Office will establish a new board of directors and gradually sell the various components of the bank on commercial terms to buyers approved by the Financial Supervisory Authority (Swedish National Debt Office, 2008).

Another major risk arises from banks being unable to acquire sufficient financing for their operations. Spillovers from increasing credit risk to inter-bank liquidity are important due to the reliance of banks on capital market funding (International Monetary Fund, 2008). However, concerns about liquidity have also risen in markets where underlying credit has not deteriorated significantly, such as mortgage bonds. The Government and the Riksbank have taken a number of measures to ease liquidity problems. The Government has offered to guarantee new borrowing by financial institutions of between 90 days and five years maturity. The guarantee will be granted for a fee: 0.5% of the guaranteed amount for instruments with less than one year to maturity and a rate based on the historic market price of credit default swaps plus 0.5 percentage point for instruments with more than one year to maturity. Conditions will be imposed to limit overall credit expansion and the remuneration of the institution's senior management. In total, the Government is prepared to guarantee up to SEK 1 500 billion in lending and the scheme is intended to run until 30 April 2009, with possibilities for extension until the end of 2009. Immediately after the announcement of this measure, there was a sharp drop in the spreads between interbank rates and rates on short-term government securities. Short-term interbank spreads have continued to ease in the following weeks. This suggests that the measure is helping to restore confidence in the markets. Furthermore, the Government has doubled the guarantee it offers for bank deposits from SEK 250 000 to SEK 500 000. The scheme has also been extended to cover all accounts, whereas the previous guarantee excluded certain fixed-interest-rate accounts. The amount of the new guarantee is slightly above the € 50 000 minimum agreed by EU Finance Ministers on 7 October.

Box 1.1. **The Swedish financial system and international financial turmoil** *(cont.)*

In addition, the Riksbank has established new Swedish kroner loan facilities to improve access to funding in the longer-duration segments of the money market and has offered a number of new loans in US dollars. The Riksbank has lifted restrictions on the use of mortgage bonds and newly-issued commercial paper as collateral for access to credit in the payment system. The minimum credit rating requirement for longer-term securities pledged as collateral in the payment system has also been reduced. The Swedish National Debt Office has increased issuance of short-maturity government debt and placed the proceeds in reverse mortgage bond repurchase agreements, to increase the supply of government securities and the demand for mortgage bonds.

The impact of the financial crisis on the real economy will partly depend on the extent of the reduction in new lending and on how much of the increase in the cost of funding by financial institutions will be passed on to their customers. The measures put in place by the Government and the Riksbank are therefore important, because they assure the market that funding is available, so that pricing of financial instruments can better reflect the underlying credit risks. So far there is little evidence that Swedish banks are constraining lending in Sweden to contract their balance sheets. As of September 2008, lending by financial institutions had slowed somewhat from the start of the year, but was still expanding at around 10% annual rates for households and 15% for corporations. It is possible that bank lending to corporations has remained high due to corporations having problems accessing other forms of funding. However, lending growth is expected to slow further in coming months. Part of the motivation behind the sharp reductions in policy interest rates in October was the recognition that the link between policy rates and rates faced by retail borrowers has become more tenuous (Riksbank, 2008d). Spreads between the interest rates on new loans to households and the repo rate had been low before the onset of the financial crisis but have risen sharply in recent months. Spreads between mortgage bond rates and the repo rate have fallen, but mortgage bond rates remain very volatile.

* Four major banks have about 80% of the Swedish banking market. About 30% of lending by Swedish banks is directed to foreign companies, while the remaining 70% is approximately equally distributed amongst lending to Swedish households, Swedish companies and foreign households (Riksbank, 2008b).

considerably. As of the end of October 2008, two financial institutions had requested loans from the Riksbank to help alleviate liquidity constraints. Subsequently, one of these institutions was effectively nationalised under new arrangements for state aid for financial institutions, since breaches of the law on risk exposures and reporting would have otherwise led to its banking licence being revoked. There remains the potential for further spill-over of deteriorating credit conditions in other countries, and the weakening domestic economy might feed back into the financial markets, compounding financial turbulence

GDP is expected to contract slightly at the end of 2008 and in early 2009, before growth begins to recover in the second half of 2009 (Table 1.1). Private consumption is projected to remain weak in coming quarters. House price growth has slowed, and house prices may yet fall, constraining the use of mortgage equity to finance consumption. Further income tax cuts and an anticipated return to more normal financial conditions should spur a recovery in consumer spending in late 2009. Export growth should remain weak before gradually recovering in line with Sweden's export markets. Business investment is likely to contract, as confidence has fallen and borrowing costs have risen, but investment is historically highly correlated with exports so should follow the export recovery. Residential investment is expected to contract in 2009, owing to weaker house prices and confidence, compounding unfavourable demographic patterns. Employment and labour force

Table 1.1. **Short-term economic outlook**

	2005	2006	2007	2008	2009	2010	08Q4	09Q4	10Q4
	Current prices SEK billion	Percentage changes, volume (2000 prices)							
Private consumption	1 328.4	2.5	3.0	1.9	0.7	2.5	1.3	0.9	3.3
Government consumption	722.7	1.5	1.1	0.6	1.0	0.5	0.4	1.4	0.0
Gross fixed capital formation	475.9	7.7	8.0	3.0	–2.7	2.0	–0.0	–1.6	3.8
Final domestic demand	2 526.9	3.2	3.4	1.8	0.1	1.8	0.8	0.5	2.5
Stockbuilding[1]	–4.2	0.2	0.7	0.3	0.2	0.0			
Total domestic demand	2 522.7	3.4	4.2	2.1	0.3	1.8	2.1	0.5	2.4
Exports of goods and services	1 333.4	8.7	6.3	3.3	0.3	3.8	0.4	0.9	5.9
Imports of goods and services	1 120.9	8.2	9.9	4.2	0.3	3.3	1.4	0.8	5.1
Net exports[1]	212.5	0.9	–1.1	–0.2	0.0	0.5			
GDP at market prices	2 735.2	4.4	2.9	0.8	0.0	2.2	–0.1	0.5	3.1
GDP deflator		1.5	2.9	3.7	2.5	1.6	4.3	1.0	2.0
Memorandum items									
Consumer price index		1.4	2.2	3.5	1.5	1.1	2.5	1.2	1.1
Private consumption deflator		0.9	1.3	2.4	1.3	1.0	2.3	1.1	1.1
Employment[2]		2.0	2.5	1.2	–1.2	–1.0	0.3	–1.6	–0.2
Labour force participation rate[2]		70.8	71.1	71.2	70.7	70.4	71.0	70.6	70.4
Unemployment rate[2]		7.1	6.1	6.1	7.0	7.7	6.4	7.4	7.7
Household saving ratio[3]		7.1	8.3	9.2	10.3	9.3			
General government financial balance[4]		2.2	3.5	2.8	0.5	0.4			
Current account balance[4]		8.5	8.4	6.5	6.5	6.9			

Note: National accounts are based on official chain-link data. This introduces a discrepancy in the identity between real demand components and GDP. For further details see *OECD Economic Outlook* Sources and Methods (*www.oecd.org/eco/sources-and-methods*).

1. Contributions to changes in real GDP (percentage of real GDP in previous year), actual amount in the first column.
2. Historical data and projections are based on the definition of unemployment which covers 15 to 74 year olds and classifies job-seeking full-time students as unemployed (Annex 1.A2).
3. As a percentage of disposable income.
4. As a percentage of GDP.

Source: OECD, *Economic Outlook* No. 84.

participation are both expected to fall and the unemployment rate rises above the estimated structural rate, implying easing wage pressures. Labour productivity growth has been negative over the last year, following very strong growth for a number of years, but should pick up strongly as the recovery in the labour market is set to lag the recovery in activity (Figure 1.9).

How should economic policies respond to the slowdown?

Sweden has put in place a strong macroeconomic policy framework since the crisis of the early 1990s. Monetary policy is conducted independently by the Riksbank, with a clear mandate to maintain price stability (Box 1.2). Fiscal sustainability has been restored and the automatic stabilisers are strong (Girouard and André, 2005).[3] This stability-oriented policy framework should be allowed to function as designed.

With zero GDP growth projected for 2009, the output gap is expected to widen considerably. Along with lower commodity prices, this should help disinflation and allow the Riksbank to cut interest rates further, following the two cuts – 100 basis points in total – undertaken in October.[4] However, there is a risk that monetary policy easing will not be as effective as normal, to the extent that lower policy rates do not ease broader monetary and

Figure 1.9. **Productivity should recover to its trend**

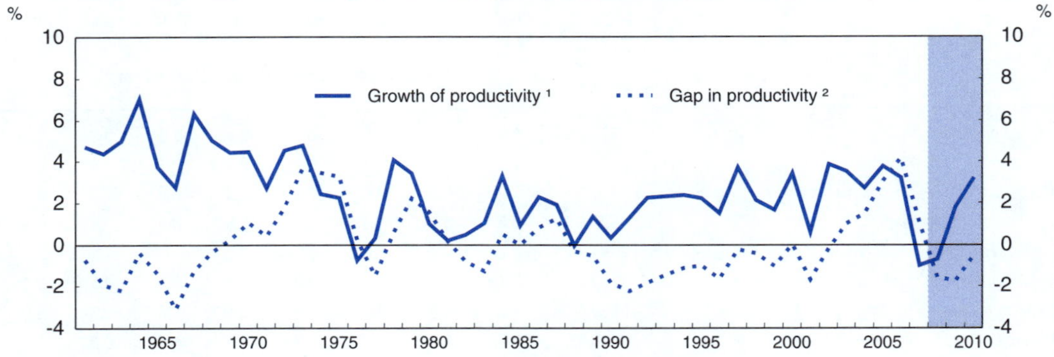

StatLink http://dx.doi.org/10.1787/485107514208

1. Productivity is measured as real GDP divided by the product of total employment by average hours worked per employed person.
2. The productivity gap is calculated by detrending productivity using a Hodrick-Prescott filter and then taking the difference between the actual and the trended series. The difference is expressed as a per cent of the trend.

Source: OECD, Economic Outlook No. 84 database.

financial conditions as much as usual due to the strained situation of financial markets. This would argue for sharper and earlier policy rate reductions than would be the case if financial markets were operating normally. Assuming financial conditions return to normal by late 2009, some increase in interest rates should be warranted in 2010 as growth picks up and the output gap starts to narrow.

The government is set to impart a fiscal stimulus of almost 1% of GDP in the 2009 Budget (Swedish Government, 2008). Two thirds of the easing relates to tax cuts and one third to additional spending (numbers in brackets indicate the lasting net budget impact). The corporate income tax rate will be reduced from 28% to 26.3% (0.21% of GDP) and the general employers' contribution rate from 32.42% to 31.42% (0.22% of GDP). These measures are financed by tighter rules for transfer pricing (0.17% of GDP) and for deduction of corporate interest expenditures (0.21% of GDP). The threshold from where the state income tax is paid will be raised and the in-work tax credit enlarged (0.45% of GDP for the two measures combined). The basic tax deduction will be raised for people aged 65 or above (0.05% of GDP). The employers' contribution rebate for youth will be enlarged (0.02% of GDP). Among the spending initiatives, the largest item is a lasting rise in investment spending on transport infrastructure (0.11% of GDP). Priority will be given to investment in roads, taking account of the impact on other forms of transport. Spending will increase in a number of other areas: research, teacher training and other education measures; new subsidies for environmentally-friendly cars and climate- and energy-related investment and research; healthcare treatment guarantee and improved mental health, which are partly financed by savings from lower replacement rates in disability benefits; police and courts; and measures for arriving immigrants. In addition, eligibility for unemployment benefits will be eased.

The Swedish fiscal policy framework and the recent strong fiscal outcomes means that Sweden is much better placed than many OECD countries to deal with the fallout of the global financial crisis. In recent years, general government net lending has been well above the target of a 1% of GDP surplus on average over the economic cycle. Long-term fiscal pressures are evident in Sweden as in most other OECD countries, but for several reasons they are not as great in Sweden. Even after the easing implied by the 2009 Budget, the

Box 1.2. **Monetary policy and communication in Sweden**

The Riksbank's aim is to maintain price stability, defined as an annual change in the consumer price index of 2%, with a tolerance band of ±1 percentage point. Riksbank forecasts are based on the assumption that the repo rate will evolve such that monetary policy is well balanced – that is, inflation is close to the target two years ahead without excessive fluctuations in inflation or the real economy (Svensson, 2008). The Riksbank explicitly states that monetary policy decisions routinely take into account changes in asset prices and other financial variables. The 2007 *Survey* reviewed Sweden's inflation performance over the last decade and the role of monetary policy (OECD, 2007).

In 2007, the Riksbank became one of only a handful of central banks to publish it own forecasts for the policy rate (three times per year). Soon after announcing this decision, the Riksbank also started to hold a press conference following each monetary policy meeting, rather than just after those resulting in a repo rate change. Also, the minutes from the monetary policy meetings now report the detailed views of each Executive Board member and not merely if they enter a reservation against the majority decision (Rosenberg, 2007). It was subsequently decided that the repo rate forecast would be published following each monetary policy meeting (six times per year).

Soon after the decision to publish the repo rate forecasts, the Riksbank announced that it would be reducing the "signaling" it provided to the market between monetary policy meetings. This meant that speeches by board members would be more focused on the reasons for previous monetary policy decisions and less on future ones (Rosenberg, 2007). However, in May 2008, an updated communication policy was released that promised that the Riksbank would be "more generous" with information between monetary policy meetings, such as commenting on the impact of new statistics on forecasts and discussing the data affecting the policy decision (Riksbank, 2008a).

There has been some market reaction to Riksbank communications, notably in relation to the February 2008 interest rate hike. This rise surprised the markets, mainly because the timing coincided with heightened concerns over international economic and financial market developments. However, the rate rise was consistent with the interest rate path published by the Riksbank in December 2007. On other occasions, the Riksbank has been criticised for the size of changes in the repo rate projection from one publication to the next (Apel and Vredin, 2007).

The publication of the interest rate path should not be viewed in isolation, but rather as a part of the broader communication strategy outlined above, which aims to facilitate the achievement of monetary policy objectives. However, it may take time for market participants and the general public to learn how to interpret the Riksbank's published views. The publication of the expected path of the repo rate bolsters policy credibility, focusing attention away from current rates toward a longer-term assessment of monetary conditions. However, its usefulness may be diminished in periods such as the current financial crisis, when rapid economic and financial developments mean that published projections of the future repo rate may be quickly out of date. The publication of the minutes of the Executive Board's monetary policy meetings, spelling out the views of each Board member, helps elucidate alternative scenarios and the risks around the outlook. In the same vein, the most recent change to the communication policy helps in that it provides the Riksbank with more scope to elaborate on the risks and possible future developments in speeches. This should lead to a more continuous assessment and so reduce the likelihood of surprises.

government considers that longer-run fiscal sustainability is safeguarded, although an exact assessment is difficult to make because the fiscal balance often worsens more during downturns than would be expected using standard cyclical-adjustment techniques. Moreover, while the spending increases in the 2009 Budget appear affordable, they reduce the scope for further tax cuts. Even if many of the new spending measures should be beneficial for longer-term growth, it would have been better to finance these priority initiatives with savings in other spending areas.

Meanwhile, a more expansionary monetary policy and strong automatic stabilisers weaken the rationale for additional discretionary fiscal stimulus to support growth. An anticipated return to more normal conditions in financial markets, further monetary easing and the already announced fiscal stimulus are expected to spur a recovery in economic growth in late 2009 and into 2010. However, if the economic situation deteriorates further and additional fiscal stimulus is deemed necessary, it should take the form of temporary measures or should continue the government's recent approach of targeting measures to boost the economy's growth potential. In this case, priority should be given to further income tax cuts (Chapter 3).

Medium-term assessment and key challenges

Potential GDP growth picked up from 2½ per cent in the second half of the 1990s to around 3% annually in the first half of the 2000s. It is expected to remain strong, at around 2¾ per cent annually, during the second half of this decade buoyed by strong working-age population growth and the effects of recent labour market reforms. Between 2011 and 2015, it is projected to slow to around 2¼ per cent per annum – still above the OECD average – primarily due to slower working-age population growth (Table 1.2). Accordingly, the medium-term reference scenario is for growth in real GDP per capita to slip from around 2¼ per cent between 2006 and 2010 to around 1¾ per cent in 2011-15 while growth in real GDP per head of working-age population would be stable at around 2%.

Table 1.2. **Potential output growth and its components**

Annual average % growth

	Potential real GDP growth	Potential labour productivity growth	Potential employment growth	Components of potential employment[1]		
				Trend participation rate	Working-age population	Structural unemployment
2006-10	2.8	2.1	0.7	–0.2	0.7	0.1
2011-15	2.2	2.1	0.1	–0.2	0.2	0.0

Note: Potential real GDP is calculated using a production function approach with capital and labour inputs, as outlined in Beffy *et al.* (2006). In this table, growth in trend average hours worked is captured in potential labour productivity growth along with capital deepening and total factor productivity.

1. Percentage point contributions to potential employment growth. The contributions do not necessarily add to the total due to an adjustment to account for differences between National Accounts and Labour Force Survey employment measures.

Source: Updated from *OECD Economic Outlook No. 83.*

The remainder of this chapter discusses the main drivers of potential GDP growth over the coming years to highlight the key challenges facing the economy and opportunities for lifting income growth. This assessment points to progress made on recommendations from previous Surveys and to the key issues to be discussed in subsequent chapters of this *Survey*. The methodology for assessing medium-term potential is based on a

OECD ECONOMIC SURVEYS: SWEDEN – ISBN 978-92-64-05423-3 – © OECD 2008

decomposition of GDP into labour supply and productivity, where labour supply is further broken down to take into account the foreseeable developments in working-age population, participation rate, structural unemployment and average hours worked (Beffy *et al.*, 2006).

Labour supply

Swedish employment rates are high, but the average number of hours worked annually by each person employed is low. Labour supply, measured as total hours worked per person by the working-age population, is therefore close to the OECD average. Most of the difference between the Swedish and the OECD average employment-to-population ratio is explained by higher participation of women across all age groups. The share of women working is higher than in any other OECD country, except Iceland, for women aged 25-54 as well as for women aged 55-64. For men aged 55-64, labour market participation is also relatively high. Moreover, the problems of early retirement draining labour supply are less pronounced in Sweden than elsewhere: over half of the 60-64 year old women are working, compared to just a quarter in the median OECD country. Meanwhile, average hours worked are well below the OECD average, notably due to longer holidays and other leave reducing the number of weeks worked per year.

About 1 million people, or almost one fifth of the working-age population, are living on income support. A key part of the government's policy programme over the past couple of years has been implementing measures to sustainably increase employment in order to boost income growth and keep up the overall level of welfare services. Key elements of this policy approach have included: the introduction (and subsequent expansion) of an in-work tax credit; tapering the unemployment benefit replacement rate as the period of unemployment gets longer; reductions in employer social security contributions for older workers, younger workers and people who have been out of work for an extended period (employer contributions are waived for the same length of time as the person was out of work); and tightening of administrative arrangements for access to sickness and disability benefits. In the 2009 Budget, the government estimates that the labour-market and tax measures introduced in 2007-08 will, *ceteris paribus*, raise potential employment by 1.8% in 2011, with measures introduced in the 2009 Budget boosting the total effect to 2.2% in 2011 and 2.8% in the long run (Swedish government, 2008). Two thirds of this effect results from tax cuts and one third from changes to unemployment benefits, sickness and labour market policies. Three quarters of the total effect is expected to come in the form of higher labour force participation, and only one quarter in the form of lower structural unemployment.

Population dynamics

Growth in the working-age population is expected to decline in coming years from the relatively high rate observed since the turn of the century. In the absence of any other change, this would imply slower growth in potential labour supply and therefore potential GDP growth. There is little policy can do to boost population growth in the short term, apart from increasing immigration.[5] However, immigrants are generally less well attached to the labour force than native Swedes (Box 1.3). Hence, policies or other changes that increase labour force participation or hours worked are required to achieve income growth closer to the rates experienced over the past decade.

Box 1.3. **Immigrants' labour market integration**

Immigration into Sweden has increased considerably since 2005, by almost 90% in net terms in 2006 and a further 6% in 2007. This reflects sharply higher humanitarian immigration but possibly also cyclically-strong demand for labour. Employment rates for foreign-born people in general are around the OECD average, although the gap between the employment rate of foreign and native-born people is amongst the highest in the OECD (OECD, 2008a).

Around three quarters of all immigrants in Sweden are refugees and persons coming to Sweden for family reasons, and many find labour market integration difficult. A large share of the recent increase in immigration is attributable to asylum seekers from Iraq, for whom Sweden has been the principal destination country. The gap in labour market outcomes between immigrants and Swedes is largest for immigrants from Africa and the Middle East. For this group, the employment rate is almost 30 percentage points lower, the participation rate almost 20 percentage points lower, and the unemployment rate almost 20 percentage points higher than for native Swedes (OECD, 2007).

In order to improve the employment prospects of immigrants, the 2007 *Survey* recommended allowing lower initial wages and stronger earnings progression during their first years of employment, introducing a special benefit regime for youth without children (aimed at all youth but likely to disproportionately benefit young immigrants), improving the provision of language training, developing procedures to avoid discrimination in employment based on name or ethnicity and speeding up asylum decisions (OECD, 2007).

Since then, subsidised employment arrangements have been introduced for asylum seekers who have received residence permits, quota refugees and their close relatives for the first 18 months after receiving a residence permit. A new labour market scheme known as "Step-in jobs" was introduced in July 2007, offering possibilities for new arrivals to combine language training with part-time employment. In early 2008, measures were announced to improve the training programme "Swedish for Immigrants" (SFI), including skills-enhancement for teachers, national tests, clearer goals, and a three-year time limit for SFI training. There are plans to introduce a special bonus for migrants achieving language proficiency in a stipulated time, as well as a bonus for municipalities when immigrants complete SFI or get into employment within 12 months after settlement. Anonymised job applications are currently being tested in the public sector. Several of the general labour market measures benefit immigrants disproportionately; in New-start Jobs, for example, one third of all participants are immigrants.

There has also been strong growth in work and study-related immigration since 2005, in particular from Poland. This may be more related to the strong labour market, although since large-scale immigration from new EU member states is a relatively new phenomenon, it is difficult to tell what proportion might be regarded as potentially long-term residents. Careful assessment of labour market demand at regular intervals is needed to ensure that there is an adequate provision of work permits and of entry possibilities to satisfy labour market requirements. Approval of single employer requests for work permits can be time-consuming and idiosyncratic (OECD, 2008a). It is therefore encouraging that the Swedish government is adopting a new approach in which residence and work permits will be issued based on employers' own assessment of their needs, rather than a Public Employment Service ruling about whether the right qualifications are already available in Sweden, other EU/EEA countries or Switzerland. Time limits for residence and work permits will be extended, so an initial two years can be prolonged to four if the individual still has a valid work contract. After four years, a permanent residence permit can be granted. In addition, asylum seekers who have found employment while their applications are being processed may be given a chance to apply for a work permit directly, meaning that a person whose asylum application has been rejected does not need to return home to apply for a permit which is likely to be granted.

Labour force participation

Sweden's overall labour force participation rate is amongst the highest in the OECD and well above the OECD average.[6] Several factors are likely to affect it going forward:

- Assuming constant participation rates by age cohort, changes in the age structure of the population imply that the participation rate will fall between 2007 and 2015. This is because the population aged 65 to 74, which has lower participation rates, is growing much faster than the rest of the population.
- The rising share of foreign-born people in the working-age population will also put downward pressure on the participation rate since, historically, foreign-born people have had lower participation rates than native Swedes.
- Recent policy initiatives (in particular the in-work tax credit and tightening of eligibility for labour market programmes) are expected to raise the participation rate.

The net impact of these forces is that the trend participation rate is likely to be lower by 2015 than it was in 2007. Demographic effects will subtract between one and two percentage points from the trend participation rate and policy initiatives are assumed to increase it by one percentage point. The key areas for potential further gains are in better integration of immigrants into the labour market and further reductions in the inflow into disability pension entitlement (Box 1.4).

Unemployment

The Swedish unemployment rate has moved relatively closely in line with the OECD average over the current decade and in 2007 was just above it. The variation in unemployment rates between people with different levels of educational attainment are not as marked in Sweden as in many other OECD countries. The incidence of long-term unemployment is fairly low: 27% of the unemployed remain so for over six months and 13% for over a year, compared with OECD averages of 43% and 29% respectively (OECD, 2008b).

Estimated structural unemployment, defined as the rate of unemployment consistent with stable inflation (the NAIRU), has fallen gradually over the past decade (Figure 1.11). It has been assumed to decline further between 2007 and 2011, reflecting *inter alia* the new policy of gradually reducing unemployment benefits over the entitlement period and the in-work tax credit. The government's estimates of the expected reduction in the structural unemployment rate due to these measures, and those introduced in the 2009 Budget, is broadly in line with the medium-term reference scenario presented above. Further details on data used to estimate the structural unemployment rate in Figure 1.11 are presented in Annex 1.A2.

While overall unemployment is only a little above the OECD average, youth unemployment is a more serious cause for concern. In 2007, 19% of the 15-24 year olds participating in the labour market were unemployed, almost three times more than in Denmark, Iceland, the Netherlands and Norway. Moreover, among OECD countries, the ratio between the unemployment rates of young and prime-age adults is less favourable to youth only in Luxembourg and Iceland. Even excluding full-time students, the unemployment rate for 15-24 year olds stood at 14.3% in 2007. Chapter 3 looks in detail at the link between youth unemployment and educational attainment and considers policy options to improve educational outcomes and youth's employment prospects.

Box 1.4. **Sickness and disability**

The share of the working-age population receiving disability pensions or on sickness absence is very high by international standards. Sickness absence has come down markedly from the exceptional heights reached in 2002, but it is difficult to know how durable these improvements may be. In contrast to previous labour market upturns, the rate of sickness absence has continued to fall despite the improvement in unemployment in recent years, suggesting that a large part of the fall may last. The inflow into disability pensions has also declined markedly, leading to an overall reduction in the stock of disability pensioners as a proportion of the working-age population (Figure 1.10). However, while disability benefit-inflows have fallen for most age groups, they have risen sharply for youth, which could have lasting effects if these young people remain in the disability-benefit system. A large share of the increase in young disability-pension recipients relates to mental health problems.

Figure 1.10. **Sickness absence and disability pensions**

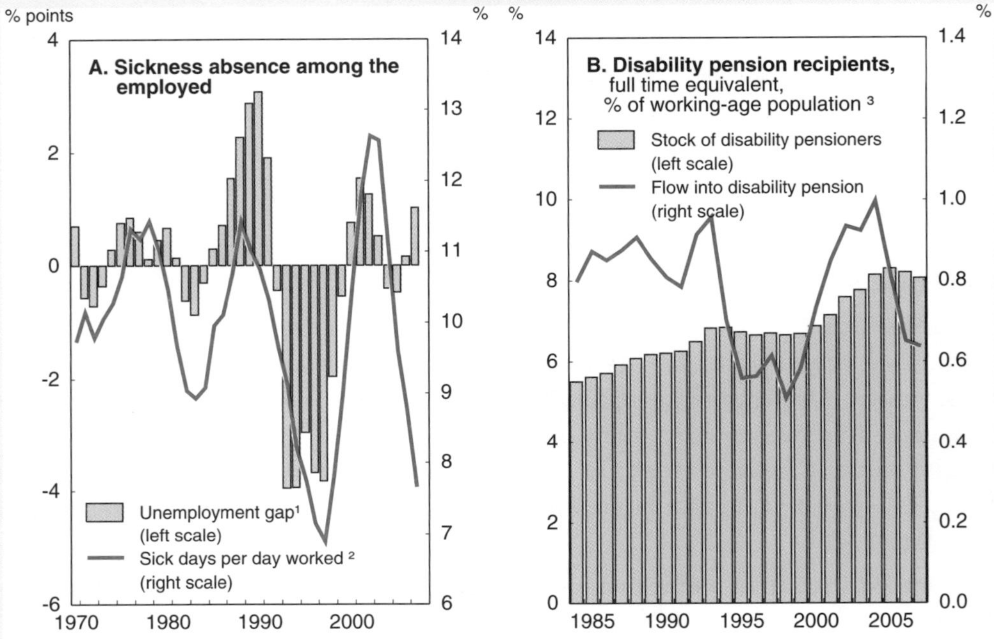

StatLink http://dx.doi.org/10.1787/485163177125

1. The unemployment gap is the difference between the structural unemployment rate (NAIRU) and the actual unemployment rate.
2. Full-time equivalent of total sick days as a per cent of total days worked in a year.
3. The working age population used in this figure covers 16 to 64 year olds.

Source: Swedish Social Insurance Agency; OECD *Analytical database*.

The 2007 *Survey* recommended continuation of improvements in the administration of social insurance offices and procedures for medical assessment; limits on the duration of sickness benefits and careful monitoring of partial disability benefits to ensure that they are not being used as an income top-up for part-time workers. Measures have been put in place over a number of years, including further measures in the 2008 budget bills. These measures include a focus on planning return to work for people on sickness absence and on an assessment of the ability to return to work in the previous or another role. The size of the benefit has been reduced for people who remain on sickness benefits over 12 months. Reduced employer social-security contributions have also been introduced for employers hiring people who have been receiving sickness benefit, rehabilitation benefit, or sickness or activity compensation for at least a year (Annex 1.A1).

There is also a link between benefit fraud, reported hours worked and income tax payments, where social norms on the appropriateness of claiming sickness and disability benefits may have slipped over time (Lindbeck, 2008). Chapter 4 discusses the links between high taxes, social benefits and combating non-reported economic activity.

Figure 1.11. **Actual and structural unemployment rates**[1]

As per cent of labour force

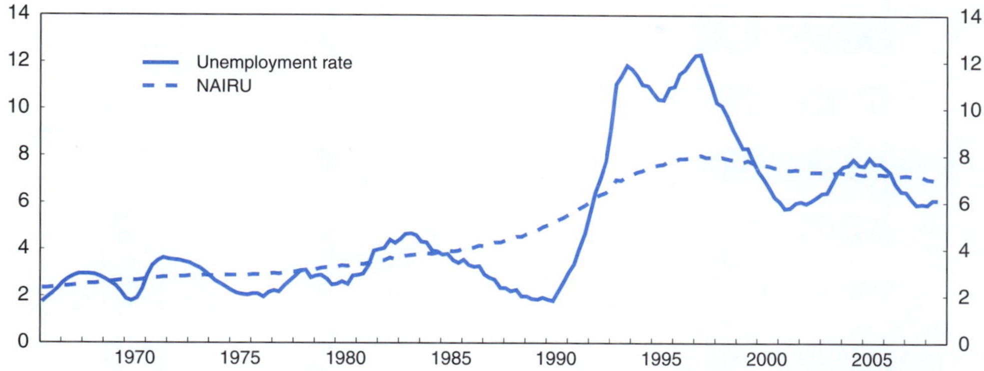

StatLink http://dx.doi.org/10.1787/485204600638

1. The structural unemployment rate is the non-accelerating rate of unemployment (NAIRU), estimated according to the methodology outlined in Gianella *et al.* (2008).

Source: OECD, *Analytical database.*

Hours worked

As noted above, average hours worked in Sweden are well below the OECD average, notably because longer holidays and other leave reduce the number of weeks worked per year. Part-time workers work considerably longer weekly hours than in other countries, but absence from work is extensive for both full- and part-time employees. The number of public holidays and vacation weeks is higher than in many other countries. Moreover, the average Swedish employee spends more weeks in maternity/parental and sick leave. Over the next few years, the trend in hours worked is likely to be boosted by the government's labour market reforms. The in-work tax credit is likely to increase labour force participation but may lower average hours worked through income effects. Changes to sickness insurance arrangements should help to further reduce sickness absence. A cumulative increase of about one percentage point in trend average hours worked is assumed between 2007 and 2013.

Across countries, there is a negative correlation between marginal tax rates and average hours worked. This may reflect a number of factors, but when controlling for employment and the average tax level for the whole economy, the marginal tax wedge is an important determinant of average hours worked by women. Chapter 4 discusses the relationship between taxes and hours worked and argues for continued focus on reducing the high marginal tax rate on labour income to help expand overall labour supply.

Productivity

Over the longer run, productivity is likely to be the main source of sustained income growth, since ultimately increases in labour supply are limited by individuals' preferences over the choice between work and leisure. As mentioned above, the number of people living on income support suggests that Sweden is still a long way from exhausting gains in additional labour supply. However, the fundamental importance of productivity growth means that policies to raise productivity should remain a priority.

Productivity growth in Sweden has been strong over the past decade and a half and appears to have been driven almost entirely by gains within each sector rather than reallocation of resources from low- to high-productivity sectors (Figure 1.12). In Sweden,

Figure 1.12. **Shift-share analysis of labour productivity**

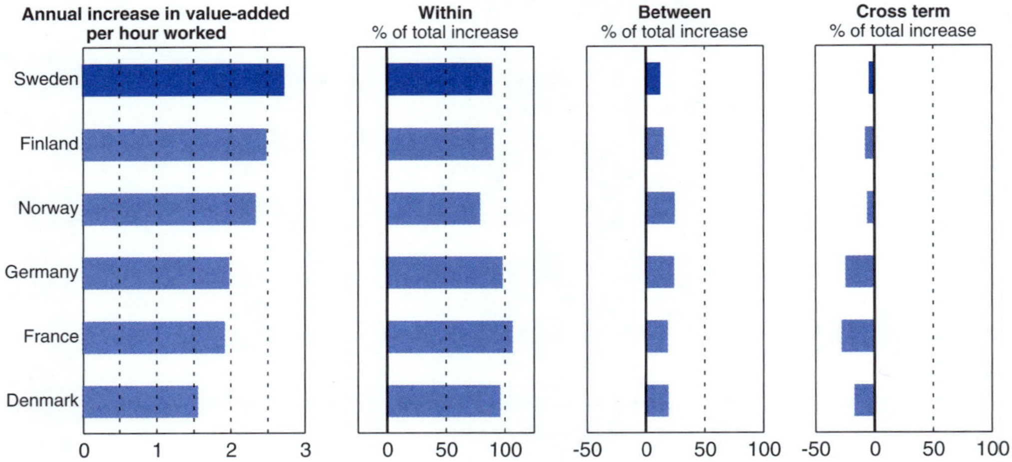

StatLink http://dx.doi.org/10.1787/485207086167

Source: OECD STAN *database* 2008.

between 1993 and 2005, the reallocations of labour between sectors were small. The largest change was a 3-percentage-point increase in the share of labour devoted to the finance, insurance, real estate and business services sector. The finance sector has above-average productivity so this resource shift boosted aggregate productivity. Similarly, there was a 1.5-percentage-point fall in the share of labour dedicated to agriculture, hunting, forestry and fishery, which has below-average productivity. These changes accounted for only one tenth of total productivity growth. The main sector contributing to productivity growth was manufacturing.

During the early and mid-1990s, a process of regulatory reform was initiated across the OECD area with Sweden being a frontrunner in several sectors at that time. A number of important services were liberalised and, along with increased market openness and integration associated with EU accession and the gradual deepening of the internal market, these reforms have paid off in terms of solid growth. Although the first generation of reforms during the 1990s did boost productivity, major challenges remain and some sectors of the economy are still subject to various barriers that stifle competition and hence innovation. A new momentum for reform is therefore needed to sustain future growth, as argued in the previous *Survey*.

Human capital

In addition to renewed regulatory reform, improvements in the education system can bring new momentum to Swedish productivity growth. Several recent studies suggest that higher education levels have been an important contributor to Swedish GDP growth over the last decade or so. The proportion of the workforce with post-secondary education rose strongly between the mid-1990s and the mid-2000s, with 28% of the workforce having a post-secondary education in 2005, up from 20% in 1997. The Swedish National Institute for Economic Research disaggregated labour inputs by gender, age and level of educational attainment and found that 0.3 percentage points of the yearly increase in labour productivity in the business sector between 1997 and 2005 can be explained by an increase in the quality of labour. This reflects the change in the composition of the labour force over this period towards groups with higher levels of productivity and an increase in the share of employees with a post-secondary education (NIER, 2008a). A broadly similar result has been derived using EU KLEMS data, which allow decomposition of the growth in value added into the contribution from changes in labour composition (a shift in the share of hours worked from low- to high-skilled labour), growth in total hours worked and ICT and non-ICT capital input growth (Van Ark *et al.*, 2007). This shows that, between 1995 and 2004, the shift in labour composition was an important contributor to growth in value added, particularly in the electrical machinery, post and communications sector, where it contributed 0.7 percentage points, but also in the finance and business services sector, where it contributed 0.5 percentage points. Of the countries where comparable data are available, only the United Kingdom recorded a larger contribution to value added growth from higher skill composition (Table 1.3).

Table 1.3. **Growth in market economy gross value added and its components**

Average annual volume growth rates, 1995-2004

	Growth in gross value added, market economy	Contribution to growth in GVA from				
		Total hours worked	Labour composition	IT capital	Non-IT capital	MFP
United Kingdom	3.3	0.4	0.5	1.0	0.5	0.9
France	2.5	0.4	0.4	0.5	0.5	0.7
Hungary	4.3	0.6	0.4	0.6	0.4	2.2
Japan	0.7	–0.7	0.4	0.3	0.3	0.4
Spain	3.6	2.2	0.4	0.5	1.4	–0.9
Sweden	**3.3**	**0.2**	**0.4**	**0.7**	**0.6**	**1.5**
Denmark	2.3	0.6	0.3	1.3	0.5	–0.5
United States	3.7	0.3	0.3	0.8	0.6	1.6
Austria	2.6	0.3	0.2	0.6	0.3	1.2
Belgium	2.4	0.5	0.2	0.8	0.6	0.3
Czech Republic	2.3	–0.5	0.2	0.8	1.7	0.1
The Netherlands	2.8	0.5	0.2	0.7	0.3	1.0
Finland	4.4	0.9	0.1	0.6	0.2	2.6
Germany	1.0	–0.5	0.1	0.5	0.5	0.4
Italy	1.4	0.9	0.1	0.2	0.9	–0.7

Source: Van Ark *et al.* (2007).

NIER projections assume that the rising trend of enrolment in post-secondary education does not continue in coming years, which would imply it cannot be relied upon to further boost income growth. However, since older persons in the labour force have lower rates of post-secondary educational attainment, their retirement will raise the average educational attainment of the workforce. This effect will contribute 0.1% per year to business-sector productivity growth between 2006 and 2020. Increasing the number of students may reduce the potential pool of employees and reduce value-added in the short term. However, in the long term, the increase in labour quality associated with extra education raises productivity and value added (NIER, 2008a).

This type of analysis does not allow for the impact of the choice of subjects on youth's employment prospects. It also assumes that there is no mismatch in the demand and supply of workers with different skills, so the additional supply of higher-educated workers does not result in a reduction in wages for this group. This is akin to assuming that industry structure will change to suit the supply of additional skilled labour that is produced by the education system. Making the most out of gains in human capital requires education choices that adapt to market demand for labour. Since additional human capital takes time to acquire, this calls for more information about current and future demands for skills available to students when they make their study choices. Swedish students currently start later and take longer to complete tertiary studies than their counterparts in neighbouring countries. Starting and completing studies earlier would raise the returns to education by increasing the number of income-producing years. Improving the quality of education would also increase the returns to education. Issues related to educational subject choice, the speed of completion of studies and the quality of education in Sweden are discussed further in Chapter 4.

Privatisation

The government's privatisation programme, involving the sale of some SEK 50 billion (€ 5.3 billion) of state-owned enterprises per year between 2007 and 2011, is welcome since there is evidence that market liberalisation and privatisation increases firm-level productivity and raises investment. There is also evidence of a macroeconomic link through the impact of market liberalisation and privatisation on capital deepening and multifactor productivity growth. Key lessons from this research are that privatisation is most effective when combined with reforms boosting competition in the market in which the privatised firm operates. Recent financial market turmoil may require some deals to be postponed, but down the road, privatisation should continue. Further progress should proceed alongside consideration of competition and regulation issues in each sector, particularly those where the State has a strong presence. The links between privatisation and productivity, as well as the government's privatisation programme, are discussed further in Chapter 5.

In addition to the large state-owned enterprise sector, there are around 300 municipal housing corporations owned by their respective municipalities. These corporations rent housing to the general public with the rents set by agreement with local tenants unions based on historic cost taking into account the age composition of the housing stock. Private sector rents are set in the same way and are often linked to public sector rents. The regulation of the housing market was extensively reviewed in the 2007 *Survey*. A key recommendation was that market conditions should be allowed to have more impact on rent determination. Recent proposals have taken steps in this direction (Box 1.5).

Conclusions

Provided the existing sound macroeconomic policy frameworks are maintained, there is little reason to suspect that the current global financial crisis and economic downturn will have a lasting adverse impact on the performance of the Swedish economy or its relative international standing. Recent gains in employment should be consolidated with further efforts to strengthen the labour market. Ensuring that budget responds to the downturn in a way that is consistent with sustainable long-term fiscal policy is a key challenge (Chapter 2). Tackling the most distortive elements of the tax system, including high marginal income tax rates, is an opportunity presented by the strong fiscal position (Chapter 3). Improving the school-to-work transition and getting the most out of human capital accumulation will also be important to boost productivity and sustain robust income growth (Chapter 4). Further income gains are also likely from the competition benefits of further privatisation (Chapter 5). The following chapters address these key challenges in turn.

Box 1.5. **Housing market deregulation**

The lack of market-determined rents means that rental housing is allocated via queuing, extensive search and, in some cases, black market trades. Some households wait up to ten years for their preferred property and some are forced into home ownership when they would prefer to rent. The 2007 *Survey* recommended allowing rents to be determined by market conditions (in particular for private rental housing), increasing competition in the construction sector and improving the land-planning process. Since 2006, rents for newly-constructed dwellings have been exempted from the review process which tied private sector rents to those set in the public municipal housing corporations. While this was a step in the right direction, without broader reform to rent regulation this measure may have made new dwelling investment more risky by increasing the disparity in rents for new and old dwellings.

In early 2008, two governmental reports were released examining the role of rent regulation and municipal housing corporations in light of EU legislation on state aid (SOU, 2008a and 2008b). They recommended removing the link between private rents and rents in the public sector. Under this proposal, the rent review process for private rentals, which previously considered the rent increases in public rental housing in the same municipality, should allow rent increases or decreases of up to 5% if there are substantial and persistent shortages or surpluses of properties in the municipality. In addition, they recommended that the rent review process should be allowed to consider rent increases in neighbouring municipalities if they are part of the same urban area. The report considered alternatives to the current form of municipal housing corporations to ensure consistency with EU rules on state aid and competition. One alternative would involve municipal housing corporations operating on a "business-oriented model", pursing the maximisation of long-term profits. Presumably, if this model were implemented, it would lead the municipal housing corporations to seek rents more in line with market prices in areas where there are supply shortages. In mid-2008, a third governmental report suggested a number of simplifications of land-planning and construction authorisations (SOU, 2008c).

Increasing the possibilities for owning an apartment is another important issue. Currently, a form of tenant-ownership exists where individual persons own a share of a cooperative which in turn owns the apartment building as a whole. The ownership right can be used as collateral for mortgage loans and can also be sold at market price, although the cooperative may reserve the right to approve the buyer. However, the ownership right is limited in the sense that the apartment cannot be sublet for more than a short period. The 2007 Survey recommended allowing owner-occupied apartments as in other OECD countries. It is therefore most welcome that, in November 2008, the government presented legislation to this effect. If adopted, owner-occupied apartments can be created via new construction from May 2009 and the government also intends to prepare legislation allowing conversion of existing properties.

The 2007 *Survey* also recommended increasing housing taxation to make it more neutral with respect to other assets. Instead, the government has cut housing taxation by replacing the national housing tax with a municipal government charge which is a fixed amount (with a limit in relation to assessed value) and increased the capital gains tax on private dwellings by 2 percentage points (Chapter 3).

Notes

1. Technological innovations make it possible to produce ever bigger volumes of ICT equipment, and this is correctly measured as GDP volume growth and thereby productivity growth. But the mirror image of productivity growth is that prices of ICT equipment continue to fall. The consequence is that aggregate real income grows less rapidly than real GDP, because the prices of the average goods and services consumed and invested in Sweden do not have a similar downward trend. In national account aggregates, this is reflected in downward-trending terms of trade, as export prices fall relative to import prices. The effect has gained potency as high-tech production expanded. Since 1999, it accounts for a steady difference of half a percentage point between annual growth rates of real GDP and a measure correcting for the terms-of-trade loss, sometimes referred to as "command GDP", as illustrated in the previous *Survey*. The term "command GDP", which has sometimes been used in the literature, conveys that the terms-of-trade adjustment leads to a measure of the volume of consumption and investment that GDP can buy or "give command over".
2. Open economy forces and human capital were key to strong Swedish growth from 1870 to 1970. From relative poverty in the mid-19th century, incomes in Sweden caught up rapidly with those in the United Kingdom, continental Europe and the United States between 1870 and 1910, and most of this catch-up can be ascribed to increased integration in the international economy, not least in the form of capital inflows, helped by comparatively strong literacy (O'Rourke and Williamson, 1995).
3. Recent income tax cuts and reductions in unemployment benefits may have weakened the automatic stabilisers, but this has not yet been quantified.
4. On 9 June 2008, the Riksbank announced that it would no longer focus on the CPIX measure of inflation in discussing monetary policy. CPIX excludes from the CPI the effects of mortgage expenditure and indirect taxes and subsidies and has been used to show inflation developments aside from the direct impact of the Riksbank's own policy actions. The key reason for de-emphasising the CPIX is that the Riksbank expects a systematic difference between the CPI and CPIX for some time in the future. This is primarily due to the fact that mortgage interest expenditure in the CPI is based partly on a house price index that only captures house price increases when houses change hands. The long period of high house price growth (averaging more than 8% per year since the mid-1990s) means that the CPI will reflect strong growth in mortgage interest expenditure in coming years regardless of the path of interest rates (Wickman-Parak, 2008). It has been argued that the move from the CPIX to the CPI will mean that monetary policy will be tighter than would otherwise have been the case, since the CPI is expected to be approximately 0.3 percentage points higher than the CPIX in coming years (National Institute for Economic Research, 2008b).
5. To the extent that policy could raise fertility, this would increase population growth, but likely reduce the labour force participation rate as parents take time out of work to raise their children.
6. International comparisons based on a working-age population of 15-64 for most countries and 16-64 for Sweden show that Sweden has a participation rate of about 80% compared to the OECD average of about 70%. The new methods for measuring the labour force in Sweden, discussed in Annex 1.A2, cover the age group 15-74 and result in a participation rate of around 70%.

Bibliography

Andersen, T., B. Holmström, S. Honkapohja, S. Korkman, H. Söderström and J. Vartiainen (2008), *The Nordic Model: Embracing Globalisation and Sharing Risks*, Taloustieto Oy, Helsinki.

Apel, M. and A. Vredin (2007), "Monetary-Policy Communication: The Experience of the Swedish Riksbank", *Czech Journal of Economics and Finance*, Vol. 57, No. 11-12.

Beffy, P.-O., P. Ollivaud, P. Richardson and F. Sédillot (2006), "New OECD Methods for Supply-Side and Medium-Term Assessments: A Capital Services Approach", OECD Economics Department Working Paper No. 482.

Bjørnskov, C. (2008), "Social Trust and Fractionalisation: A Possible Reinterpretation", *European Sociological Review*, Vol. 24, No. 3.

Borg, A. (2008), *Re-establishing the Swedish Model*, Presentation at the Economists Conference on Sweden, Stockholm, 5 March.

Finansinspektionen (2008a), "Finansinspektionen Stress Tests Large Banks", 15 October.

Finansinspektionen (2008b), "Finanssektorns stabilitet" (The Finance Sector's Stability), 2008:18, 15 October.

Gianella, C., I. Koske, E. Rusticelli and O. Chatal (2008), "What Drives the NAIRU: Evidence from a Panel of OECD Countries", OECD *Economics Department Working Paper*, No. 649.

Girouard, N. and C. André (2005), "Measuring Cyclically-Adjusted Budget Balances for OECD Countries", OECD *Economics Department Working Paper* No. 434.

Institute for Management and Development (2008), *World Competitiveness Yearbook 2008*, CD-Rom version, Institute for Management and Development, Lausanne.

International Monetary Fund (2008), "Sweden: 2008 Article IV Consultation – Staff Report", IMF Country Report No. 08/278, August.

Johansson, M. (2006), "Inkomst och ojämlikhet i Sverige 1951-2002" (Income and inequality in Sweden 1951-2002), Institute for Futures Studies Working Paper, Stockholm.

Lindbeck, A. (2008), "Prospects for the Welfare State", Seminar Paper, No. 755, Institute for International Economic Studies, Stockholm University.

National Institute for Economic Research (2008a), "Hours, Capital and Technology – What Matters Most?", *Occasional Studies*, No. 18, Stockholm.

National Institute for Economic Research (2008b), *The Swedish Economy*, June.

OECD (2006), *Society at a Glance: OECD Social Indicators*, Paris.

OECD (2007), *OECD Economic Surveys: Sweden*, Paris.

OECD (2008a), *International Migration Outlook – SOPEMI 2008*, Paris.

OECD (2008b), *OECD Employment Outlook 2008*, Paris.

O'Rourke, K. and J. Williamson (1995), "Open Economy Forces and Late 19th Century Scandinavian Catch-up", NBER Working Paper No. 5112.

Pettersson, T. and T. Pettersson (2007), "Lifetime Redistribution Through Taxes, Transfers and Non-Cash Benefits", in Harding, A. and A. Gupta (eds.), *Modeling Our Future – Population Ageing, Social Security and Taxation,* Elsevier.

Riksbank (2008a), "Updated Communication Policy for the Riksbank", Press release, 7 May, *www.riksbank.com/templates/Page.aspx?id=27931*.

Riksbank (2008b), *Financial Stability Report,* 2008: 1, June, Stockholm.

Riksbank (2008c), "Minutes of the Executive Board meeting No. 7, 2 July 2008", 16 July, *www.riksbank.com/templates/Page.aspx?id=28523*.

Riksbank (2008d), *Monetary Policy Report,* 2008:2, October, Stockholm.

Rosenberg, I. (2007), "Changes in Monetary Policy Communication", Press release, 11 May, *www.riksbank.com/templates/Page.aspx?id=24741*.

SOU (2008a), *EU, allmännyttan och hyrorna* (EU, public housing and rents), Swedish Government Official Reports, No. 2008:38.

SOU (2008b), *Frågor om hyra och bostadsrätt* (Issues of rental accommodation), Swedish Government Official Reports, No. 2008:47.

SOU (2008c), *Bygg – helt enkelt* (Build – simple as that), Swedish Government Official Reports, No. 2008:68.

Svensson, L. (2008), "Transparency under Flexible Inflation Targeting: Experiences and Challenges", Presented at the Riksbank Conference "Refining Monetary Policy: Transparency and Real Stability", Stockholm, 5-6 September.

Swedish Government (2008), *Budget Bill 2009*.

Swedish National Debt Office (2008), "Swedish National Debt Office assumes control over Carnegie", Press Release, 10 November.

Van Ark, B., M. O'Mahony, and G. Ypma (2007), "The EU KLEMS Productivity Report: Issue 1 March 2007".

Wickman-Parak, B. (2008), "The Riksbank's Inflation Target", Speech delivered at Swedbank, Stockholm.

World Economic Forum (2008), *Global Competitiveness Report 2008-2009*.

ANNEX 1.A1

Progress in structural reform

This table reviews action taken on recommendations from previous *Surveys*. Many of the recommendations were made in the 2007 *Survey*, but key recommendations made earlier are also included. Recommendations made in this *Survey* are shown in the boxes at the end of each chapter.

Recommendations made in previous Surveys	Action taken since the latest *Survey* (February 2007)
LABOUR MARKETS AND INTEGRATION OF IMMIGRANTS	
Increase job search obligations by those receiving unemployment and similar benefits, and use moderate sanctions to support these requirements. Ensure adequate coaching and job search assistance for those at the margin of the labour market.	A Job and Development Guarantee was introduced in June 2007, involving three phases: 1. intensified jobseeker activities, including coaching; 2. offering access to a range of labour market programmes, including work training, workplacement, subsidised employment and skills enhancement; 3. after 450 days, full-time community service employment.
Reduce the generosity of part-time unemployment benefits.	The number of benefit days that can be used in case of part-time unemployment has been limited to 75.
Better adapt the welfare model and labour market institutions to the increased diversity associated with immigration. Undertake general reform or targeted measures to avoid unemployment and inactivity traps: social assistance and housing benefits for families with numerous children seem particularly problematic.	The possibility of a general social insurance review is occasionally discussed, but no action has been taken yet.
Introduce a special benefit regime for youth without children, coupled with enhanced training offers. Even if all irrespective of origin are treated equally, it would benefit immigrants and their offspring disproportionately.	A Job Guarantee for Young People was introduced from December 2007, providing support and increased incentives for unemployed youth to obtain work or engage in further education.
Allow, in collective agreements, for lower initial wages followed by stronger progression during the first years of employment; this would make it easier for immigrants to get established on the labour market while improving their knowledge of the Swedish language and other local conditions.	As a substitute for wage differentiation, subsidised "Step-in Jobs" have been introduced for asylum seekers who have received residence permits, quota refugees and close relative immigrants during the first 18 months after receiving a residence permit.
Ease job security rules for regular contracts, and consider in particular if the criteria for what is fair dismissal are too strict in order to reduce the risk for employers hiring immigrants and others whose capabilities can be difficult to gauge. Abolish the last-in-first-out rule so employees risk less by taking another job.	The duration of temporary contracts has been extended, but this has not been paralleled by any easing of the rules for regular contracts (Chapter 3). Firms with less than ten employees have been exempted from the last-in-first-out rule for the first couple of layoffs.
Improve language training for newly-arrived migrants *inter alia* by improving teachers' capabilities and integrating language training on the workplace. Introduce early childhood action for migrants' children with language problems.	In early 2008, improvements were announced to the "Swedish for Immigrants" initiative, including skills-enhancement for SFI teachers, national tests, clearer goals for SFI and a three-year time limit for SFI education.
Pilot more non-bureaucratic procedures for filling job vacancies in large as well as small firms in ways that avoid possible discrimination based on name and ethnicity.	Anonymised applications are currently being piloted in the public sector.
Shorten the time of reaching a final decision on asylum applications so that full economic integration can start earlier.	Two investigations have been initiated since February 2007. The first evaluates the new organisational framework for handling appealed asylum and citizenship cases. The responsibility for such decisions was transferred to the regional migration courts in Stockholm, Malmö, and Gothenburg in 2006. The second investigation regards how the reception of asylum-seekers can be improved, thereby making the asylum-process more effective.

 OECD ECONOMIC SURVEYS: SWEDEN – ISBN 978-92-64-05423-3 – © OECD 2008

Recommendations made in previous Surveys	Action taken since the latest *Survey* (February 2007)
SICKNESS AND DISABILITY	
Continue to improve administration in social insurance offices and the procedures for medical assessment. Limit the duration of sickness benefits to ensure early rehabilitation.	A range of measures were introduced from July 2008. A return-to-work plan should be drawn up in cases where there is a risk of long-term sickness absence. After no more than three months of sick leave, an assessment must be made of the person's ability to work in another role with the current employer. If the employer cannot offer suitable work and the case of sickness risks becoming long-term, contact must be made with the Employment Service. Sickness benefit (payable at 80% of previous income but with a ceiling) will generally remain in place for no more than 12 months. If work capacity is then still reduced, the person will be moved on to "extended sickness benefit", with lower compensation, payable for a maximum of 18 months. "Well again jobs" were introduced for people who have been receiving sickness, rehabilitation or disability benefits for at least a year, with a large rebate on employer social security contributions. Under a two-year pilot scheme, private employment services agencies will participate in action to enable people on long-term sick leave to regain their work capacity and return to work.
Monitor carefully how partial disability benefits are being used to ensure that they are not just an income top-up for people who wish to scale back their working hours. Revisit the many cases where disability pension has been granted during the past five years to assess options for rehabilitation to bring the person back to some form of work.	Disability benefits will only be granted when it can be established that work capacity is unlikely to improve. To extend the possibilities for disability benefit recipients to try out their work capacity, individuals will retain 25% of their compensation for the first twelve months of gainful employment. Those receiving disability benefits with no time limit, granted before September 2007, will be able to continue claiming partial benefits even after one year if taking up work, and they will have a lasting right to return to full benefits.
TAXATION	
Continue to cut income taxes in ways that maximise the effect on employment rates and hours worked. Raise the threshold for where the state income tax applies or cut its rate.	The in-work tax credit, introduced in 2007, was enlarged in 2008 and is set to be enlarged further in 2009. A small reduction in the state income tax is planned for 2009 (Chapter 3).
Raise the effective rate of VAT to make room for greater income tax cuts.	In the 2008 Budget, a number of taxes were increased to help finance other measures in the budget, including taxes on tobacco, alcohol and carbon dioxide.
FISCAL FRAMEWORK	
Augment the surplus target with a medium-term debt target to reduce the risks of slippage from year to year.	The fiscal rules have not been changed, but slippages have been avoided with actual surpluses exceeding targets.
Operate the ceiling for operational expenditures and non-entitlement transfers as a hard budget constraint on a three-year-ahead basis. Introduce a specific margin that is ring-fenced from anything but business-cycle related spending changes.	Binding three-year expenditure ceilings were reintroduced in the 2007 Spring Fiscal Policy Bill.
Reduce the pro-cyclicality of the balanced-budget requirement for local governments by basing it on average taxable income over a number of years. Alternatively, central government grants could be adjusted counter-cyclically.	No action.
HEALTHCARE	
Improve access to healthcare by strengthening incentives for family doctors and treating those in most need first. Ensure the quality of healthcare provision across regions through greater benchmarking, improved co-ordination between municipalities and county councils and fewer counties. Encourage more private service provision in the hospital sector and in long-term care for older persons. Abolish the state-owned monopoly in pharmaceutical retailing, at least for non-prescription drugs.	The government has proposed free right of establishment in primary care. Rules restricting county councils from transferring the operation of regional hospitals, regional clinics and hospitals to non-public actors have been abolished. An inquiry has been launched to consider wider choice for those receiving publicly-funded elderly and disabled care. The state monopoly for pharmaceutical retailing will be abolished from January 2009, including for prescription drugs.
Increase the role of user charges.	No action.

Recommendations made in previous Surveys	Action taken since the latest *Survey* (February 2007)
EDUCATION	
Identify and pursue cost-effective ways of improving the performance of the education system, particularly in mathematics and science. Develop better indicators of school performance to raise transparency and help identify the factors that influence outcomes.	A new reading-writing-arithmetic initiative was announced in 2008. Moreover, national tests will be advanced to start at the third year of compulsory education from 2009. National tests become mandatory at the fifth year of compulsory education also in English. Science tests will be introduced at the ninth year of compulsory education. A government report in early 2008 on upper secondary education recommended increased use of performance indicators such as the share of students attaining eligibility for entering higher education after three years. A legislative proposal has been presented with a new scale for marking students to be introduced from the academic year 2011/12.
Look at ways of reducing the years spent in school by raising the number of hours spent in instruction towards international averages. Re-examine the balance between instruction time and after-school care.	No action.
Adjust admission rules so as to advance the start of tertiary education: reduce the option for improving upper-secondary grades in municipal adult education so that extra points could be awarded for relevant work experience only. Tuition fees combined with income-contingent loans could also be introduced, or some of the student's loans could be converted into grants if studies are finished within the prescribed period.	An admission reform is to take effect from autumn 2010. Persons basing their application solely on upper secondary grades will be given some priority over applications based on grades that have been improved in adult education.
INNOVATION AND ENTREPRENEURSHIP	
Strengthen incentives to commercialise publicly-funded research by sharing intellectual property rights between the researcher and the institution. Develop the organisational structure and expertise to effectively commercialise research.	An inquiry is considering tax deductions for contributions to the non-profit sector to stimulate research. The government will abolish the VAT on contributions to research at academic institutions and is considering introducing intellectual property protection insurance for patents.
Remove quantitative restrictions on venture capital investments by institutional investors, including private pension funds.	No action.
Eliminate wealth taxes, or at least raise their thresholds. Reform the elements of the tax system that discourage wealth accumulation outside of pension plans. Adjust the 3:12 rules for closely-held companies, so that high earnings to a larger extent are recognised as entrepreneurial in nature and taxed as such rather than as income from work.	From 2007, the wealth tax was abolished. The 3:12 rules for closely held companies were simplified in 2007 and the thresholds from which the rules apply were raised, lowering the tax payable for closely-held companies with few employees (Chapter 3).
Adjust how previous earnings enter the calculation of unemployment insurance benefits to give failed entrepreneurs a more neutral treatment taking into account their earnings in previous employment.	A committee has been set up in order to review the issue.
COMPETITION	
Strengthen the Competition Authority's capacity to combat hard-core cartels and other serious breaches of competition law. Strengthen the leniency system by providing for substantial, non-criminal sanctions on individuals. Streamline the process and reduce the time for dealing with competition cases. Reconsider the need for two separate judicial reviews of the rulings of the Competition Authority.	Following an inquiry into the Competition Act, the government intends to submit a bill in 2008 to make it more effective. The inquiry proposed harmonising market concentration testing with EU law, clearer rules for determining the size of damages, and changing the thresholds for competition testing.
Strengthen the legal framework governing market activities of municipalities and other public institutions, bringing them within the scope of the Competition Act and providing greater opportunity for competitors to seek redress. Rationalise the present supervisory structure for public procurement into a single agency with scope to impose sanctions, and ensure that tenders from internal and external suppliers are treated equally. Increase outsourcing of public services. Specify clearly in government mandates to the agencies what are their core activities and place limits on expansions in other directions. Improve efficiency via dissemination of best practices in the public sector by further developing comparative datasets at all levels of government.	The Competition Authority has recommended the introduction of a national law on free choice in primary care and home help in elderly care, with open reporting of quality indicators at care-giver's level. The Authority has also recommended making sanctions stiffer in cases of non-compliance with the procurement rules. New legislation came into effect in January 2008 on public procurement and procurement in water, energy, transport and postal services. The National Board For Public Procurement was made part of the Competition Authority on 1 September 2007 as a step towards improving oversight of public procurement.
Reduce state ownership, with emphasis on separating natural monopolies from competitive activities. Privatise government-owned companies currently operating in competitive markets.	The government has sold its interest in Vin&Spirit, OMX and Vasakronan, and it has reduced its holdings of Teliasonera. Parliament has approved the sale of Nordea and further sales of Teliasonera shares.
Expose all the activities of the state-owned passenger rail company to competition and require it to operate under a hard budget constraint with no prospects of further government capital injections to bail it out.	No action.

Recommendations made in previous Surveys	Action taken since the latest *Survey* (February 2007)
Consider alternative regulatory mechanisms that would allow the introduction of competition in alcohol retailing without sacrificing control over access to liquor.	No action.
HOUSING	
Introduce legislation to allow owner-occupied apartments as an alternative to the current tenant-ownership.	The government has presented legislation for the introduction of owner-occupied apartments starting in May 2009. Initially, they can only be created via new construction, but the government also intends to prepare legislation allowing conversion of existing properties.
Rent regulation should be phased out to make the market function better. Regulation of rents in municipal housing companies should be reformed, and closer co-operation between concerned parties should be encouraged. Malmö's example of gradually introducing rent differentiation according to demand and supply should be considered as a model for Stockholm.	In April 2008, a government report proposed easing the regulation of private rentals. Rents would be allowed to increase or decrease by up to 5% if there are substantial and persistent shortages or surpluses of properties in the municipality. Moreover, rent comparisons should take a wider perspective including neighbouring municipalities if they are part of the same urban area.
Increase housing taxation. Base the taxation of tenant-owned housing on property value assessments that reflect the value of each individual apartment. Raise the real-estate tax rates for owner-occupied and tenant-owned housing to levels that are neutral *vis-à-vis* other asset classes. Strengthen capital gains taxation: an interest liability on accrued (but not realised) capital gains could be considered, or the effective tax rate on realised capital gains could be increased, *e.g.* by basing the tax on the full capital gain, rather than two thirds as currently. Moreover, deferral should not be granted when the owners die and the house or apartment is inherited. Reduce the value of interest deductibility, *e.g.* by lowering the threshold for the 21% rate so that it applies for all negative net capital income. Review capital market regulations to facilitate reverse mortgages easing the liquidity constraint when house prices (and thereby mortgage equity) grow leading to higher recurrent housing taxes.	The national real estate tax was abolished in 2008 and replaced by a municipal government charge with a relatively low cap per dwelling. Although the tax on capital gains on the sale of private dwellings was raised by 2 percentage points, the net effect of the two measures has been a reduction in housing taxation.
Make housing allowances dependent on income and personal and family characteristics rather than the level of housing expenditures.	No action.
Carry on with the phasing out of the interest subsidy scheme.	Completed.
Abolish the credit guarantee scheme as it might encourage risky lending by the banking sector.	No action. By contrast, the government has proposed introducing state credit guarantees to facilitate first-time buyers' acquisition of housing.
Enhance competition in the construction sector: change the public procurement process to reduce participation costs and thereby increase the number of companies bidding. Municipalities should allocate land on a competitive basis, rather than selling land through a direct transfer combined with counter-demands.	Efforts are being made to strengthen competition policy in general.
Make land planning processes more efficient. Municipalities should increase the speed with which cases are processed. Allow private developers to go to court to challenge a negative municipal planning decision.	A committee was appointed in June 2007 with the task to, among other things, analyse existing planning regulation and organisation and propose changes that would increase efficiency and quality.
PROMOTING ENVIRONMENTALLY SUSTAINABLE GROWTH	
Ensure that rigorous cost-benefit analysis is systematically used to evaluate environmental policy options.	A public investigation has been set up to evaluate existing work on environmental economics and propose improvements.

ANNEX 1.A2

Labour force data

With this Survey and *OECD Economic Outlook* No. 84, the OECD adopts Statistics Sweden's new Labour Force Survey. The new methodology introduced two key changes. First, the age coverage of the population was widened to 15-74 from 16-64. Second, to be consistent with international standards, students who are looking for work are now included among the unemployed. Formerly, they were classified as outside the labour force. These changes have raised the level of employment and unemployment, increased the unemployment rate and lowered the labour force participation rate. For 2007, the new methodology gives an unemployment rate of 6.2% compared to 4.6% on the previous definitions; the participation rate is 71.1% compared to 79.3%.

At present, data on the new definition are only available from Statistics Sweden starting in 2005. However, a much longer time series is needed for seasonal adjustment and for estimation of the structural unemployment rate (non-accelerating inflation rate of unemployment or NAIRU). Therefore, quarterly series for 1976-2005Q1 have been constructed by the OECD Secretariat as described below; these series will be used until data covering a longer historical time span become available from Statistics Sweden.

Quarterly data for 1976-2005Q1 are based on estimates for employment and unemployment from the National Institute of Economic Research (KI) presented in the August 2007 issue of *The Swedish Economy* for the 16-64 year olds. To extend these series to the 15-74 year olds, the following assumptions have been used. It is assumed that the participation rate of the 65-74 year olds was 8%. As very few of the oldest age group are unemployed, their unemployment rate is assumed to be a third of that for the 16-64. For the 15 year olds, a participation rate of 11% is assumed and the unemployment rate is assumed to be five times that of the 16-64 year olds. These assumptions were based on the observed participation and unemployment rates between 2005 and 2007, effectively assuming that there has been no trend change in the unemployment or participation rates of these groups. The unemployment and participation rates are then used to derive levels of employment and unemployment for 15 and 65-74 year olds which are added to the KI figures for the 16-64 year olds. Finally, the figures for 1976 to 2005Q1 are combined with the Statistics Sweden figures for 2005Q2 to 2008 and the combined series are seasonally adjusted.

The unemployment rate constructed as described above for the 15-74 year olds for the years prior to 2005 is virtually identical to that for the 16-64 age group published by the National Institute for Economic Research. However, the participation rate is on average around 10 percentage points lower. This reflects the fact that most of the people added to the working-age population by expanding the age coverage are outside the labour force.

The unemployment and participation rate series constructed for 1976-2005 are relatively insensitive to the assumptions made for unemployment and participation rates of the 15 year old and 65-74 year age cohorts. A 1 percentage point change in the assumed participation rate of 65-74 year olds changes the participation rate for 15-74 year olds by 0.13 percentage point on average between 1976 and 2005. Assuming that the 65-74 population had the same unemployment rate as the 16-64 population increases the unemployment rate for 15-74 year olds by, on average, 0.05 percentage points between 1976 and 2005. A 1 percentage point change in the assumed participation rate of 15 year olds changes the participation rate for the 15-74 group by 0.02 percentage point on average over the period 1976-2005. Assuming the 15 year olds had the same unemployment rate as the 16-64 population would have lowered the unemployment rate by 0.06 percentage point on average between 1976 and 2005.

The OECD's NAIRU series has been re-estimated (see Figure 1.10 in the body of Chapter 1). It follows the methodology outlined in Gianella *et al.* (2008), using a Philips curve and Kalman Filter (Table 1.A2.1).

Table 1.A2.1. **Philips curve estimation results**

Philips curve					
$\Delta\pi$	1961Q2-2007Q4		S.E.	0.8552	
	COEF	*T-STAT*	R2 adjusted	0.4259	
CST	0.0086	0.1371		*Test statistic*	*PROB.*
$\Delta\pi(-1)$	–0.816151	–11.7784	Heteroskedasticity	0.2283	0.9223
$\Delta\pi(-2)$	–0.6499	–8.3111	Serial correlation (1)	0.6736	0.4129
$\Delta\pi(-3)$	–0.3682	–5.2990	Serial correlation (4)	6.7073	0.0000
u-u*	–0.0582	–1.4671	Normality	44.8048	0.0000
			Sacrifice ratio	3.0457	.
Kalman filter					
Variance of error term in signal equation		0.60			
Variance of error term in first state equation		0.035			
Variance in error term in second state equation		0.15			
Parameter values of second state equation		0.90			

Source: OECD Secretariat calculations.

ISBN 978-92-64-05423-3
OECD Economic Surveys: Sweden
© OECD 2008

Chapter 2

Fiscal policy: What should the targets be?

The current fiscal policy framework was introduced after the crisis of the early 1990s as part of a stability-oriented macroeconomic policy framework. The simple but clear surplus target has been successful at achieving fiscal consolidation, but it may now be time to refine the fiscal strategy to ensure that the sound fiscal position can be sustained in the long term. This chapter assesses the achievements of the current framework and suggests more clearly underpinning the fiscal targets by long-term sustainability and intergenerational equity considerations. Key questions are what future fiscal pressures should be expected and to what extent alternative policies can be used to deal with them: pre-funding, increased labour utilisation, raising efficiency in public service provision via competition and user choice and shifting the balance between public and private funding.

The current fiscal framework

The central government budget process was tightened in the mid-1990s, at a time of extensive fiscal consolidation, following the economic crisis of the early 1990s, which had led to increased government spending, large deficits and rising debt. The new approach introduced a medium-term fiscal framework (previously budgeting was only for a single year) and a top-down budgeting process. In 1997, multiple-year expenditure ceilings were adopted, and in 2000 a budget surplus target and balanced-budget requirement for local governments were implemented (Box 2.1).

What has the fiscal framework achieved?

The net lending targets and spending ceilings have been met. Net lending has averaged 1.4% of GDP from 2000 to 2007 (Table 2.1). The indicator showing the average value of net lending since 2000 has exceeded 1% since 2006, and the seven-year moving average indicator has been close to or above 1% since 2003. Estimated structural budget balances show that, unlike in many other OECD countries, discretionary policy has acted counter-cyclically (Ahrend, *et al.*, 2006). The balanced-budget rule for local governments has not been met every year since its inception, with the local government sector as a whole running deficits between 2001 and 2003. However, the rule that local government deficits should be corrected within three years appears to have been met at the aggregate level. The expenditure ceilings have not been breached but the budget margin (the difference between the ceiling and actual spending) has been eroded by additional outlays after the expenditure ceiling was fixed. Moreover, tax expenditures have been used to reduce the risk of the expenditure ceilings being breached. Also, borrowing from the National Debt Office to finance investment spending has been used to avoid breaching the expenditure ceilings since this defers parliamentary appropriation (limited by the expenditure ceiling) from the time that the investment takes place until the time the debt is amortised (Hansson Brusewitz and Lindh, 2005).[1]

The improvement in net lending has been achieved through expenditure restraint rather than higher taxes. The share of public spending in GDP is still the highest in the OECD, for a variety of reasons. A large proportion of individuals' smoothing of their income over their lifetime is carried out through the public sector and a significant share of private services are provided by the public sector. In addition, transfers are higher than in many other countries, although they are generally taxed like earned income. Taking account of taxation of benefits and mandatory private social spending, Sweden's net publicly-mandated social spending is some 7 percentage points of GDP less than gross public social expenditure, and lower than in France and Germany. The trend decline in spending has largely been driven by reduced interest expenditure, in line with lower debt, and a reduction in transfers, particularly in relation to housing, support for the unemployed and labour market measures (Figure 2.1). In recent years, lower transfers have reflected a fall in the number of people excluded from the labour market due to sickness and disability,

 OECD ECONOMIC SURVEYS: SWEDEN – ISBN 978-92-64-05423-3 – © OECD 2008

Box 2.1. **Key elements of Sweden's fiscal policy framework**

The main fiscal target is a general government surplus of 1% of GDP over the business cycle (Swedish government, 2008a).* It is motivated by the following goals:

- Public finances should be sustainable in the long term.
- Fiscal resources should be distributed evenly across generations.
- Economic efficiency should be promoted through a predictable development of taxes and expenditures.

Three indicators are used by the government to assess performance against the surplus target:

- Average net lending from the year 2000, the year in which the target was first applied, combined with information about the estimated output gap over the same period.
- Average net lending over a seven-year period, including the current year, the next three and the previous three, combined with information about the estimated output gap over the same period (introduced in the 2007 Spring Fiscal Policy Bill).
- The structural balance, *i.e.* cyclically-adjusted net lending adjusted for one-off and temporary effects.

The expenditure ceilings are designed to support the surplus target and prevent temporary revenue from being used to finance permanent expenditure. They take into account economic developments to avoid pro-cyclical fiscal policy and include a budget margin to cope with uncertainties. The aggregate expenditure ceilings are broken down into 26 expenditure areas, covering central government expenditures and the spending of the income pension system, but do not cover interest or local government expenditures. When first introduced, the expenditure ceilings were intended to be set three years in advance. However, for a number of years, the ceilings were only set two years in advance. The three-year-ahead ceiling was re-instated in 2007.

The balanced-budget requirement for local governments applies to the aggregate position of all local governments and calls for any deficits to be offset by surpluses within three years.

In 2007, the government established a Fiscal Policy Council (*Finanspolitiska Rådet*), to monitor the fulfilment of fiscal targets. It's role includes examining the clarity of budget documents and quality of the data on which they are based, and whether developments are in line with long-term sustainable growth and high employment. The establishment of the Council was also intended to foster public debate on economic policy. The government has begun work on a comprehensive review of the fiscal framework aimed at increasing its clarity and strengthening it to face future challenges.

* The surplus target was initially 2% of GDP but was reduced to 1% when the premium pension system, introduced in the reforms of the late 1990s, was reclassified to the private sector in 2007.

which to some extent may have been cyclical. Government investment spending as a share of GDP has fallen since the 1970s but is not evidently low by international standards (see below, Box 2.2).

A key motivation for the general fiscal policy framework was to strengthen the fiscal position following the economic crisis of the early 1990s. Swedish general government gross debt has fallen from a peak of almost 85% of GDP in 1996 to about 47% of GDP in 2007.

Table 2.1. **Fiscal balance and expenditure: have the targets been met?**

As per cent of GDP

	2000	2001	2002	2003	2004	2005	2006	2007	2008 *est.*	2009 *est.*
Net lending	3.7	1.7	–1.4	–1.2	0.6	2.0	2.2	3.5	2.8	1.1
Central government	4.0	7.3	–1.9	–1.9	–0.5	0.4	0.8	2.1	1.6	0.5
Local government	0.2	–0.2	–0.5	–0.2	0.2	0.6	0.3	0.3	0.3	0.1
Pension system	–0.4	–5.4	1.0	1.0	0.9	1.0	1.0	1.1	0.8	0.4
Net lending average from 2000 to given year	3.7	2.7	1.3	0.7	0.7	0.9	1.1	1.4	1.5	1.5
7-year moving average of net lending				0.9	0.9	1.0	1.4	1.8	2.1	
Cyclically-adjusted net lending	3.0	1.8	–0.9	–0.6	0.7	1.7	1.3	2.8	3.2	2.1
Structural balance	1.9	2.2	–0.7	–0.4	0.4	1.1	0.8	2.1	2.8	1.9
OECD cyclically-adjusted net lending	*2.4*	*1.0*	*–1.7*	*–0.8*	*0.9*	*2.4*	*1.7*	*3.0*	*3.2*	*2.2*
Expenditure ceiling	34.0	34.0	33.5	32.7	32.7	31.8	31.3	30.5	30.0	30.0
Actual spending subject to ceiling	33.8	33.8	33.5	32.6	32.6	31.6	30.9	29.6	29.4	28.8
Budget margin	0.2	0.2	0.0	0.1	0.1	0.2	0.4	0.9	0.5	1.1

Note: The 7-year moving average is calculated using the given year, the three years prior and the three following years. Cyclically-adjusted net lending is calculated using net lending and the "adjustment for the economic cycle" from Table 20 of Annex 2 to the 2009 Budget Bill and the equivalent table in the 2008 Budget Bill for figures relating to 2000 and 2001.

Source: Swedish government (2007, 2008a), *OECD Economic Outlook No. 84 database*.

Figure 2.1. **Government spending as a share of GDP has fallen**

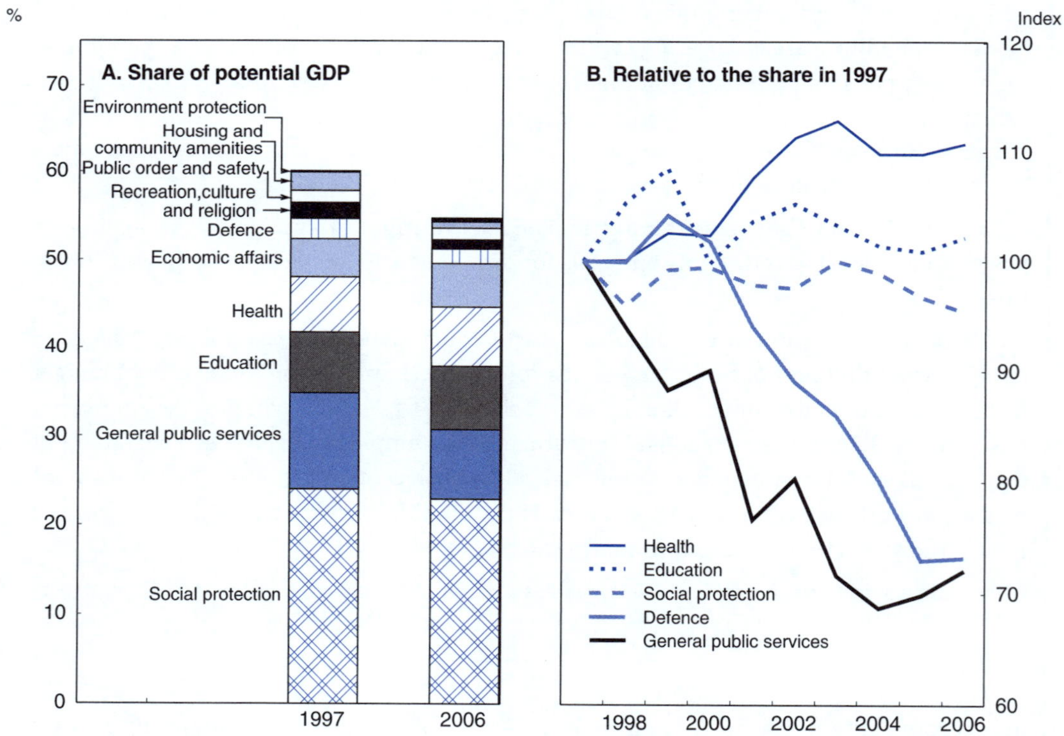

Source: OECD, *National Accounts* and *Analytical database*.

StatLink http://dx.doi.org/10.1787/485214200188

Net debt had deteriorated from a small net asset position in the early 1990s to 27% of GDP in 1996 but the government had restored a net asset position of 20% of GDP by 2007 (Table 2.2).[2] The framework appears to have been successful in helping to restore local government finances, since local government net financial position has also improved. In addition, the stock of physical assets, which are not included in the net assets measure, amounts to some 40 to 50% of GDP. The overall improvement in the government's balance sheet has not been driven solely by net lending: more than half of the increase in net financial assets since the mid-1990s can be ascribed to GDP growth and valuation effects (Swedish Fiscal Policy Council, 2008). Sweden is one of only a few OECD countries that has financial assets in excess of liabilities. In comparison to other OECD countries, it has also achieved one of the largest improvements in net financial assets over the last decade (Figure 2.2).

Table 2.2. **General government balance sheet**

Consolidated, per cent of GDP

		1996		2007	
		Assets	Liabilities	Assets	Liabilities
General government	Net financial position	–26.6		19.9	
	Total financial instruments	72.4	99.0	70.5	50.6
	Debt	45.3	90.3	29.2	45.8
	Equity	20.6		36.4	
	Other	6.5	8.7	4.9	4.9
of which:					
Central government	Net financial position	–61.5		–10.3	
	Total financial instruments	27.8	89.4	32.3	42.5
	Debt	9.2	84.2	11.9	40.0
	Equity	15.6		17.7	
	Other	3.1	5.1	2.6	2.6
Local government	Net financial position	–0.9		1.2	
	Total financial instruments	8.7	9.6	8.8	7.6
	Debt	4.2	6.1	5.9	5.6
	Equity	1.2		1.3	
	Other	3.3	3.5	1.6	2.0
Social security funds	Net financial position	35.8		29.0	
	Total financial instruments	35.9	0.0	29.5	0.5
	Debt	31.9	0.0	11.3	0.2
	Equity	3.8		17.4	
	Other	0.1	0.0	0.7	0.3

Source: *Statistics Sweden Financial Accounts* and *National Accounts*.

The government has introduced measures in the 2009 Budget Bill that will reduce net lending by almost 1% of GDP. These measures cover three broad areas: investment in infrastructure and research, lower income taxes, and increased spending on pensioners and psychiatric care. Cyclically-adjusted net lending would be reduced to around 2% of GDP in 2009 although slower GDP growth may bring headline net lending close to balance (Chapter 1).

Figure 2.2. **Government net financial assets is improving in Sweden**[1]

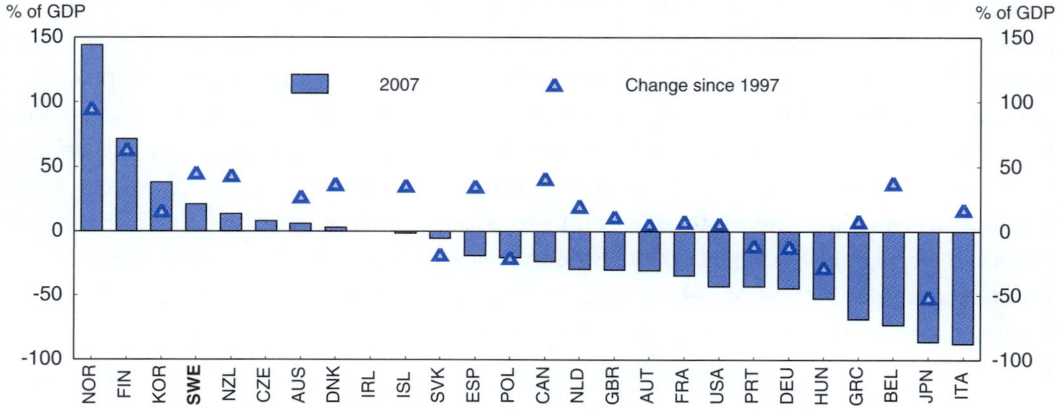

StatLink http://dx.doi.org/10.1787/485245441302

1. General government net financial assets are financial assets less liabilities (usually debt). It is the negative of net financial liabilities or net debt.

Source: OECD, *Analytical database*.

What should guide the choice of future fiscal targets?

While the fiscal targets have helped restore public finance sustainability, they have been criticised on a number of points. The surplus target was set to achieve fiscal consolidation but the level of 1% of GDP is largely arbitrary. The expenditure ceilings have been met, but they have also been circumvented by the use of tax expenditures and borrowing to finance investment, and they are not clearly linked to the surplus target (Swedish National Audit Office, 2008; European Commission, 2008a; Swedish Fiscal Policy Council, 2008). These problems, and the approach of the demographic transition that the surplus target was intended to facilitate, has led the government to initiate a review of the fiscal framework. This was announced in the Budget Bill for 2007 and the outcomes of this review will be reported by 2010.

The ultimate goal of fiscal policy targets should be to ensure sustainability, meaning that current tax and spending policy settings can remain unchanged in the future without generating an explosive path for government debt, which could ultimately lead to higher interest rates and cause macroeconomic as well as financial market instability. The standard approach to fiscal sustainability rests on the idea that government debt should be stable as a proportion of GDP at some finite horizon (often 50 years). A strict approach to ensuring sustainability would be to set the target to maintain the current financial position. A net lending surplus of about 1% per year would be sufficient to stabilise net assets at their current level of around 20% of GDP, given the government's projections of GDP growth and interest rates. However, this approach hinges on an essentially arbitrary level of net assets. Also, setting a fixed target to maintain net financial assets, even if expressed as an average over the economic cycle, constrains the use of pre-funding or tax-smoothing as a long-term policy tool, implying perhaps temporary changes in tax rates or spending. Also, this approach does not ensure a particular level of intergenerational distribution of resources, which is currently stated as an ambition in the government's fiscal policy statements. Finally, it has been argued that the factors that can affect net financial assets which are not included in net lending (the so-called stock-flow adjustment) could be manipulated to help achieve fiscal targets (Buti *et al.*, 2006).

A more rigorous forward-looking approach would be to set short-run fiscal targets with reference to the existing stock of assets and liabilities, the expected path of revenues and expenditures, and fiscal sustainability calculations based on these projections. This could incorporate an assessment of the uncertainty around long-term projections and an analysis of the risks to the budget resulting from the composition of the balance sheet (for example, the likelihood of default on government-provided loans) and other transactions (for example, government guarantees). The expected paths of balance sheet items and revenues and expenditures are important, in addition to net present values. The intertemporal budget constraint may be satisfied (the net present value of future budget surpluses may be enough to cover existing net debt), but with a trajectory that involves sharply increasing debt initially followed by a strong fiscal improvement. Such a trajectory would leave the budget more susceptible to the effects of a negative economic shock than a sustainable path with a smoother trajectory for net debt.

Fiscal targets should also take into account the fact that parts of the general government balance sheet will evolve over time according to factors that are exogenous to fiscal policy. For example, higher returns on assets in the pension system would likely reduce future government spending related to the basic age pension. Similarly, higher investment returns on state-owned enterprises would reduce the need to raise taxes to finance a given path of expenditure. However, in both cases, if the higher return was achieved through a more risky investment strategy, the budget may also be more exposed to occasional losses. In addition, a decision to invest in physical capital may increase the required ongoing investment to maintain the asset as it depreciates (Box 2.2). Loans to the private sector increase government assets and interest income but the principal is not captured by net lending. Publication of a full balance sheet with a reconciliation of changes in net worth due to net lending and other factors would make it easier to assess the extent to which a net lending target would need to be adjusted to take these factors into account. Full accrual balance sheets are currently published in the United Kingdom, New Zealand and Australia.

The government also sees a role for fiscal policy in promoting an equitable distribution of resources across generations. To monitor achievement of this goal, generational accounts should be produced on the same basis (*i.e.*, with the same assumptions and methodologies) as fiscal sustainability calculations. Generational accounts can be used to assess the distribution of public sector activities by mapping the taxes paid and public benefits received across age cohorts. They do come with a number of caveats, however. They ultimately rely on the lifecycle consumption model and require assumptions about the extent of intergenerational altruism. They may not be as familiar to policymakers, potentially increasing the risk of mis-interpretation. They treat government payments made today on par with payments to be made in the future, which may be considered uncertain due to the possibility of policy change (Auerbach, 2008). Expenditures that cannot be specifically linked to a particular generation are assumed to benefit all generations equally. This means that expenditures whose costs and benefits do not occur in the same period may be misallocated in the generational accounts (Heijdra and van der Ploeg, 2002). This is a risk with capital investment, where the expenditure is incurred in one period but the benefits are spread out over time. Finally, generational accounts do not capture non-tangible assets such as environmental amenity, so cannot give a complete picture of intergenerational redistribution (Productivity Commission, 2005). Despite these drawbacks, they can usefully inform target setting and assessment of policy achievement.

Box 2.2. **Is a golden rule necessary?**

A risk with a strict rule-based fiscal framework with a net lending target and expenditure ceilings is that these rules may discourage physical capital investment. Such expenditures may be politically easier to defer in order to meet a net lending or expenditure target, because they are discrete and often one-off. It can be argued that government investment is different from other types of spending because the benefits are spread further over time and investment increases private sector output (Fatas, 2005). Hence, a number of countries (the United Kingdom, Germany) have adopted a "golden rule", where budget deficits are allowed but only up to the amount of capital spending (that is, debt issuance can finance investment). Such a rule provides for the costs and benefits of an investment to be spread over a similar period, rather than the costs being borne upfront and the benefits accruing later.

Over a long time span, government investment as a share of GDP has fallen, but it has been stable since the mid-1990s, suggesting that the fiscal framework introduced in the late 1990s did not induce a fall in public investment (although it is possible that the investment share of GDP would have increased in the absence of the rule). Estimates of the stock of public capital suggest that Swedish public capital may be low by international standards (Kamps, 2004).

Excluding investment from the fiscal target could make fiscal policy more volatile and loosen control over the aggregate budget position. If capital spending is politically easy to defer in order to meet a target, it may not have the same public value as other types of spending so loosening the budget constraint for capital spending and not other spending may not be consistent with public preferences. The definition of investment (expenditures that result in the acquisition of physical capital) most likely would exclude expenditures providing long-term benefits, such as education or research and development. In addition, a golden rule may create incentives to artificially reclassify certain types of spending as investment in order to bypass the budget constraint.

In addition, a golden rule might create a bias in favour of purchasing physical capital over other forms of capital service provision. Government can either buy capital outright, affecting net lending upfront, or it can contract a private enterprise to construct the capital and pay a rental fee or service charge as the infrastructure is used by the public. Such an arrangement would be classified as consumption for the purposes of net lending. A golden rule loosens the budget constraint for purchasing but not for renting capital.

Reporting a balance sheet including physical assets would improve coverage of the government asset position and could prompt further analysis of the role of government-owned assets and how they are expected to develop over time. The use of an accrual-accounting flow measure for the budget target, incorporating depreciation as an expense, would replace the upfront cost of investment by the depreciation of the asset over time in the fiscal target. This would facilitate the choice between purchasing and renting capital and create an explicit link between the fiscal flow target and government net worth. However, using an accrual measure for the budget flow target raises a number of complex issues which would need to be carefully considered, such as the cash management implications of budget allocations for accruing expenses like depreciation and civil servant pension liabilities (OECD, 2007a).

Adopting an approach to setting fiscal policy with reference to projected long-term developments would be more complex than the current surplus target. In particular, it could be argued that the government could manipulate the underlying modelling and assumptions. This may weaken the discipline imparted by the fiscal targets. To guard against this, the Fiscal Policy Council should be required to formally verify the assumptions and methodologies used to determine the targets.[3] The targets could be re-affirmed or adjusted at regular intervals, based on updated long-term projections and refinement of the estimation methodologies, to allow for early action if the impact of demographic or other changes turned out to be larger than expected.

A number of OECD countries, particularly those which have recently recorded budget surpluses, have adopted policy targets derived from projections of future fiscal developments. In New Zealand, the government is required by law to produce a long-term fiscal outlook every four years and a fiscal strategy report each year. The latter report demonstrates how fiscal targets are linked to long-term developments. The budget is prepared on an accrual basis, and the target is for operating surpluses (accrued revenues must exceed accrued expenses, regardless of the actual cash flow) over the economic cycle consistent with increasing net worth. The exact level of the surplus is determined by what is required to achieve the long-run objectives (New Zealand government, 2008). In Denmark, the budget target is for structural surpluses of ¾-1¾ per cent of GDP per year to 2010 and then the budget should at least be balanced from 2011 to 2015. These targets were set with reference to the expected future development of public finances, to ensure fiscal sustainability measured using a variant of the inter-temporal budget constraint (OECD, 2008a). The sustainability indicator is also used to assess the long-term implications of major policy measures. Such an approach could be usefully applied in Sweden, building on the long-term projections already presented each year in the Budget Bills (Swedish National Audit Office, 2007b).[4]

The link between the expenditure ceilings and the net lending target should be clarified. With a target for net lending tied to the development of the balance sheet, the purpose of an expenditure ceiling would be to constrain the overall size of government. If tax smoothing is pursued, the expenditure ceiling becomes the control variable to ensure that the net lending target is met given the anticipated path of revenue. The expenditure ceiling has been an important fiscal control mechanism in recent years and has been met every year since its introduction. The level of ceiling is currently set to allow for cyclical fluctuations in spending, with the three-year-ahead ceiling set to be 3% above the estimate of ceiling-restricted expenditure. However, in the past, the budget margins have been fully used during upswings, forcing cuts in expenditures during downturns. This could be addressed by increasing the size of the budget margins, although larger margins might be interpreted as additional scope for permanent spending increases. Alternatively, consideration could be given to excluding cyclically-sensitive expenditures from the expenditure ceiling to prevent them from limiting the operation of the automatic stabilisers. Consideration could also be given to introducing a formal assessment of new tax expenditures as part of the budget decision-making process, in order to prevent their use as a means to bypass the expenditure ceilings (Swedish National Audit Office, 2007a). This would ensure that tax expenditures at least receive the same scrutiny as direct expenditures in the budget process. Similarly, arrangements for borrowing from the National Debt Office to finance capital investment should also be eliminated. It is therefore welcome that the 2009 Budget states that government investment should be financed from general revenue, like other expenditures, rather than by separate borrowing. Part of the 2008 surplus (0.75% of GDP) will be allocated to repayment of loans previously taken out by the National Rail Administration and Swedish Road Administration. Loan financing will not be considered for new investment projects unless the costs are to be recovered by user charges (Swedish government, 2008a).

The local-government balanced-budget rule should be amended to reduce the risk of pro-cyclical local fiscal policy. The balanced budget rule for local governments is a minimum requirement and is often interpreted by local governments as requiring a small surplus. However, if a deficit does emerge the requirement that the financial position is to be restored within three years raises the possibility that local governments may need to tighten fiscal policy during economic downturns. Local governments should have the incentive to save during economic upswings to avoid having to raise taxes during slowdowns, as happened in the early 2000s. The 2005 *Survey* recommended reforming the balanced-budget requirement so that revenue for the purposes of the target is calculated with reference to the average taxable income over a number of years, creating a form of over-the-cycle target (OECD, 2005).

Consideration could also be given to formalising periodic reviews of the overall allocation of spending, to supplement reviews of the effectiveness of particular programmes. The Swedish annual budget process is incremental, considering new policy proposals although often with a requirement that new spending is offset with savings elsewhere in the budget. While it would be resource-intensive, multi-year reviews could free up resources from low-priority areas to ensure overall spending restraint and comply with the fiscal targets. The Canadian government has recently introduced a four-year spending review cycle with a view to freeing resources for reallocation to other priorities, although to date this process has not yielded significant savings (OECD, 2008b). The UK government conducted comprehensive spending reviews in 1998 and 2007, which examined all government programmes from a zero-base perspective, helping to reallocate spending towards higher priorities, in health and education in particular. Bi-annual spending reviews were conducted in the interim setting out three-year spending plans for departmental expenditures. However, actual real spending has exceeded that planned in all spending reviews since 1998 and a considerable fiscal deficit has emerged (OECD, 2007b). Thus, spending reviews do not automatically deliver spending control; they are not a substitute for fiscal discipline.

Are current policies sustainable given future fiscal pressures?

The government's long-term fiscal projections indicate that the general government budget balance will strengthen to about 2.5% of GDP in 2011 (the last year of budget forecasts) and is then projected to deteriorate progressively to 1% of GDP by 2015. Beyond that horizon, net lending is driven by demographic changes, deteriorating to deficits of around 1.5% of GDP in the 2040s before recovering slightly to a deficit of 1.2% of GDP in 2050 (Figure 2.3). Accordingly, the net financial asset position is projected to improve as a share of GDP until about 2020, and then to deteriorate, to net debt of 3.3% of GDP by 2050.

Based on a number of technical assumptions,[5] including that of an unchanged retirement age despite the foreseeable increase in longevity, the government projects transfers and consumption combined to decline by about 1.5 percentage points of GDP between 2008 and 2050. The fiscal gap opens up because of a technical adjustment – a transfer of 3.3% of GDP to households – phased in between 2011 and 2015. This adjustment is introduced in order to reduce the surplus from its level in 2011 to the target of 1% of GDP by 2015, after which the projections are based on demographics. This technical adjustment changes with the projection for the surplus at the end of the budget forecast horizon. For example, in the 2008 Spring Fiscal Policy Bill, the surplus in 2011 was estimated to be 4.1% of GDP, and the technical adjustment required to reduce the surplus to 1% in 2015 was therefore 5% of GDP per year (Swedish government, 2008b).

Figure 2.3. **The fiscal position is expected to deteriorate**

As per cent of GDP

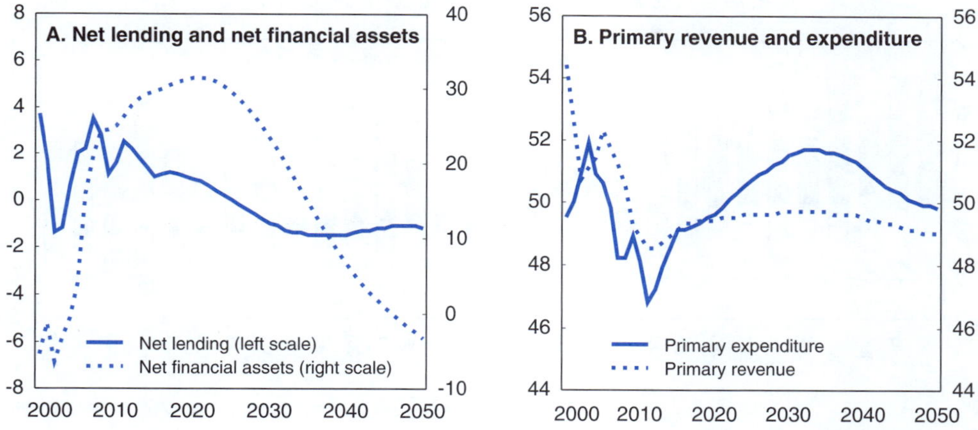

StatLink http://dx.doi.org/10.1787/485261713886

Source: Swedish Government (2008a).

Demographically-driven pressures are mainly in elderly care. The government projects consumption related to elderly care to rise by about 2 percentage points of GDP between 2008 and 2050. Consumption of medical services is expected to rise by about one-half a percentage point and transfers related to health are expected to fall by about one-half a percentage point of GDP, based on a fixed standard of care. Pension expenditure is projected to be broadly stable as a share of GDP until 2040, falling thereafter, due largely to the pension reforms of the late 1990s, which reduced pension entitlements and introduced the self-balancing income pension system. Through the universal guarantee pension, the government retains the risk that retirement income from the new income pension system is inadequate. Education spending is projected to decline by about 1 percentage point of GDP between 2008 and 2050 due to demographics.

OECD projections of growth in health and long-term care spending based on demographics alone are lower than those of the government. They take into account an adjustment for healthy ageing, and an income effect for age care which assumes that the income elasticity of demand for aged care services is zero, so income growth drives down long-term care spending as a share of GDP. Even projections that take into account non-demographic factors, combined with measures to contain the growth in costs (the cost-containment scenario in Figure 2.4), suggest that Sweden faces the lowest increase in health and long-term care spending in the OECD, in part due to a relatively small increase in the old-age dependency ratio. However, expectations for standards of care will almost certainly rise, and much larger increases in spending are projected in the absence of cost-containment measures – public spending on health and long-term care could rise by more than 4 percentage points of GDP between 2005 and 2050 relative to the impact of demography alone (OECD, 2006).

Projections produced by the European Commission, which cover pensions, education and labour market measures in addition to health and age care, are more pessimistic than the government's. That said, even these projections show that Swedish public finances face a smaller demographic challenge than in many other European countries. These estimates take account of reduced care needs due to improved health accompanying

Figure 2.4. **Health and long-term care expenditure is not expected to rise as much as in other countries**[1]

Projected increase between 2005 and 2050, per cent of GDP

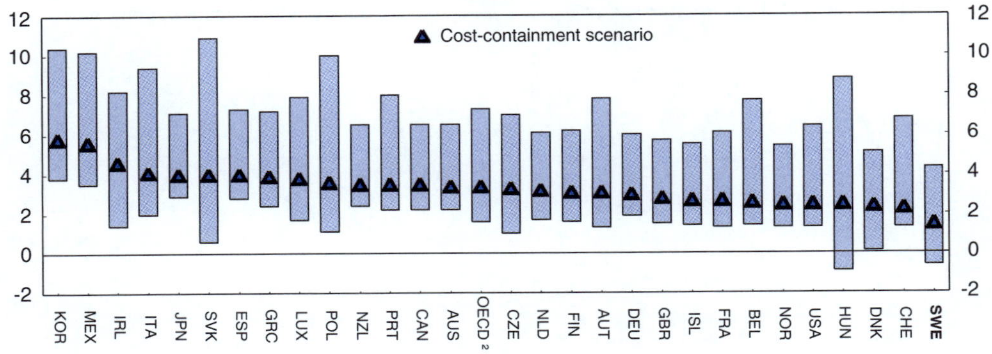

StatLink http://dx.doi.org/10.1787/485270408646

1. The vertical bars correspond to a range of alternative scenarios. Countries are ranked by the increase of expenditures between 2005 and 2050 in the cost-containment scenario.
2. OECD average excluding Turkey.

Source: OECD (2006).

increased life expectancy. However, the government expects larger falls in both pension and unemployment benefit spending.

Using internationally comparable figures, Sweden is one of a handful of European countries which are considered to have sustainable fiscal positions. This is based on an indicator which shows how much the budget balance would need to change each year in order to satisfy the inter-temporal budget constraint. A negative value of the indicator suggests that the fiscal stance can be permanently loosened and fiscal policy would still be sustainable (European Commission, 2004). In Sweden's case, the sustainability indicator value is –1.2; that is, the primary budget surplus (total budget surplus less net interest) could be permanently reduced by 1.2% of GDP and the fiscal position would still be sustainable. This result is achieved because the starting surplus and initial debt position are sufficient to offset the impact of the fiscal deterioration associated with demographic change (Figure 2.5).[6]

Figure 2.5. **Sweden's public finances appear sustainable**[1]

As per cent of GDP

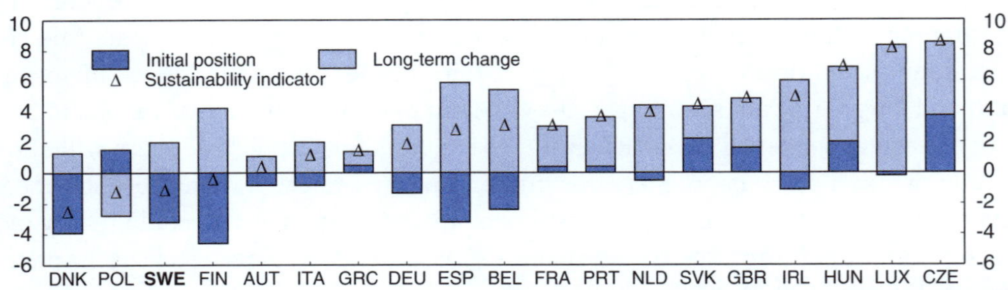

StatLink http://dx.doi.org/10.1787/485278518671

1. The sustainability indicator measures by how much net lending must increase to ensure that the inter-temporal budget constraint is met – that is, the net present value of future budget surpluses is enough to offset initial gross public debt. The "initial position" measures the change in the budget required to balance the inter-temporal budget constraint assuming the budget balance in 2007 is maintained indefinitely. The "long-term change" measures the required change in the budget balance to offset the impact of expected future developments in spending and revenue.

Source: European Commission (2008b).

The government's calculations of fiscal sustainability show a less positive picture, but still point to long-term sustainability. The central scenario yields a sustainability indicator value of –0.1. The calculations are based on the European Commission indicator of sustainability but more optimistic projections for long-term spending, as outlined above. In addition, the projections cover a longer time horizon, which allows them to take on board a projected improvement in the fiscal position beyond 2050. However, as noted above, the government's projections also incorporate an *ad hoc* technical adjustment of 3.3% of GDP, designed to bring net lending to the 1% surplus target by 2015.[7] Without this adjustment, surpluses would deteriorate from around 4% in 2015 until the early 2030s, but even at the height of the impact of demographic change, the budget would most likely still be in surplus. Calculations made prior to the fiscal measures announced in the 2009 Budget indicated that, without the technical adjustment, the fiscal stance could be permanently loosened from its 2007 level by nearly 4 percentage points and still be considered sustainable, assuming no other adjustment to the projections (Swedish Fiscal Policy Council, 2008). There is clearly a need to refine the approach to moving from the current path of net lending to the 1% target (Swedish Fiscal Policy Council, 2008; Swedish National Audit Office, 2008).

At present, there is no formal reporting of whether fiscal policy is achieving the government's intergenerational aspirations. Generational accounts have been produced for Sweden, however, they are based on different assumptions from the government's.[8] These accounts show that all generations born between 1930 and 2009 are to receive a net transfer from the government. This comes about because government debt has been accumulated since 1930, and the share of debt to GDP is posited to be the same at the end of the projection period in 2110 as in 2006. Thus, the accounts support for the idea that current generations are receiving benefits that are being financed by future generations (Pettersson *et al.*, 2007).

How should public spending growth be tackled?

As outlined above, future fiscal pressures are likely to derive from two main sources: the impact of demography on age care and health spending, which is already high in comparison to other OECD countries, and the impact on public spending of technological change and increasing service demands. There are several policy approaches to dealing with these fiscal pressures. Tax rates could be raised as budget pressures arise to ensure that the budget remains balanced. However, the impact of globalisation on tax bases and the incentive effects of high labour taxes are likely to put downward pressure on tax rates. While Sweden was an early mover in reducing corporate income tax rates, there has recently been further pressure for further tax cuts, culminating in the government announcing a reduction in the corporate income tax rate in the 2009 Budget. High marginal tax rates on labour are likely a contributing factor behind relatively low average hours worked. These issues are taken up in more detail in Chapter 3. The alternatives to higher taxes are pre-funding, measures to increase the growth of tax bases and measures to address the expected growth in spending or reduce spending in other areas to create room for additional demands. These are discussed below.

Pre-funding

The current fiscal target, and projected surpluses in excess of the target, implies that fiscal policy is currently pre-funding, or saving, to meet future fiscal pressures. Pre-funding is appropriate from an efficiency perspective when it results in smoothing tax rates through time. That is, a temporary period of surpluses can finance a subsequent temporary period of deficits while maintaining constant tax rates throughout. This is efficient since the deadweight costs of taxation are posited to be more than proportional to the tax rate – stable tax rates produce lower deadweight losses than near-term falls followed by future increases in tax rates. Pre-funding is not appropriate for dealing with permanent increases in spending, such as those associated with higher service demands or future technological change. The gains from tax smoothing compared to a balanced-budget strategy may be small, possibly less than 1% of GDP, but could be significantly larger, up to over 5% of GDP, if the initial surpluses are invested in assets earning a higher rate of return than government debt (Davis and Fabling, 2002)[9]. The benefits are also larger the greater the expected increase in government spending and the higher the initial tax rates.

However, there are reasons – notably political economy ones – to be cautious about the extent of pre-funding. Pre-funding might create the perception that the government has excess resources in the short term, creating incentives for additional public spending and reducing incentives to address spending growth. This would exacerbate the fiscal problem pre-funding was designed to help alleviate (Pinfield, 1998). If pre-funding involves asset accumulation, these problems can be partly mitigated by specifically linking the assets to already committed future expenditures and ensuring a strong governance framework for the management of the assets. This "expenditure creep" may not be a major problem in Sweden's case since the fiscal surpluses are being applied to reducing gross debt and accumulating assets in the income pension system, which has clear rules for how and when the assets can be used. Also, clearly explaining the rationale for surpluses in the near term to help meet longer-term fiscal pressures should reduce the demands for higher spending in the short run. However, the higher the degree of pre-funding in the short term, the larger the risk that it would lead to increased spending pressures.

The intergenerational equity implications of pre-funding also need to be further investigated. Scenario analysis conducted with the generational accounts shows that replacing the 1% surplus target by a balanced-budget rule results in generations born before 1960 receiving higher net transfers from the government and generations born after 1960 receiving lower net transfers – sharply lower in the case of those born since 1990. This supports the view that a strategy of near-term surpluses should be maintained (Pettersen *et al.*, 2007). However, it does not show the intergenerational effects of surpluses of more than 1% in the coming years or higher spending in the long term. There would be more transparency if generational accounts were produced with the same projections and assumptions as sustainability analysis. From an *ex post* perspective, too little pre-funding implies that current generations receive benefits paid for by future generations, while too much pre-funding generates the opposite effect. This calls for regular review of estimates of the long-term fiscal trends and regular re-assessment of the required extent of pre-funding.

The sustainability analysis outlined earlier suggests that the modest easing in the fiscal stance in the 2009 Budget is unlikely to jeopardise long-term sustainability even though it will reduce pre-funding (Chapter 1). Indeed, the strong fiscal framework and improved fiscal position means that Sweden is much better prepared than many OECD countries to deal with the current downturn. If the economic situation deteriorates further in the wake of the global financial crisis and additional fiscal stimulus is deemed necessary, it should be designed to avoid negative long-term fiscal implications. As recognised in the Budget documentation, fiscal balances often worsen more during

 OECD ECONOMIC SURVEYS: SWEDEN – ISBN 978-92-64-05423-3 – © OECD 2008

downturns than anticipated using standard cyclical-adjustment techniques. Any new measures should either be temporary or aimed at boosting the economy's growth potential. The high marginal tax rates and the associated deadweight costs (discussed in Chapter 3) suggest that income tax reduction should continue to have priority. Some areas of public spending have been linked to higher national income, *e.g.* education, childcare, research and development and infrastructure (Afonso *et al.*, 2005) and so the 2009 Budget's focus on infrastructure and research is welcome. However, not all of the new spending measures in the Budget will be growth enhancing and these measures reduce the scope for further tax cuts. In addition, what ultimately matters is not the level of spending but the outcomes achieved and, in some cases, such benefits could be reaped without additional funding, through efficiency measures or increased private contributions towards currently publicly-funded services (see below).

Increasing labour utilisation

Further increases in labour utilisation would expand the tax base and reduce public social spending.[10] This has been the government's focus in recent years. The Fiscal Policy Council estimates that larger-than-anticipated effects of the recent labour market policies could allow for a permanent relaxation of the fiscal stance of about half a per cent of GDP (Swedish Fiscal Policy Council, 2008). There is, of course, a natural limit to the expansion of employment, since ultimately individuals' decisions about whether to work or not are based on their preferences with respect to leisure and the consumption of goods purchased with the returns from supplying labour. That said, the current level of hours worked per person and the extent of exclusion from the labour market, described in Chapter 1, suggest that there is a long way to go in raising labour supply before these natural limits would be binding.

Increasing the statutory retirement age may reduce expenditure on the basic pension and generate additional tax revenue. Raising the average retirement age would reduce the longevity risk borne by the government in the income pension system (the risk that the income pension system will not deliver "sufficiently" high retirement income due to longer life). Finland, Germany, and Portugal have linked pension benefit levels to life expectancy. In Denmark, a decision has been taken to index the retirement age to life expectancy, although this will not apply until 2024 (Denmark faces a much larger problem with early retirement than Sweden, as documented in OECD, 2008a). The Swedish income pension system already entails some incentives to extend working life, since additional years of work raise the replacement rate in retirement. Also, the system allows pensioners to access part of their savings while still working. This eases the transition from work to retirement and in principle could extend people's working lives. The Fiscal Policy Council estimates that gains from increasing the retirement age could be enough to permanently reduce the budget surplus by around 1% of GDP (Swedish Fiscal Policy Council, 2008).

Raising public sector efficiency

The efficiency of public service delivery could be increased through greater use of contracting out and increasing the degree of user choice. Such mechanisms have been shown to lower the cost of service delivery, improve outcomes (for example in education), and increase the flexibility and tailoring of services to consumer needs (Lundsgaard, 2003). Sweden ranks around the middle of a sample of OECD countries for the extent of user choice and competition in local government service provision and at the top in terms of private provision and contracting out (Figure 2.6).

Figure 2.6. **User choice and competition in public services could be improved**

Use of market mechanisms in public service provision in sub-central governments, indices[1]

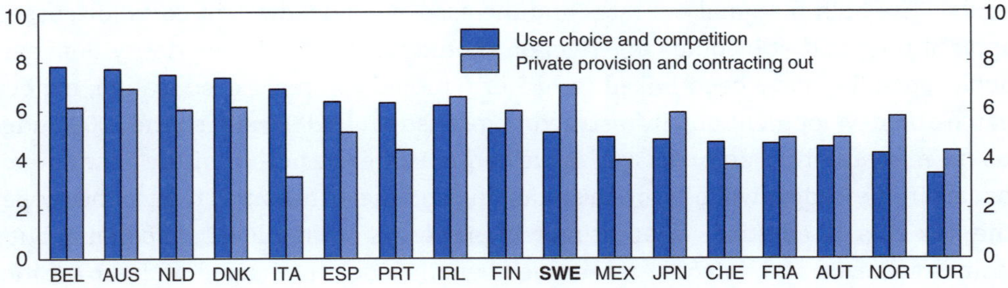

StatLink http://dx.doi.org/10.1787/485307844714

1. The "User choice and competition" index is higher when there are fewer restrictions on residents choosing providers within and outside their own jurisdiction, when there are fewer restrictions on residents outside the jurisdiction accessing services within the jurisdiction and when private providers face fewer restrictions on market access. The "Private provision and contracting out" index is higher the higher the percentage of private providers, the higher the number of outsourced services, the fewer are the restrictions on tendering and the more the government promotes private provision.

Source: Blochliger (2008).

The Swedish Competition Authority has argued that competition in public procurement in Sweden appears to be moving in the wrong direction. In a growing number of instances, procurement entities are receiving fewer tenders. Requirements that government agencies post public notification of contracts which have a value exceeding particular thresholds are being disregarded. In addition, there is a tendency to use the lowest price as a selection criterion, which may adversely affect incentives to improve service content (Swedish Competition Authority, 2007). There may be reluctance on the part of municipalities and state institutions to change the way they operate to facilitate more competitive tendering (OECD, 2007c). Recently, a proposal has been put forward to expand user choice in social services and health care. This would involve setting a contract with a fixed price and fixed quality standards and allowing the beneficiary to choose amongst alternative providers (SOU, 2008). However, the proposal does not require municipalities and county councils to use such a system. Although mandatory action might be seen as impacting on the autonomy of local governments, it may be necessary in order to bring about desired changes in the implementation of public procurement. Mandation would need to be accompanied by effective sanctions for non-compliance (OECD, 2007c).

Shifting the balance between public and private funding

Requiring individuals to finance more of the consumption elements that are currently publicly provided would reduce pressure on the spending side of the budget. Currently, some 80% of all government redistribution is over the lifetime of the same individual (Pettersson and Pettersson, 2007). Increasing private provision of some services that are currently publicly provided, but are not pure public goods, may reduce over-consumption and help contain costs. User fees are also a complement to choice and contestability in public service delivery, in the sense that better-tailored and higher-quality public service delivery may simply create more demand for these services. Price signals are needed to keep demand under control. At present, user fees at the local government level, where many public services like sub-tertiary education, health and medical care are delivered, are used only moderately compared to other OECD countries (Figure 2.7).

Figure 2.7. **User fees are only moderately used at the local government level**

Price signals in funding in sub-central governments, indices[1]

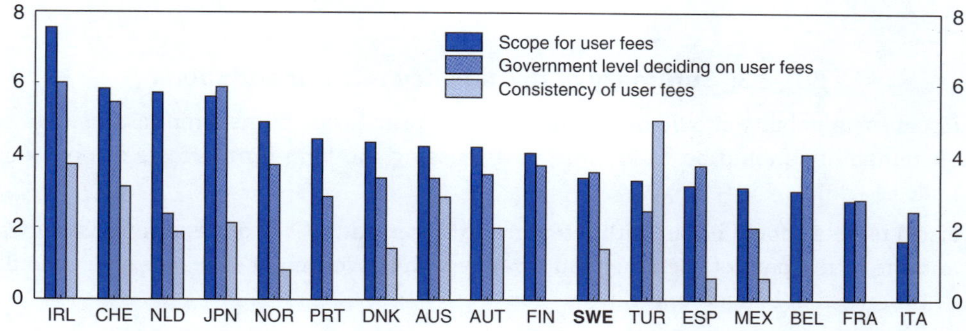

StatLink http://dx.doi.org/10.1787/485317153830

1. The "Scope for user fees" index is higher when the share of costs covered by user fees is higher. The "Government level deciding on user fees" index is higher if the provider decides or if the local government unit decides, relative to the central government deciding. The "Consistency in user fees" index is higher if the body that decides on the level of the fees gets the revenue and if the provider or local government tenderer decides on the fees.

Source: Blochliger (2008).

There are a number of areas where further user charging could be considered. Public spending on long-term care is high by international standards and is the area of spending that is set to rise most due to demographic change. More private contributions towards elements of age-care expenditures, such as home care, may be warranted. Currently, around 4% of municipalities' costs for health and social care for the elderly are financed by charges. In 2007, the highest charge for home aged-care services was SEK 1 612 (around € 175) per month. Around 22% of all people granted home care received between 10 and 25 hours per month and 39% received between 1 and 9 hours a month. The public sector share of total health expenditure is the fourth highest in the OECD and fees play a relatively limited role in financing health and medical care. Within certain limits, county councils are free to decide how much patients must pay but a high-cost protection scheme exists, ensuring that no patient ever needs to pay more than a total of SEK 900 (around € 100) over a 12-month period. Greater private contributions to health and age-care funding could take the form of higher user charges, reducing the need for pre-funding, or introducing a form of individual accounts, as in the pension system, aimed partly at pre-funding, as outlined in the 2005 *Survey* (OECD, 2005). Public spending on tertiary education as a per cent of GDP is fourth-highest in the OECD, but private funding of tertiary education is very low by international standards suggesting scope to raise education funding with greater private contributions, as discussed in Chapter 4.

Conclusions

The fiscal policy framework in Sweden has helped lower public debt and smooth the economic cycle. The fiscal surplus will be reduced by the current economic downturn but the cyclically-adjusted surplus is expected to remain above the target of 1% of GDP in the next few years. This is likely to lead to pressure for permanent increases in spending. The question of how quickly the surplus should be returned to target is intertwined with the issue of what the target should be. A way forward is to develop a full government balance sheet and consistent fiscal sustainability and intergenerational equity calculations. These could then be used to guide the setting of the fiscal targets over a number of years. Using these calculations more actively and publicly to explain the benefits of various policy options would help ensure that fiscal policy retains a long-run focus (Box 2.3).

Box 2.3. **Summary of fiscal policy recommendations**

- Fiscal sustainability should be emphasized as a prime goal. Transparent assessment of sustainability should be used more in discussing the long-term effects of proposed policies.
- Fiscal targets should be set with reference to the existing stock of assets and liabilities, and the future path of spending and revenues. The government's balance sheet should be presented in budget reporting.
- To better appreciate the implications of fiscal policy for intergenerational distribution, generational accounts should be produced and published using the same data and assumptions as the fiscal sustainability calculations that are already produced.
- In the process of establishing a new set of fiscal targets, the Fiscal Policy Council should be required to formally verify the assumptions and methodologies used.
- Periodic reviews of the overall allocation of spending could be considered to assess how new spending pressures arising from greater service demands or technological change could be financed either *via* private spending or *via* savings on existing programmes.
- Consideration should be given to formally linking the retirement age to life expectancy.
- User choice and contestability in publicly-funded services should be expanded.
- User charges and other forms of private funding should be given a bigger role in many parts of the services that are publicly funded today in order to limit excessive use and free up resources for other priorities.

Notes

1. It should be noted that borrowing for investment through the National Debt Office is permitted by the budget laws.
2. Since the early 1970s, the government has held 50 to 70% of GDP in financial assets, including a large state-owned enterprise sector and assets in the social security system. Following the pensions reforms of the late 1990s, the assets in the social security sector mainly relate to the income pension system.
3. An alternative approach would be to require an independent authority to provide the government with a path of net lending which ensured fiscal sustainability and information on the implications for intergenerational equity. The government would be expected to implement a fiscal policy that achieved this path of net lending, but with a tax and spending mix of its choice (Eichengreen *et al.*, 1999; Wyplosz, 2002). This model has not been implemented in any OECD country and would imply a considerable strengthening of the role of the Fiscal Policy Council.
4. In Norway, which is a somewhat special case, the policy framework aims to spread the benefits of future oil extraction evenly over generations. The main fiscal target is for the central government non-oil structural budget deficit to equal 4% of the asset value of the Government Pension Fund (subject to some specific exceptions). Budget documentation reports structural fiscal balances including and excluding oil revenue and generational accounts are updated each year (Norwegian Ministry of Finance, 2001).
5. The old-age dependency ratio is posited to rise from 30% in 2007 to 44% in 2050 while the youth-dependency ratio remains stable at around 40%. Average working hours, the employment rate and the unemployment rate are constant in groups defined by sex, age and country of birth, so population structure change drives potential employment. Tax receipts evolve with constant tax rates for each tax base. Tax bases grow according to the underlying economic assumptions and the implicit tax rate is calculated as the ratio of tax revenue to the tax base applying in 2011. Public

consumption expenditure is based on age- and sex-disaggregated unit costs for childcare, education, medical care, elderly care and labour market measures. Volume projections are based on the population projections, implying that public service provision is carried out with the same staffing ratio as at present. Other public consumption elements (general administration, judiciary, defence, etc.) follow the change in total population. Productivity growth in the public sector is assumed to be zero, but public sector wages grow in line with private sector wages (which in turn are driven by private sector productivity). Public transfers are assumed to grow in line with wages, even where this is not the case under current policy (Swedish government, 2008a).

6. Technically, a negative figure for the sustainability indicator suggests that policy is unsustainable in the sense that it would eventually lead to explosive asset accumulation.
7. The strength of the surpluses in the period to 2011 may partly reflect the fact that not all expenditure programmes are automatically indexed to prices or wages. The surpluses (and hence the required technical adjustment) may be reduced if there are decisions to increase the fixed nominal value of such programmes.
8. These results were obtained assuming a 1% of GDP surplus through 2015. Thereafter, spending was to be driven by demographic change, but the budget deficit was limited to 2% of GDP. This was achieved by allowing taxes to vary. The calculations are not directly comparable to the sustainability calculations presented in the budget documents since they do not take into account recent above-target surpluses and incorporate a limit on budget deficits.
9. This is based on a simulation using historical rates of return on various asset classes. It is possible that reduction in government debt and government purchases of private financial assets could change these rates of return, which would affect the calculated gains from tax smoothing.
10. Higher productivity growth would also increase the growth of tax bases, but would add to growth in public spending, since some public benefits (like old-age pensions) are linked to growth in average wages.

Bibliography

Afonso, A., W. Ebert, L. Schuknecht and M. Thone (2005), "Quality of Public Finances and Growth", ECB Working Paper No. 438.

Ahrend, R. P. Catte, and R. Price (2006), "Interactions Between Monetary and Fiscal Policy: How Monetary Conditions Affect Fiscal Consolidation", OECD *Economics Department Working Paper* No. 521.

Auerbach, A. (2008), "Long-term Objectives for Government Debt", Paper prepared for the Fiscal Policy and Labour Market Reforms conference organised by the Swedish Fiscal Policy Council, Stockholm, 29 January.

Blochliger, H. (2008), "Market Mechanisms in Public Service Provision", OECD *Economics Department Working Paper* No. 626.

Buti, M., J. Nogueira, and A. Turini (2006), "From Deficits to Debt and Back: Political Incentives Under Numerical Fiscal Rules", *Fiscal Indicators*, Proceedings of the conference of the Banca D'Italia Workshop on Public Finance, 30 March-1 April 2006.

Davis, N. and R. Fabling (2002), "Population Ageing and the Efficiency of Fiscal Policy in New Zealand", New Zealand Treasury Working Paper No. 02/11.

Eichengreen, B., R. Hausmann, and J. Von Hagen (1999), "Reforming Budgetary Institutions in Latin America: The Case for a National Fiscal Council", *Open Economies Review*, No. 10.

European Commission (2004), "The Long-Term Sustainability of Public Finances in the European Union", *European Economy* No. 4/2006, Brussels.

European Commission (2008a), "Sweden: Macro Fiscal Assessment", ECFIN/REP50205/08-EN, Brussels.

European Commission (2008b), *Public Finances in the EMU 2008*, Brussels.

Fatas, A. (2005), "Is There a Case for Sophisticated Balanced-Budget Rules?", OECD *Economics Department Working Paper* No. 466.

Hansson Brusewitz, U. and Y. Lindh (2005), "Expenditure Ceilings and Fiscal Policy: Swedish Experiences", *Public Expenditure*, Proceedings of the conference of the Banca D'Italia Workshop on Public Finance, 31 March-2 April 2005.

Heijdra, B. and F. van der Ploeg (2002), *Foundations of Modern Macroeconomics*, Oxford University Press, Oxford.

Kamps, C. (2004), "New Estimates of Government Net Capital Stocks for 22 OECD Countries 1960-2001", IMF Working Paper No. 04/67.

Lundsgaard, J. (2003), "Competition and Efficiency in Publicly Funded Services", *OECD Economic Studies* No. 35, 2002/2.

New Zealand Government (2008), *Budget 2008: Fiscal Strategy Report*, 22 May.

Norwegian Ministry of Finance (2001), "Guidelines for Economic Policy", Report No. 29 to the Storting.

OECD (2005), *OECD Economic Surveys: Sweden*, Paris.

OECD (2006), "Projecting OECD Health and Long-term Care Expenditures: What are the Main Drivers?", *OECD Economics Department Working Paper* No. 477.

OECD (2007a), "Performance Budgeting and Accrual Budgeting: Decision Rules or Analytic Tools?," Paper prepared for the Working Party on Senior Budget Officials, 11 January, Paris.

OECD (2007b), *OECD Economic Surveys: United Kingdom*, Paris.

OECD (2007c), *Sweden: Achieving Results for Sustained Growth*, OECD Reviews of Regulatory Reform.

OECD (2008a), *OECDEconomic Surveys: Denmark*, Paris.

OECD (2008b), *OECD Economic Surveys: Canada*, Paris.

Pettersson, T., T. Pettersson, and A. Westerberg (2007), "Intergenerational Distribution In a Growing Welfare State", Paper presented at the 1st General Conference of the International Microsimulation Association in Vienna, 20-22 August.

Pettersson, T. and T. Pettersson (2007), "Lifetime Redistribution Through Taxes, Transfers and Non-Cash Benefits", in Harding, A. and A. Gupta (eds.), *Modeling Our Future – Population Ageing, Social Security and Taxation,* Elsevier.

Productivity Commission (2005), "Economic Implications of an Ageing Australia", Productivity Commission Research Report, 24 March.

Pinfield, C. (1998), "Tax Smoothing and Expenditure Creep", New Zealand Treasury Working Paper No. 98/9.

SOU (2008), *Lag om valfrihet* (Law about choice), Swedish Government Official Reports, No. 2008:15.

Swedish Fiscal Policy Council (2008), *Svensk Finanspolitik* (Swedish Fiscal Policy), Stockholm.

Swedish Competition Authority (2007), *Competition in Sweden 2007*, Stockholm.

Swedish Government (2007), *Sweden's Economy: From the Budget Bill for 2008*, Stockholm.

Swedish Government (2008a), *Budget Bill 2009*, Stockholm.

Swedish Government (2008b), *Spring Fiscal Policy Bill 2008*, Stockholm.

Swedish National Audit Office (2007a), "The government's Preparation and Statement of Tax Expenditure", RIR 2007:3, Stockholm.

Swedish National Audit Office (2007b), "The government's Analysis of the Long-Term Sustainability of Fiscal Policy", RIR 2007:21, Stockholm.

Swedish National Audit Office (2008), "Tillämpningen av det finanspolitiska ramverket – Regeringens redovisning i 2008 års ekonomiska vårproposition" (Adjustment of the Fiscal Policy Framework – the government's reporting in the Spring Fiscal Policy Bill 2008), RIR No. 2008:15, Stockholm.

Wyplosz, C. (2002), "Fiscal Policy: Institutions *vs.* Rules", HEI Working Paper No. 03/2002, Graduate Institute of International Studies, Geneva.

ISBN 978-92-64-05423-3
OECD Economic Surveys: Sweden
© OECD 2008

Chapter 3

Taxation and growth: What direction should Sweden take?

In recent years, Sweden has implemented ambitious tax cuts aimed at boosting growth: it used to have the highest tax-to-GDP ratio in the OECD but is now starting to edge down the list. Yet, further reform may be needed. From income not much above average full-time earnings, the total marginal tax wedge on labour (contributions, income and consumption taxes combined) still reaches 70%. This probably helps explain short average working hours and hinders entrepreneurship, human capital formation and retention or attraction of highly-skilled staff from abroad. Corporate income taxes might also be under growing pressure from increasing capital mobility. Based on the recent OECD Taxation and Economic Growth study, this chapter assesses the Swedish tax system and the need for further tax reforms, focusing on some of the features of the tax system that matter most for longer-run growth.

Sound tax reforms have to balance a number of concerns. Revenues are needed to finance public spending priorities in infrastructure, education, health and other areas which are important for economic growth and social cohesion. But tax systems must be growth-friendly while being fair and not excessively complex. Following a review of trends in tax revenues, this chapter identifies the worst distortions in corporate and personal income taxation where cuts would be warranted. Capital mobility, labour supply and, as discussed in Chapter 4, incentives to accumulate human capital, are key when designing corporate and personal income tax reforms. Finally, housing taxes and environment and climate-related taxes, areas that could generate financing for growth-enhancing tax reforms, are reviewed.

Tax revenue trends in an international perspective

During the second half of the past century, the tax-to-GDP ratio increased steadily in most OECD countries. Although the tax-to-GDP ratio as an aggregate measure has no clear relationship to growth performances, this development nevertheless indicates potential problems as far as efficiency is concerned. The rise was particularly pronounced in Sweden: in the late 1950s, the tax-to-GDP ratio stood less than five percentage points above the US and EU15 ratios. By the late 1980s, the gap had widened to over 15 percentage points *vis-à-vis* the EU15 average and over 25 percentage points *vis-à-vis* the United States (Figure 3.1). Since then, Swedish policies have focused on avoiding any further increase. Yet, the tax-to-GDP ratio remains very high, even compared with nearby countries. Finland experienced a smaller rise in the tax burden during the 1970s and 1980s, and has managed to cut taxes more since the tax-to-GDP ratio peaked at 47% in 1995. The Netherlands, where developments paralleled Sweden's in the 1960s and 1970s, managed to end the rise in the tax burden already in the 1980s and has reduced it considerably since the early 1990s. With the recent tax cuts, Sweden has gone below Denmark, but that country aside, Sweden's tax-to-GDP ratio remains the highest in the OECD. The size of the gap *vis-à-vis* other countries is boosted by technical differences, notably that income benefits have been taxable since the beginning of the 1970s in Sweden. If correcting for this, the tax-to-GDP ratio, projected to be 46.3% in 2009, would be 42.8% (Ministry of Finance, 2008a). With this correction, the gap is smaller, but Sweden still belongs among the OECD countries with the highest tax pressure, not least reflecting that only Germany and France have higher net public social expenditure than Sweden.[1]

The bulk of Sweden's high tax revenue comes from labour taxes, in the form of social security contributions and personal income taxes. Since the late 1970s, these sources combined have accounted for at least two thirds of total revenue, as against one half on average in the OECD (Figure 3.1; Table 3.1). Like in other countries, efforts have been made to reduce personal income taxation over recent decades but with a tendency for this to be offset by increased social security contributions, leaving the average tax wedge on labour unchanged.

Figure 3.1. **Trends in tax revenue**

As per cent of GDP

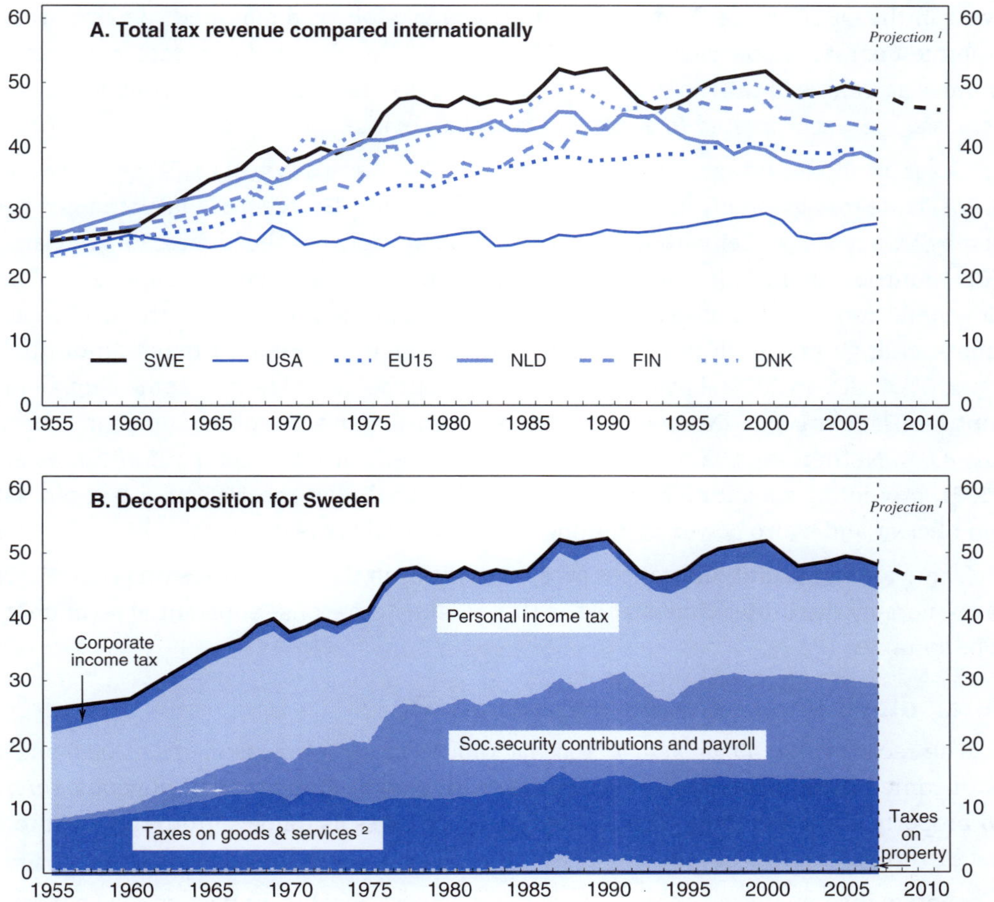

StatLink http://dx.doi.org/10.1787/485340448136

1. 2009 Budget Bill.
2. Includes value added tax and import duties etc. paid to the European Union.

Source: OECD, *Revenue Statistics* and Ministry of Finance.

Table 3.1. **Composition of tax revenue across OECD countries**

Per cent, 2006

	Denmark[1]	Finland	Netherlands	**Sweden**	EU15	United States	OECD
Corporate income tax	9	8	9	8	9	12	11
Personal income tax	50	30	19	32	25	36	25
Social security contributions and payroll tax	3	27	34	31	29	25	27
Taxes on good and services	32	31	32	26	30	17	30
Taxes on property	4	3	5	3	5	11	6
Other	0	0	1	0	1	0	3

1. In addition, 2% of total tax revenue are income taxes that cannot be allocated between corporate and personal.

Source: OECD, *Revenue Statistics*.

Corporate income taxes contribute about as much to fiscal revenues as elsewhere. In the 1980s Sweden had one of the highest corporate tax rates in the OECD, although the effective tax burden was much lower due to very generous reserve provisions (immediate depreciation of investment expenditures and possibilities for writing down the value of stocks). The tax reform in the early 1990s broadened the corporate tax base by scaling down these reserve provisions and brought the statutory tax rate down to among the lowest in the OECD; since then, other countries have followed suit, and the 28% Swedish corporate tax rate is now close to the OECD average. Despite the lower rate, corporate tax revenues as a share of GDP have grown, reflecting base broadening and, possibly, that small businesses get incorporated to a larger extent than before.

Taxes on goods and services have increased slightly as a share of GDP. The value-added tax (VAT) rate rose gradually from 17.6% in 1975 to 25% in 1995, where it has remained since. Thereby, Sweden (together with Denmark and Norway) now has the highest VAT rate among OECD countries. Environmental concerns are also on the agenda in most countries and there is a general consensus that taxes are an efficient instrument to address the challenges of climate change and pollution. Sweden's environmentally-related taxes amounted to around 3% of GDP in 2005, above the OECD average but below the level in some neighbouring countries (Denmark 4.6%, Norway 3.7%, Finland 3.3%) and in some other European countries (Italy 4.0%, Netherlands 3.6%, Portugal 3.5%). Sweden introduced a carbon tax as early as 1991, promoting substitution away from fossil fuels. Today, most electricity is generated from nuclear and hydro power, stemming environmental tax revenue.

There are important differences across countries in the use of taxes on property. Only a few – notably the United States and the United Kingdom – raise substantial revenue from property taxes.

What overall direction should tax reforms take?

The recent OECD *Taxation and Economic Growth* study (Johansson *et al.*, 2008) showed that income taxation has more adverse effects on growth than taxation of goods, services and property. It ranked the four main categories of taxes as follows, from the most to the least distortive in terms of reducing GDP:

- Corporate income taxes appear to have the strongest negative impact on GDP per capita. Lowering corporate taxes spurs investment. It also raises TFP growth, in particular for the most dynamic and innovative firms, by boosting entrepreneurship, innovation and foreign direct investment.
- Personal income taxes affect labour supply both quantitatively *via* participation in the labour market and average hours worked, and qualitatively *via* human capital formation, effort, and willingness to take less interesting jobs. Entrepreneurship may also be affected insofar as entrepreneurial income, in excess of returns on the invested capital, is taxed as personal income.
- Consumption taxes and other taxes on goods and services affect growth less. Moreover, the structure of taxation of goods and services can be used to promote environmental objectives.
- Finally, recurrent taxes on immovable property are the least harmful for growth, partly because housing is tax-favoured in virtually all OECD countries, meaning that higher property taxes imply moving closer to neutrality. Other property taxes, such as transaction taxes, may be more distortive than income taxation.

This ranking is a useful first guide for where to focus tax reforms, subject to two caveats. *First*, the estimation results apply to the average country. Thus, for example, if a particular country relies less on income taxation than the OECD average, then shifting taxation further away from income might be less beneficial than the estimation results would indicate. Hence, each country's starting position has to be taken into account. *Second*, adjustments within each tax category can hold a lot of potential beyond the prospects of reallocation between broad tax categories captured by the regression analysis.

Capital and business taxation

Given the above ranking, it is welcome that a reduction of the corporate tax rate from 28% to 26.3% is now planned for 2009. The ensuing revenue loss would be about 0.2% of GDP which would be financed by tougher tax rules, partly relating to deduction of corporate interest expenditures where these are judged to reflect tax planning (Swedish Government, 2008).[2] Aside from making Sweden a more attractive investment location, a lower corporate tax rate would help to balance the tax treatment of debt and equity finance for domestic companies raising funds from domestic investors.[3]

For entrepreneurs and closely-held companies, a set of important tax cuts have been made in recent years. The position of these companies can often be affected considerably by personal taxation of the owner. It was therefore an important step that wealth taxation (*förmögenhetsskatten*) was abolished in 2007. This comes on top of the ending of the gift and inheritance taxes a few years ago, which have made it easier to transfer small companies from one generation to the next.

Different proposals for cuts in employer contributions for specific types of firms have been mentioned in the Swedish debate. Lowering employer contributions for marginal labour market groups can be justified as a way to compensate for collectively-agreed wages, which allow too little dispersion, to reflect differences in individual productivity. However, lowering employer contributions specifically for small and medium-sized enterprises, as sometimes discussed, does not have a similar justification. Moreover, it would distort competition and hinder the natural selection process of the most efficient players in the market place, thus hindering economic growth.

It is not small companies as such, but rather innovative ones that need attention to promote economic growth. In this context, it is important to ease the process of firm creation without creating disincentives for firms to expand. It is therefore welcome that changes are now being discussed to promote entrepreneurship further by making it easier for individuals to become taxed as self-employed entrepreneurs (*F-skatt*). The changes are particularly important for those starting with one or a few customers (SOU, 2008a).[4] In particular, it is expected that female entrepreneurs will benefit from this. For example, it could be easier for someone working in municipal long-term care to start her own business with her previous employer as a key customer. If adopted, the suggested changes are expected to take effect from January 2009.[5]

Social security contributions and personal income taxation

Employment rates are high, but the average number of hours worked annually by each person employed is low, leaving labour supply, measured as total hours worked per person in the working-age population, close to the OECD average (Figure 3.2). Most of the difference in the aggregate employment-to-population ratio is explained by higher participation of women across all age groups. Moreover, the problems of early retirement draining labour supply elsewhere are less pronounced in Sweden: over half of the 60-64 year olds are working. Meanwhile, long holidays and other forms of leave reduce the number of weeks and thus the total number of hours worked per year.[6]

Figure 3.2. **Total labour supply is around average**

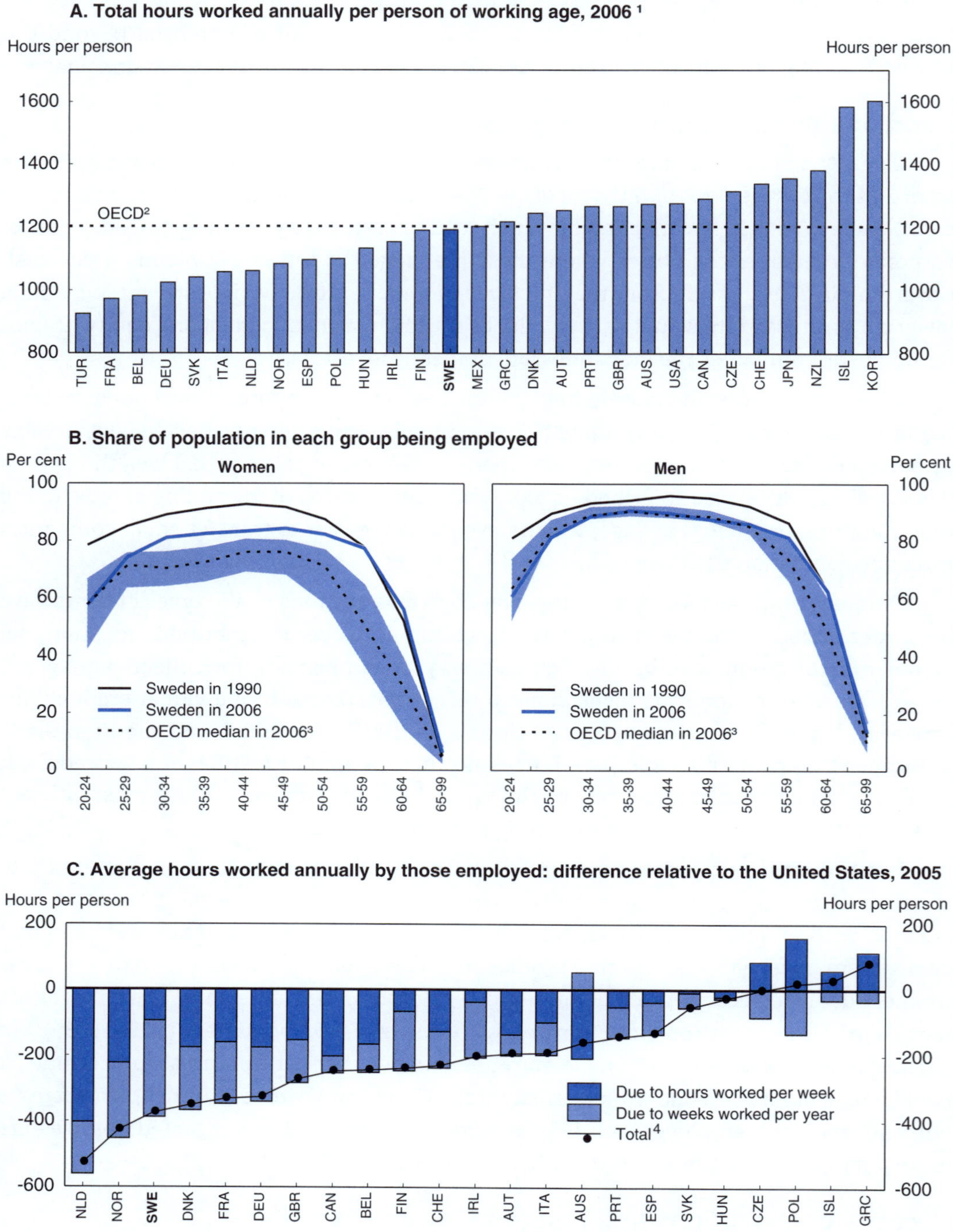

StatLink http://dx.doi.org/10.1787/485341023848

1. National statistics do not use the same age intervals for working-age population in all countries. For consistency, the data shown here are total hours worked relative to size of the population aged 15-64.
2. Considering the OECD as whole, but excluding Luxembourg.
3. The shaded area shows the range of the two central quartiles (*i.e.* half of the countries fall in this range).
4. Because of interaction between deviations in hours worked per week and weeks worked per year, the total deviation in hours worked per year *vis-à-vis* the United States is different from the sum of the two components.

Source: OECD, *Economic Outlook 83 database*, *Productivity database* and *Labour Force Statistics database;* OECD (2008a), *Going for Growth* 2008.

A striking feature of average hours worked in Sweden is the small difference between full and part-timers. Indeed, at 28 hours per week, part-timers work much longer in Sweden than elsewhere (Box 3.1). This would suggest that the main lever to raise labour supply is to elicit more working weeks per year and more hours per week from the full-time employees rather than to try and increase labour market participation or hours worked of part-timers.

Box 3.1. **Decomposing the international comparison of average annual hours worked**

A recent OECD study has established standardised measures that facilitate a detailed decomposition of how Swedish working times differ from those in other OECD countries (Table 3.2).*

- For full-time employees, the number of hours worked per week is about the same as in Denmark and Germany. *vis-à-vis* the United States, the difference is three hours: usual weekly working time is two hours shorter than in the United States and there is one hour less overtime in Sweden.
- By contrast, part-timers work considerably longer weekly hours than in other countries, including the United States.
- Absence from work is extensive for both full-time and part-time employees. The number of public holidays and vacation weeks is slightly higher than in Denmark and Germany, and much higher than in the United States. Moreover, the average Swedish employee spends more weeks on maternity/parental leave and sick leave.

Average working hours should be seen in the context of how much women and people in their late 50s and 60s participate in the labour market. The share of women working is higher than in any other OECD country, except Iceland, for prime-aged women (25-54) as well as for older women (55-64). For older men, labour market participation is also relatively high. Against this background, it could have been expected that many would be working part time, but this is not the case. With 19% of female employment being part time, Sweden is below the OECD average, and also below the average for the other Nordic countries; for men, 9% of employment is part time, slightly above the OECD average but equal to the average for the other Nordic countries.

Table 3.2. **The anatomy of a work year**

Standardised measures, 2005

	Full-time employees					Part-time employees				
	USA	AUS	DEU	DNK	SWE	USA	SWE	AUS	DNK	DEU
Annual hours worked per employee	2 097	2 073	1 756	1 710	1 622	1 093	1 072	863	826	776
Total weekly hours on all jobs	44.9	43.4	42.0	41.2	41.8	24.5	28.1	18.5	20.3	18.7
Usual weekly hours on main job	42.0		40.1	39.4	39.9	22.4	25.3		18.2	17.4
Overtime on main job	2.9		1.8	1.1	1.6	2.1	1.6		0.9	0.9
Hours on additional job			0.2	0.7	0.4		1.2		1.1	0.4
Annual weeks worked (= 52 – sum of below)	46.7	47.8	41.7	41.6	38.8	44.6	38.2	46.7	40.8	41.5
Public holidays and statutory minimum paid leave	4.0		8.1	7.8	8.4	4.0	8.4		7.8	8.1
Maternity/parental leave			0.4	0.9	1.6		1.6		0.6	0.3
Sickness and disability leave	0.6		1.1	0.9	2.4	1.3	2.8		1.0	0.8
Leave for other reasons	0.7		0.7	0.8	0.8	2.0	1.1		1.8	1.2

Source: OECD (2008a), *Going for Growth* 2008.

* Previously, OECD data on average hours worked published in the *OECD Employment Outlook* were adjusted for perceived underreporting of absence due to sickness and parental leave. This adjustment has been shown to be misleading in the case of Sweden (Holmlund, 2007). The new standardised measures reported in the OECD's *Going for Growth* do not adjust for perceived underreporting of sick and parental leave.

The total tax wedge on labour is among the very highest in the OECD for above-average incomes. Personal income taxation consists of two layers. The municipal income taxation is levied at a flat rate which varies across municipalities but averages 31.6% in 2008. The so-called state income tax, which accrues to the central government, constitutes the progressive element: it sets in at a 20% rate just above average full-time earnings and rises to 25% from one-and-a-half times average full-time earnings. In combination with employer contributions (32.4%), employee contributions (7%) and relatively high consumption taxes, the total tax wedge on labour varies between 56% and 71% for incomes exceeding the basic personal deduction (Figure 3.3). These high wedges should be seen in the light that pension entitlements are linked to the contributions made during the individual's working life. However, for the 11% pension contribution paid by employers, this link is capped at about 90% of average full-time earnings; above that threshold, the contribution is a pure tax. Effectively, the marginal wedge is lower for below-average earners and progression stronger than indicated by the schedule in Figure 3.3. Spouses are taxed separately, helping to reduce the marginal rates faced by second earners. All forms of capital income are taxed at a flat 30% rate, except for pension saving schemes, where the rate is 15%.

Recent cuts in income taxation have taken the form of an in-work tax credit. It was first introduced in 2007, then enlarged in 2008, and with the third step included in the Budget Bill for 2009, its budgetary cost has reached 2% of GDP. The aim is to make work more attractive relative to benefit recipiency, but as the size of the credit rises with earned income, it has also lowered the marginal tax wedge for persons with incomes below average (Figure 3.3).

From 2009, employer contributions will be cut by 1 percentage point across the board. Like the in-work tax credit, this cut lightens the tax wedge on earned income relative to that on income from benefits, but the long-run effects on employment are likely to be weaker than for the in-work credit. The immediate effect will be to make hiring more profitable. Indeed, the government hopes that the move can stem the likely decline in employment as economic growth slows (Swedish Government, 2008). In the long run, however, equilibrium would re-establish in the labour market with higher wages partly or fully offsetting the cut in contributions. Higher wages would elicit more hours from those already employed, and also make work more attractive relative to social assistance and other benefits where the recipient is entitled to a fixed amount. By contrast, unemployment insurance benefits and sickness benefits are calculated as a share of previous earnings, meaning that higher wages would not make these benefits less attractive – except for persons with earnings above three quarters of average full-time earnings where a benefit ceiling sets in.[7]

Lowering the overall tax burden via the in-work tax credit and cuts in employer contributions have beneficial effects, but the dynamic effects would be stronger from other income tax cuts. As explained in the previous *Survey*, owing to the narrow Swedish earnings distribution, an in-work tax credit is less straightforward to apply than in a British or American context where earned-income tax credits have had much success. Cutting the state income tax would be more cost effective: starting from a very high level, reductions in the marginal tax wedge would imply a considerable increase in how much the person retains when gross income rises. Consequently, the static revenue loss is relatively small compared to the magnitude of the change in incentives. This is particularly pronounced at incomes moderately above the point where the state income tax sets in: the density of the income distribution is still high, but declines rapidly as income rises. Thereby, a lot of taxpayers face the very high marginal wedge, but pay only very small amounts in state

Figure 3.3. **Total marginal tax wedges**

Income taxes, employer and employee contributions and consumption taxes combined for a single person without children having income at 50-200% of average full-time earnings[1]

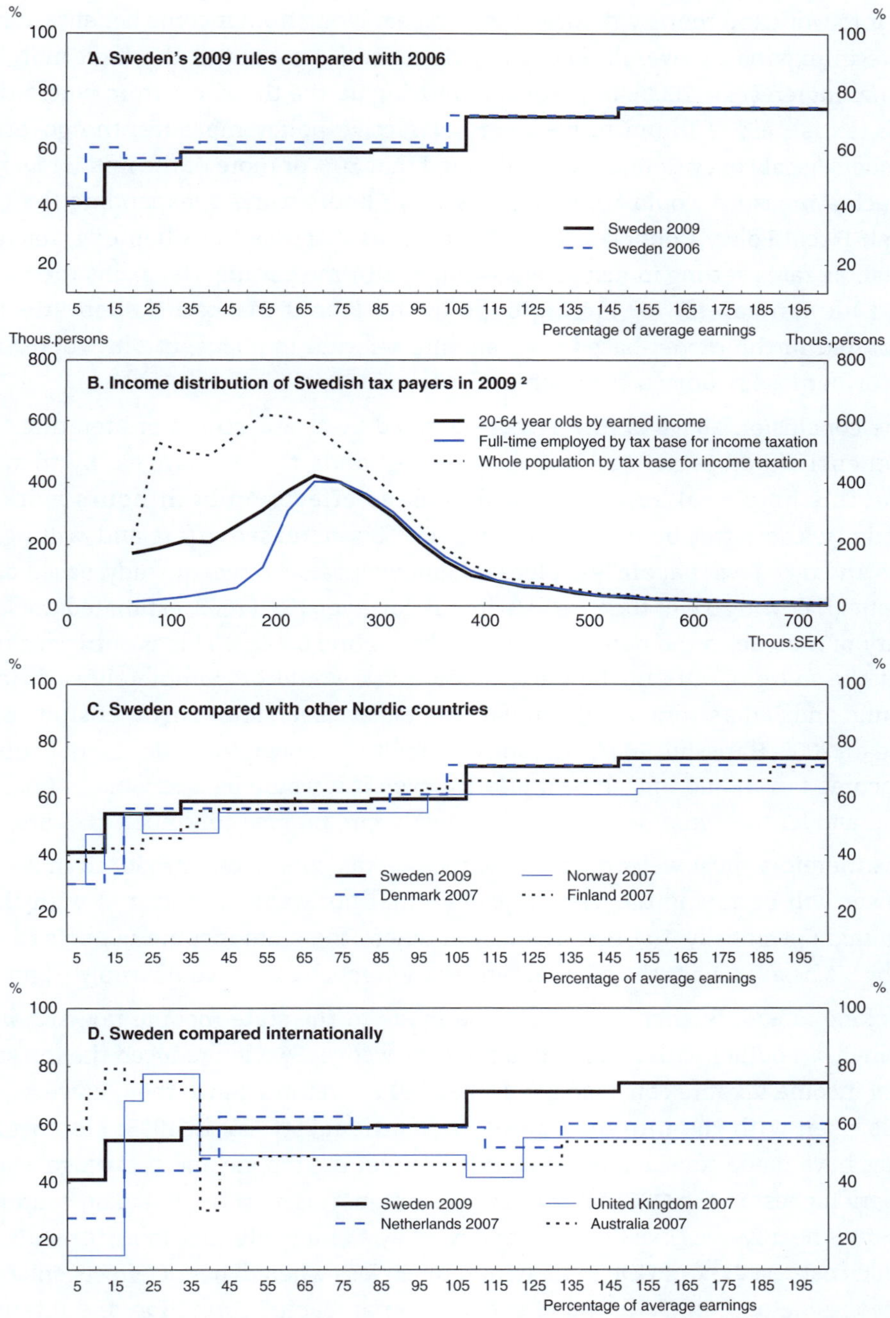

StatLink http://dx.doi.org/10.1787/485342255263

1. Average consumption taxes are 29.9% for Sweden, 30.7% for Denmark, 26.1% for Norway, 22.2% for Finland, 22.2% for the Netherlands, 17.6% for the United Kingdom and 20.1% for Australia in 2007. In Sweden, the family situation only matters for benefits entitlements, whereas social contributions and taxes are strictly individual. The Swedish tax schedule shown in the figure therefore applies to everybody.
2. The income distributions are based on the FASIT model and the 2006 HEK household survey uprated to 2009 levels. The horizontal scale is matched across the four panels as average full-time worker earnings are estimated to equal SEK 364 300 in 2009. The tax base for income taxation includes earnings, fringe benefits, unemployment and other income support and pensions etc. It does not include capital income which is taxed separately.

Source: OECD, *Taxing wages database* and the associated tax equations; OECD, *Analytical database*; Ministry of Finance, Statistics Sweden and OECD calculations.

income tax (Figure 3.3; OECD, 2007a). During the past year, models have been developed that incorporate detailed information about Swedish households' income and tax position. Results from these models confirm that although the in-work tax credit helps to draw more people into work and thereby reduces the numbers living from income benefits, it is not as effective in expanding overall labour supply as cuts targeted at the high marginal tax wedge (Lundgren *et al.*, 2008). In particular, moving up the threshold from where the state income tax is paid is found to be a very attractive policy measure: the government-established Fiscal Policy Council has estimated that 80% or more of the initial revenue loss from such a measure would come back *via* more hours worked, expanding the tax base (Swedish Fiscal Policy Council, 2008). Moreover, as discussed in Chapter 4, having high marginal tax rates setting in just above average full-time earnings weakens the incentives to build human capital for large groups in the labour market. If such effects were incorporated in the model-based assessments referred to above, the in-work tax credit would further lose relative attractiveness.

The conclusion above is further corroborated by a new strand of literature taking a comprehensive perspective at how income responds to tax changes. By focusing on income, this empirical approach encompasses effects on both hours worked and productivity, the latter being affected *inter alia* by increased effort and willingness to relocate and take jobs that are less pleasant, but well paid.[8] A recent study, based on a very large panel following 3% of the Swedish population over 1991-2002, estimated the long-run elasticity of income to the net-of-tax rate to be around 0.2-0.3. This is sufficient to imply that, at the margin, cuts in the state income tax would be completely self financing (Holmlund and Söderström, 2007). Similar results have been found in other studies (Ljunge and Ragan, 2005; Hansson, 2007). The implication to be drawn for policy is that cutting the state income tax should indeed be a priority, even if it would be advisable to finance cuts up front, and let the dynamic effects, once they occur, finance continued tax cuts.

It is therefore most welcome that the income tax cuts to be introduced in 2009 imply that fewer will be facing the very high marginal tax wedge associated with the state income tax. Specifically, the threshold from where the state income tax sets in is to be raised by 5% beyond what the standard indexation mechanism would imply (Figure 3.3).[9]

Looking ahead, further cuts should be made to the state income tax, as Sweden is increasingly an outlier with its high marginal tax wedge. Sweden reduced the top statutory personal income tax rate considerably in the 1990 tax reform. Since then, however, the top rate has risen with the introduction of an additional 5% tax in 1995. Moreover, other countries have made considerable reductions so that the top income tax wedge is now one of the very highest in the OECD; it is thus large not just *vis-à-vis* Anglo-Saxon countries, but also *vis-à-vis* nearby ones like Germany and Norway. Completely abolishing the state income tax would cost just 1.3% of GDP initially, and much less when dynamic effects enlarging the tax base are factored in. With the effects on human capital formation and international mobility likely to become gradually more important, reducing the state income tax should be a priority in the future. Such cuts are often contested as the state income tax is one of the few remaining elements creating progression in the Swedish tax system. However, equity is better served by policies to promote learning outcomes for children of all backgrounds and widen labour market inclusion than by retaining very high marginal taxes for high-income earners or the wealth tax which was recently abolished. Moreover, there would still be ample redistribution in the form of publicly-funded services like child care available to all and relatively generous social security. A socially acceptable – and efficient – approach could be to further move up the threshold from where the state income tax is paid. An efficiency-oriented income tax reform with an acceptable equitable outcome would make the Swedish welfare state considerably more robust in a context of globalisation.

The effect on hours worked from a financed reduction in the marginal tax wedge can be illustrated based on a recent OECD study of hours worked. When controlling for relevant factors, including employment and the average tax level for the whole economy, the marginal tax wedge appears a significant and important determinant of average hours worked by women. There is a clear negative substitution effect: higher taxes reduce the income from working an extra hour and so induce more consumption of leisure (Box 3.2). For men, the effect is smaller. To illustrate the implications of these estimation results, it can be instructive to simulate the effect of reducing marginal tax rates in Sweden to the level in Australia – a country with a relatively low marginal tax

Box 3.2. **Estimated cross-country effects of taxes on hours worked**

Econometric analysis of hours worked was conducted on a panel of 22 OECD countries, including Sweden, with data for 1991-2005 (OECD, 2008a; Causa, 2008). The equations also included employment rates (instrumented), educational and family patterns as control variables as well as time and country fixed-effect dummies. The main result is as follows (omitting the other explanatory variables):

For men: log (usual weekly hours worked) = -0.136^{**} marginal tax wedge + ...

For women: log (usual weekly hours worked) = -0.730^{***} marginal tax wedge +...

where ** denotes statistical significance at the 95% level and *** at the 99% level. The estimated semi-elasticities imply that a one percentage point increase in the marginal tax wedge is associated with a 0.73% decline in the usual weekly hours worked by women in the average OECD country.

These estimates confirm that marginal tax wedges are an important determinant of variation in hours worked across countries and over time, even if the exact magnitude of the effect can only be estimated with some uncertainty. In some specifications, the coefficient is not statistically significant for men. The effect tends to be stronger for married than single men and for persons with tertiary education than for those without.

Working hours data come from the labour force survey: respondents are asked to state how many hours they work in a usual week not affected by holidays, sickness absence or similar. As this excludes "unusual" overtime and second jobs, the difference between total annual hours worked in the United States *versus* Europe may not be fully captured in the dataset. Marginal tax wedges are calculated based on OECD *Taxing Wages* models which include the combined effect of direct income taxes, social security contributions paid by employers and employees, child benefits and in-work tax credits, but not consumption taxes (indirect taxes). Wedges are averages over 6 household types and gross earnings at each percentile from 61% to 200% and 33% to 99% of average production worker earnings, for first and second earners respectively.

Factors other than marginal taxes also affect average hours worked, but less. The availability and costs of childcare matter a lot, but here Sweden is already well equipped. Regulations that restrict weekly working time explain part of the variation across OECD countries for men, whereas women tend to work fewer hours and so are less constrained by maximum working-time limits.

rate. For women, the usual weekly working time would increase by over 2 hours (Figure 3.4). As always with cross-country panel estimates, it should be kept in mind that the strength of the effect might vary considerably across countries *inter alia* due to different institutional features not fully controlled for in the analysis: the estimated coefficients reflect the strength of the effect of a change in the marginal tax rate in the average country. For example, taxation of spouses individually, not combined, and differences in family and gender roles in the labour market might imply that there is less of a gap between the size of elasticities for women and men in Sweden than in the average OECD country. The simulation is therefore only illustrative.

Figure 3.4. **Illustrative simulation: women's labour supply if marginal tax rates were at Australian levels**

Simulation for total hours worked per week including effects on both usual weekly hours worked and share of women working, but not effects of the number of weeks worked per year[1]

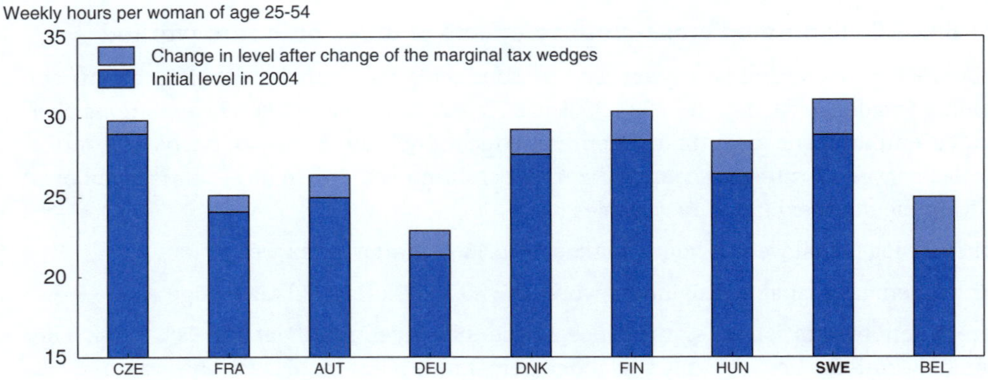

StatLink http://dx.doi.org/10.1787/485350334761

1. Countries are ranked according to change in hours worked after change of the marginal tax wedges.

Source: Calculations based on Causa (2008).

Do-it-yourself work

Doing household work oneself or purchasing help from outside is an important way in which hours worked can adjust. High marginal income tax wedges imply that even highly skilled people have an incentive to do clothes washing, cleaning, etc., themselves, even though they would be considerably more productive at other activities. It will therefore be interesting to follow how the recent Swedish tax deduction for purchase of household work will function in practice. Since July 2007, each adult can claim a tax deduction worth half of what is paid for household work in the person's own or parents' home up to a limit of 15% of average full-time earnings.[10] Coming on top of Sweden's comparatively ample provision of publicly-funded child care facilities and long-term care at home and in institutions, the scheme is intended to make it easier for both women and men to combine work and family life while increasing the jobs available for the low-skilled. Services must be acquired from a company or someone registered as self-employed, and the service purchase is liable for VAT. These safeguards are meant to prevent unreported work from growing under the scheme. In 2007, about 1% of Swedish households made use of the scheme, and the initial experience seems relatively positive. To increase user friendliness, a recent review recommended that the tax deduction be granted upfront, when the services are purchased, rather than after year-end (SOU, 2008b), a change that is likely to take effect in 2009.

 OECD ECONOMIC SURVEYS: SWEDEN – ISBN 978-92-64-05423-3 – © OECD 2008

Tax and benefit fraud

The informal economy in Sweden is smaller, relative to GDP, than in some other countries, but surveys indicate that tax evasion is a key factor underpinning undeclared work. The Swedish tax authorities estimate that it implies a total revenue loss equal to 4½ per cent of GDP, of which about half is related to unreported income from work. International studies indicate a larger shadow economy in Sweden, represent close to one fifth of GDP, broadly similar to what is estimated for Denmark, Finland, Germany and Norway (Schneider, 2004). When asked to identify the main reason for doing undeclared work in a recent Eurobarometer survey, 32% of the Swedish respondents pointed to high taxes, the third-largest share among EU27 countries (European Commission, 2007), and 84% said that there was only a small risk that tax and social-security authorities would detect undeclared work – more than in any other EU27 country. Moreover, tax ethics appear to have deteriorated as younger generations find it more socially acceptable not to declare income: almost 4% of those born in the 1970s don't report any income at all to the tax authorities despite being economically active, as against 2¼ and 1½ per cent for those born in the 1960s and 1950s respectively. Most of these people live in and around the larger cities and are men.[11]

A comprehensive approach is needed as underreporting of income is often linked to fraudulent receipt of income benefits. Raids on taxi cabs have shown that even in well-established taxi companies, up to 40% of the drivers did not declare their income to the tax authorities while, at the same time, they claimed unemployment insurance benefits, sickness benefits or social assistance. This undermines public support for sustaining these social insurance programmes and strongly distorts competition, making it hard for law-abiding firms to stay in business. A government-established commission recently estimated that 4% of all welfare benefit payments were in some way erroneous (SOU, 2008c). Half of this reflects intentional fraud on the part of recipients. The commission's main proposal is closer integration of public registers. Today, welfare benefits are paid out on the basis of information provided by the recipient about her or his work, income, assets and housing situation. Instead, the commission proposes that the information collected by one authority should be available to the other authorities needing it. The tax authorities would have a central position, collecting information from employers about each individual's income on a monthly basis and establishing a register of individuals' major assets and liabilities. In addition, the tax authority would be given a mandate to check that the information about the place of residence is correct by visiting the person concerned. The commission also recommends extended possibilities for the tax authorities to control the construction sector, which appears to have particular problems, similar to those in cleaning and transport.[12] These are confirmed by the Eurobarometer survey: 31% of the Swedes responding that they had commissioned undeclared work said that construction was the most important area, compared with just 16% on average for EU27 countries (European Commission, 2007).

Stronger sanctions might also be considered to stem tax and benefit fraud. Indeed, it is striking that people in Sweden consider the risk of being caught for undeclared work smaller than in other European countries. The commission's proposal to introduce administrative fines for benefit fraud is therefore welcome. Such administrative sanctions are possible today for tax fraud, but not for benefit fraud where sanctions can only be applied in court cases. The commission's proposals to oblige municipal case workers to report when they spot wrong information could also be an important step forward – similar obligations exist for civil servants in other areas.

Housing taxation

Housing taxation is the form of taxation involving the smallest economic distortions, it is little used and it could therefore be given a larger role. In fact, Sweden had a well-functioning real estate tax until the end of 2006: owner-occupied housing was taxed at an annual effective 0.7% of the market value, based on frequently-updated value assessments. As analysed in the previous *Survey*, the rate should have been higher to ensure neutrality *vis-à-vis* other parts of capital taxation, but the tax advantage for housing was not alarmingly large (OECD, 2007a). It is therefore regrettable that this value-based housing tax has been replaced by a fixed fee per house (Box 3.3). With the recent rise in house prices, this shift has implied a revenue loss of around ¼ per cent of GDP.

Box 3.3. From a proportional value-based state housing tax to a capped municipal fee

Housing taxation has changed in two steps. From 2007, property valuations were frozen at the level applied for taxation in 2006, and the part of the tax relating to land value was capped at SEK 2 per square metre, with an additional cap for the total at SEK 5 000. For multi-dwelling houses, the tax rate was reduced from 0.5% to 0.4% and imputed rent taxation was abolished (OECD, 2007a). From 2008, a complete reform was implemented. The state housing tax was abolished. A municipal fee was introduced of SEK 6 000 for one-family houses and SEK 1 200 per dwelling in multi-dwelling houses, but with the restriction that the fee cannot exceed what the state housing tax would have been under the previous system. To finance this second step, the effective tax rate for housing capital gains taxation was raised from 20 to 22%, and access to deferred taxation of realised capital gains was reduced by limiting the maximum deferral to SEK 1 600 000, not allowing it when the owner dies, and charging interest on realised but deferred gains (Ministry of Finance, 2007a).

The shift from a value-based tax to a capped fee implied very large tax cuts for owners of large and well-located houses – benefiting first and foremost those living in the Stockholm region. In effect, the change in the housing tax has weakened the tax system's overall capacity to redistribute resources down the income scale (LO, 2008; Figure 3.5). Whether that is desirable is of course a political choice, but it should be seen in the context of reforms of the distortive state income tax that will inevitably imply less redistribution via income taxation. One way to offset this with minimal distortions would be to reinstate a housing tax levied in proportion to home value.[13]

Two further changes to housing taxation are now being discussed, but in some respects they would create new distortions. One suggestion is to introduce a 1% tax on the part of the house's value that exceeds SEK 5 million. This would restore some of the 2006 system's redistributive capacity. Another proposal is to extend the current pensioner rule, which limits housing taxes to 4% of the household's income, to apply irrespective of age. This proposal would not cost much revenue, but it would imply that the estimated 100 000 persons concerned by the extension of the rule would see their effective marginal tax rate rise by four percentage points, thereby creating a low-income trap.

Figure 3.5. **Distributional effects of the housing tax cut**

Change in disposable income by decile, 2008[1]

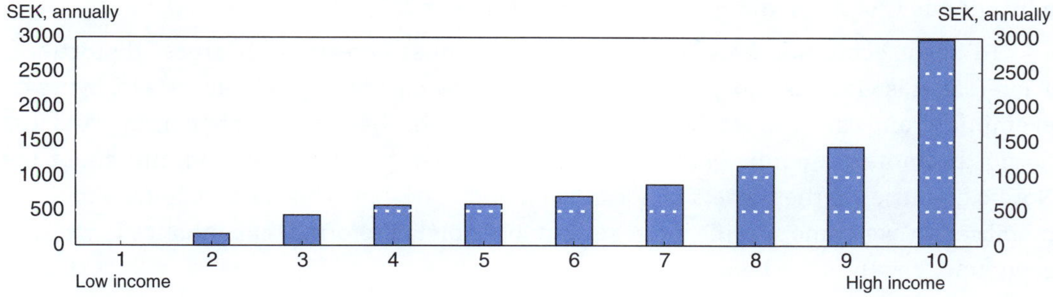

StatLink http://dx.doi.org/10.1787/485353177780

1. No assessments are available for the combined effect of the changes implemented in 2007 and 2008. Therefore, the figure shows only the effect of the changes implemented in 2007, comparing what housing taxes would have been in 2008 under the 2006 rules *versus* the 2007 rules. The effect of taxation of tenant-owned apartments is not included. The distributional effects of the changes implemented in 2008 were relatively small, as the tightening of capital gains taxation tends to weigh most on the highest-income deciles.

Source: Statistics Sweden (2007).

Climate and environmental taxation

Environment and climate-related taxes would be a natural source for additional revenue to finance cuts elsewhere. Indeed, to curb greenhouse gas emissions at affordable costs, it is vital to expand the role of economic instruments, such as carbon taxes or emissions trading schemes. By putting a "price" on greenhouse gas emissions, such instruments ensure that mitigating action takes place where it is cheapest and creates incentives for R&D and clean technology adoption (OECD, 2008b). Thereby, broad market-based measures are more growth-friendly than complex regulations or tax instruments targeting specific modes of transport, energy production or home insulation.

One important caveat for the use of carbon taxes is how they interact with emission trading schemes. Raising carbon taxes in one EU country will reduce emissions there, but the effect tends to be offset by increased emissions in other EU countries in response to the lower equilibrium prices on emission permits – unless the total volume of permits is reduced. This means that the use of carbon taxes on firms covered by the emission scheme could result in efficiency losses. Once the post-2012 climate policy architecture has taken shape within the European Union and internationally, it will be easier to design climate-related tax measures.

Nevertheless, certain aspects could be improved already now. For example, the rebates and exemptions from Sweden's CO2 tax do not all seem to be warranted by interactions with the EU Emission Trading Scheme. For diesel used to fuel machinery in agriculture and forestry, 79% of the standard CO2 tax is reimbursed upon application (Ministry of Finance, 2007b). Such exemptions raise the economic costs for society as a whole of achieving targets for reductions in CO2 emissions.

Conclusions

When taxes amount to about half of national income, as in Sweden, a number of distortions are bound to arise holding back businesses and people's productive drive. To achieve a marked reduction in these distortions, Swedish tax reforms should aim not just at fine-tuning, but at genuine tax cuts backed by spending restraint. Social objectives can be achieved in ways that require less public funding than today, as discussed for higher education in Chapter 4 and more generally in Chapter 2.

To boost economic growth, tax reductions must address the largest distortions. Therefore, it is vital that tax policy is not captured by narrow special interests lobbying for exemptions and caveats, which end up complicating the system or implementing cuts that do not promote economic growth, such as on housing. What many admire about the Nordic countries is their levels of social trust and cohesion. This social capital should be mobilised to overcome specific interests and focus on tax reforms that enhance longer-run economic growth to the benefit of all.

Box 3.4. **Summary of tax recommendations**

- Continue with reductions of the corporate income tax rate.
- Continue the cuts in taxation of income from work, focusing on reducing the very high marginal tax wedge setting in not much above average full-time earnings. As the adverse effects on human capital formation and international mobility of highly-skilled professionals are likely to become more important, a future priority could be to phase out the state income tax, in the absence of which the highest marginal wedge from contributions and income taxes combined would be just below 50%.
- Consider tougher sanctions for tax and benefit fraud without adding to the system's complexity.
- Reinstate a housing tax levied in proportion to home value.
- Consider shifting more of the tax burden onto environment and climate taxes. Reconsider current non-neutralities such as the option for farmers to have CO_2 taxes on diesel reimbursed.

Notes

1. In 2005, net public social expenditure stood at 27.6% of GDP in Sweden, compared with 20.9% on average for the 26 OECD countries for which comparable data are available (provisional figures from the OECD's SOCX 2008 database, available at *www.oecd.org/els/social/expenditure*).
2. The tax authorities estimate that there is a growing tendency of such tax planning which is akin to transfer pricing. Via internal loans, multinational companies can deduct interest expenditure in Sweden while obtaining the interest income in low-tax jurisdictions. To counter such practices, the tax authority has proposed that interest deductibility should not be allowed where the transactions are considered to have a tax-planning rather than a commercial purpose (Skatteverket, 2008). Critics argue that it will be cumbersome to administer such a differentiation and, thus, it would entail considerable compliance costs for companies.
3. Based on industry-level data, the OECD *Taxation and Economic Growth* study has estimated that, for the average country, a reduction in the corporate income tax rate from 35% to 30% would increase the long-run investment-to-GDP ratio by 0.2-0.5 percentage points (Vartia, 2008). Assessing the planned 2009 corporate tax cut on this basis is complicated by two factors: Sweden's corporate tax rate is lower to start with, and the measures to limit the deduction of interest expenditures are likely to attenuate the boost to investment.
4. The main proposal is that the assessment of whether the activity is an independent entrepreneurial activity (not a *de facto* employment relationship) would be more clearly based on the extent of dependence on the key customer, integration in this customer's organisation and the content of agreements existing between the self-employed and the customer. With this clarification it will be more predictable for potential entrepreneurs whether they would qualify for being taxed as a business.

5. Another area that might warrant attention is the length of time during which creditors have a claim on the assets of a failed entrepreneur. As discussed in the previous *Survey*, this period is ten years in Sweden, compared to just one in the United States (OECD, 2007a).
6. On the back of strong growth, average hours worked have risen, but only by about 1% from 2005 to the first half of 2008. Given the magnitude of cross-country differences, this does not change the comparison in Figure 3.2 to any noticeable degree.
7. Benefits that are adjusted over time not only for inflation but also for growth in real wages will also rise following the transition to a new labour market equilibrium. However, this does not matter much in a Swedish context: only the old-age pension is indexed by earnings, whereas social assistance and ceilings for unemployment insurance, sickness and disability benefits are indexed by consumer prices.
8. To what extent these studies capture the positive effects from human capital formation is unclear: increased incentives to study would boost incomes in the long run, but reduce incomes in the short run in so far as working hours are reduced to attend training or staff accept less wage growth in return for more employer-paid training.
9. The threshold is raised from nominally SEK 28 400 a month in 2008 to 31 700 in 2009. Another option was also discussed in the memorandum calling for public comments ahead of implementation in the 2009 budget, namely to introduce an initial 10% bracket in state income taxes, starting where the 20% rate sets in currently (Ministry of Finance, 2008b).
10. The services accepted under the scheme include cleaning, clothes washing, cooking, gardening and care for children or adults such as the elderly or disabled. The maximum annual tax deduction is SEK 50 000 which would apply for purchases worth SEK 100 000. The deduction is based on spending including VAT, but excluding materials, travel, etc.
11. The information has come up in an ongoing effort of the tax authorities to scrutinise cases where individuals' consumption and capital transaction indicates considerable income but where the individual pays little or no taxes. In total, 520 000 individuals aged 20-61 (10.3% of the population in the age group) had no reported income at all from work, social benefits or capital returns. In other economic registers, however, 115 000 (2.3% of the population in the age group) appeared as economically active in various ways. During the autumn, the tax authorities will review the individual cases (*Dagens Nyheter*, 5 July 2008,"Skattemoral hos 70-talister granskas").
12. Ongoing efforts by the tax authorities to combat tax fraud have uncovered a series of cases where temporary work agencies hired out construction workers to well-established large companies, while systematically paying these workers undeclared income. Eighty per cent of the cases concern activities in and around Stockholm, possibly reflecting the city's easy accessibility from the Baltic states via ferry, and that it is easier to hide such practices in a large city. Criminal gangs have increased their control of large parts of the construction, cleaning and transport sectors, and their activities in these sectors are often linked to other criminal activities such as drugs trade and human trafficking (*Dagens Nyheter* STHLM, 10 July 2008, "Svartarbetare hyrdes ut till kända byggföretag").
13. As discussed in the previous *Survey*, the problems that made the previous housing tax unpopular could be resolved in better ways than through the current capped fee. For example, financial innovation in mortgage markets (in the form of the introduction of reverse mortgages) could relieve the much-discussed liquidity problems arising for low-income pensioners living in owner-occupied housing in areas where valuations go up.

Bibliography

Arnold, J. (2008), "Do Tax Structures Affect Aggregate Economic Growth? Empirical Evidence from a Panel of OECD Countries", OECD *Economics Department Working Paper*, No. 643.

Causa, O. (2008), "Explaining Differences in Hours Worked Among OECD Countries: An Empirical Analysis", OECD *Economics Department Working Paper* No. 596.

European Commission (2007), "Undeclared Work in the European Union", *Special Eurobarometer*, No. 284, October.

Hansson, Å. (2007), "Taxpayers' Responses to Tax Rate Changes and Implications for the Cost of Taxation in Sweden". *International Tax and Public Finance*, Vol. 14, No. 5.

Holmlund, B. (2007), "Hur mycket arbetar vi egentligen i Sverige?" (How Much do Swedes Work?), *Ekonomisk Debatt*, No. 6.

Holmlund, B. and M. Söderström (2007), "Estimating Income Responses to Tax Changes: A Dynamic Panel Data Approach", Uppsala University Department of Economic Working Paper No. 2007:25.

Johansson, Å., C. Heady, J. Arnold, B. Brys and L. Vartia (2008), "Taxation and Economic Growth", OECD *Economics Department Working Paper* No. 620.

Ljunge, M. and K. Ragan (2005), "Labour Supply and the Tax Reform of the Century", Working Paper, University of Chicago.

LO (2008), *Vad händer med skatterna? – Kommentarer till skatteförändringar år 2007 och 2008* (What Happened with Taxes? – Comment on Changes 2007 and 2008), report from the LO Economists.

Lundgren, S., L. Behrenz, H. Edquist and L. Flood (2008), *Vägar till full sysselsättning* (Paths to Full Employment), Konjunkturrådets Rapport 2008, SNS, Stockholm.

Ministry of Finance (2007a), *Avskaffad statlig fastighetsskatt, m.m.* (Abolished state housing tax, etc.), legislative proposal 2007/08:27 of 29 October, *www.regeringen.se/sb/d/108/a/91113*.

Ministry of Finance (2007b), *Budgetproposition för 2008* (Budget Bill for 2008), Stockholm.

Ministry of Finance (2008a), *Budgetproposition för 2009* (Budget Bill for 2009), Stockholm.

Ministry of Finance (2008b), *Sänkt skatt på förvärvsinkomster* (Lower Tax on Earned Income), 17 June.

OECD (2004), *OECD Employment Outlook*, Paris.

OECD (2007a), *OECD Economic Surveys: Sweden*, Paris.

OECD (2007b), "Fundamental Reform of Corporate Income Tax", *OECD Tax Policy Studies*, No. 16, Paris.

OECD (2008a), *Going for Growth: Economic Policy Reforms*, Paris.

OECD (2008b), *Outreach, Reform and the Economics of Climate Change*, Key Information for the Meeting of the OECD Council at Ministerial Level 2008, Paris.

Schneider, F. (2004), "The Size of the Shadow Economies of 145 Countries all over the World: First Results over the Period 1999 to 2003", IZA Discussion Paper No. 1431.

Skatteverket (2008), *Förslag om begränsningar i avdragsrätten för ränta m.m. på vissa skulder* (Proposal for Reduced Deductibility of Interest Expenses, etc., for Certain Types of Debt), *Promemoria* of 23 June, *www.regeringen.se/sb/d/10041/a/107833*.

SOU (2008a), *F-skatt åt flera* (Making Taxation as Self-Employed Accessible for More), Swedish Government Official Reports, No. 2008:76, Stockholm.

SOU (2008b), *Skattelättnader för hushållstjänster* (Tax Relief for Purchase of Household Services), Swedish Government Official Reports, No. 2008:57, Stockholm.

SOU (2008c), *Rätt och riktigt – Åtgärder mot felaktiga utbetalningar från välfärdssystemen* (Right and Lawful – Action Against Erroneous Payments of Welfare Benefits), final report from the Delegation against Erroneous Payments, Swedish Government Official Reports, No. 2008:74, Stockholm.

Statistics Sweden (2007), *Fastighetsskattens förändring* (Changes in Housing Taxation), Stockholm.

Swedish Fiscal Policy Council (2008), *Svensk Finanspolitik* (Swedish Fiscal Policy), Stockholm.

Swedish Government (2008), *Bättre villkor för företagande och konkurrens* (Better conditions for business and competition), 8 September.

Vartia, L. (2008), "How Do Taxes Affect Investment and Productivity? – Industry-Level Analysis of OECD Countries", OECD Economics Department Working Paper, forthcoming.

ISBN 978-92-64-05423-3
OECD Economic Surveys: Sweden
© OECD 2008

Chapter 4

Education and youth employment

The Swedish labour market functions well for core workers, but the inclusion of youth could be improved. The unemployment rate for youth is four times higher than for prime-age adults, reflecting both deficiencies of the education system and some specific features of the Swedish labour market. Learning outcomes in compulsory schooling are above-average in reading, but not in mathematics and science. In secondary school, the programme structure is fragmented, and youth completing a vocational programme appear to lack important skills: they are not "job ready". This is problematic in the context of a labour market characterised by high minimum wages, set in collective agreements, and stringent employment protection rules: those with low productivity have little chance to find a job, and employers are cautious about hiring youth whose skills are often hard to assess, in particular youth with an immigrant background. This chapter reviews recent proposals for education reform. It also examines how recent tax and benefit changes might be supplemented to ensure that job-search is genuinely attractive without deterring youth from entering and completing further studies early on.

Education and youth employment must be seen together in a wider economic perspective. This holds especially in an economy like Sweden's where high income taxes and generous benefits shape not just labour market outcomes but also the relative attractiveness of different educational choices. For example, the most effective solutions to skill shortages resulting in unemployment spells for adults might be to improve the early stages of education. Increasingly skill-intensive labour demand requires larger investments in education to create a matching supply. But if this were to be all met *via* current arrangements, relying on public funding, it would add to the fiscal challenges of ageing and drive up taxes. Those taxes, however, are already an important reason behind labour market exclusion and generate some of the adverse incentives in the education system. Therefore, this chapter analyses education and youth employment with an emphasis on the economy-wide linkages (Box 4.1). After disentangling labour market outcomes for youth, it reviews learning outcomes and policies in compulsory education, *i.e.* age 7-16. The chapter then turns to upper secondary education and thereafter higher education. Finally, the role of labour market institutions, including minimum wages, employment protection rules, activation programmes and benefits is analysed.

Human capital and youth employment outcomes

By international standards, educational attainment is high in Sweden. Over 90% of the younger cohorts have completed upper secondary education, a share among the highest in the OECD and above the other Nordic countries (Figure 4.1, panel A). The share of adults having completed tertiary education is closer to the international average, but the share of each youth cohort graduating from tertiary education is now rising rapidly following strong expansion of higher education since the 1990s. In 2006, the number of new graduates was equivalent to 40% of a youth cohort; more than the OECD average, but less than in the other Nordic countries (Figure 4.1, panel B). But with around 80% of each cohort entering higher education in the most recent years, the supply of graduates is set to rise further.

Changes in workforce skill composition are shaped not just by the educational attainment of the young flowing into the labour market, but also by those retiring. There is a sizeable gap between the 91% upper secondary attainment rate of the 25-34 year olds who recently joined the labour market and the 73% rate of the 55-64 year olds who will retire from the labour market over the coming ten years (Figure 4.1). This gap means that the average educational attainment of the labour force is growing, enabling Sweden to benefit from technological change that raises skill-intensive labour demand. However, the gap is set to narrow in the future: the upper secondary attainment rate is stable for the inflow, being virtually the same for the 35-44 year olds as for the 25-34 year olds, but the cohorts moving towards retirement in the coming decades are considerably more qualified than those retiring today. At that horizon, it could become challenging to continue raising the average educational attainment of the labour force at the current pace.

Box 4.1. **Education and youth employment policies in a Swedish economic context**

Official Swedish education policy documents mostly state the learning objectives in the various areas of education. Meanwhile, to analyse the economy-wide linkages that are relevant for education and youth employment, it is useful to lay out the core objectives and interactions that seem central in an economic perspective. The central policy ***objectives*** might be summarised as:

- ***Equal opportunities.*** Realising the potential of all to be employable in a modern workplace gives people the possibility to improve upon their situation *via* working. Being employable is also a key step towards social integration and participation, including for immigrants. And it gives individual independence, not least for women.
- ***Economic growth.*** Human capital and skills in a wide sense are essential for economic growth, since they are necessary in order to adopt technological advances and complementary organisational changes. Hence, the educational achievement of youth cohorts entering the labour market is one of the most important areas of government policy influence over business competitiveness. Indeed, companies typically cite human capital as a major determinant of international location choices.

Meanwhile, some features of the Swedish economy, combined with a strong preference for equal opportunities and equity, mean that certain ***interactions*** warrant particular attention, possibly more so than in some other OECD countries:

- ***The composition of labour supply.*** Each person's choice of skill formation affects the relative earnings of others *via* the labour market equilibrium. This matters because of the equity preference and the labour market institutions which limit the availability of low-skilled jobs. If those who have the cognitive capabilities to study abstain or wait too long while taking low-skilled jobs, it will be harder to find employment for those who don't have the cognitive capability to study. This holds provided there is some complementarity between high- and low-skilled labour demand or that consumption includes demand for non-tradable low-skilled services. Similarly, boosting average hours worked for the high-skilled would raise demand for low-skilled labour.
- ***Fiscal externalities.*** Choosing education with good labour market prospects has a large positive impact on public finances by boosting the tax base and reducing outlays on income-replacing benefits. By contrast, if more prospective students shift towards education choices driven by consumption aspects (leisure and other non-pecuniary benefits), the capacity to finance a welfare state would be weakened.

Youth unemployment is a cause for concern. In 2006, more than one in five 15-24 year olds participating in the labour market were unemployed, a proportion four times higher than for the 25-54 year olds. Among OECD countries, apart from Finland, youth unemployment rates above 15% are only found in Central, Eastern and Southern European countries. By contrast, in Denmark, Iceland, the Netherlands and Norway, where social preferences are much the same as in Sweden, the unemployment rate of the 15-24 year olds is just a third of the Swedish rate. Moreover, among the OECD countries with high youth unemployment rates, the ratio between the unemployment rates of young and prime-age adults is nowhere more skewed to the disadvantage of youth than in Sweden (Figure 4.2). On the back of buoyant economic growth, youth unemployment has declined in recent years from 22.8% in 2005 (3.7 times the rate for 25-54 year olds) to 19.2% in 2007

Figure 4.1. **Educational attainment compared with other Nordics**

Per cent, 2006

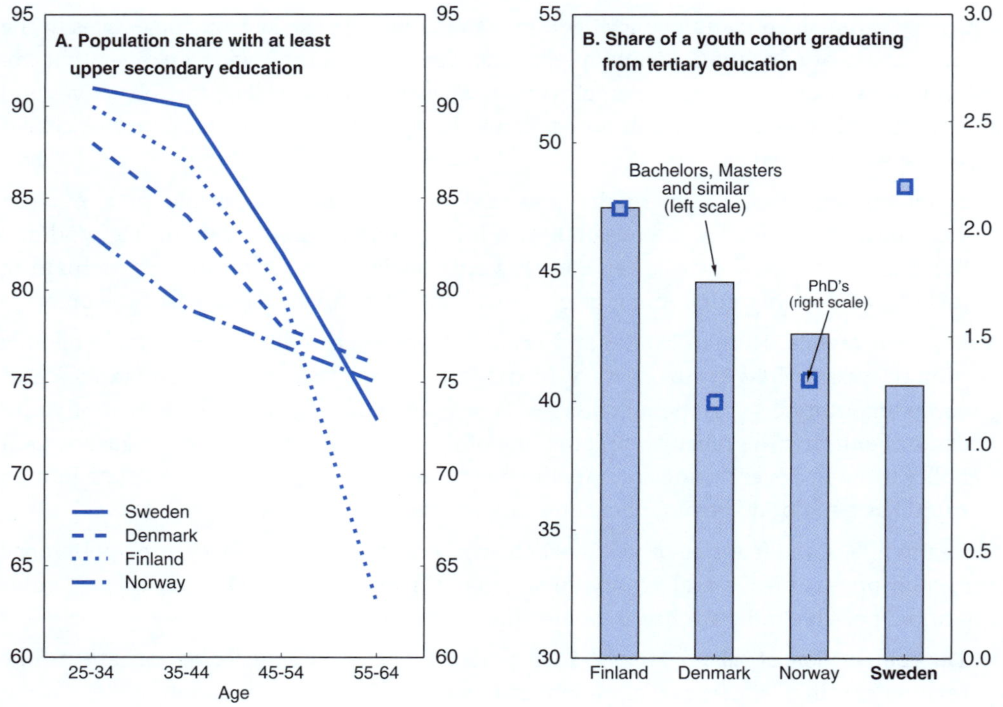

StatLink http://dx.doi.org/10.1787/485361817521

Source: OECD (2008b).

(4.3 times the rate for 25-54 year olds), but that is still high compared to other countries. Even excluding full-time students, the unemployment rate for 15-24 year olds stood at 14.3% in 2007.[1]

Short duration mitigates the economic and social costs associated with youth unemployment. In fact, two thirds of Swedish youth unemployment is due to spells of three months or less (Figure 4.2). On that score, youth unemployment may be considered less of an issue than in Germany and the United Kingdom, even if the youth unemployment rate is higher in Sweden. By contrast, the incidence of youth unemployment is higher across all durations when compared to Denmark and Norway.[2]

At the core of the youth unemployment problem are the long-lasting unemployment spells affecting certain groups. Immigrants and youth who fared poorly in school are particularly at risk (Box 4.2). Morover, unemployment spells early in life may affect motivation and self confidence or be seen as a bad signal by future potential employers: even spells shorter than three months following graduation from Swedish upper secondary education give rise to long-run negative effects persisting for at least five years (Skans, 2004).

While a fairly high proportion of youth are unemployed, few are inactive. Indeed, the share of youth that are neither in employment, education or training (the so-called NEET rate) is a bit below the OECD average (OECD, 2008a).[3] This suggests that lack of education or training places is not the main source of the Swedish unemployment problem. The root cause might rather be inadequate quality in education and training or labour market distortions – the issues reviewed in the rest of this chapter.

Figure 4.2. **Youth unemployment**

2006

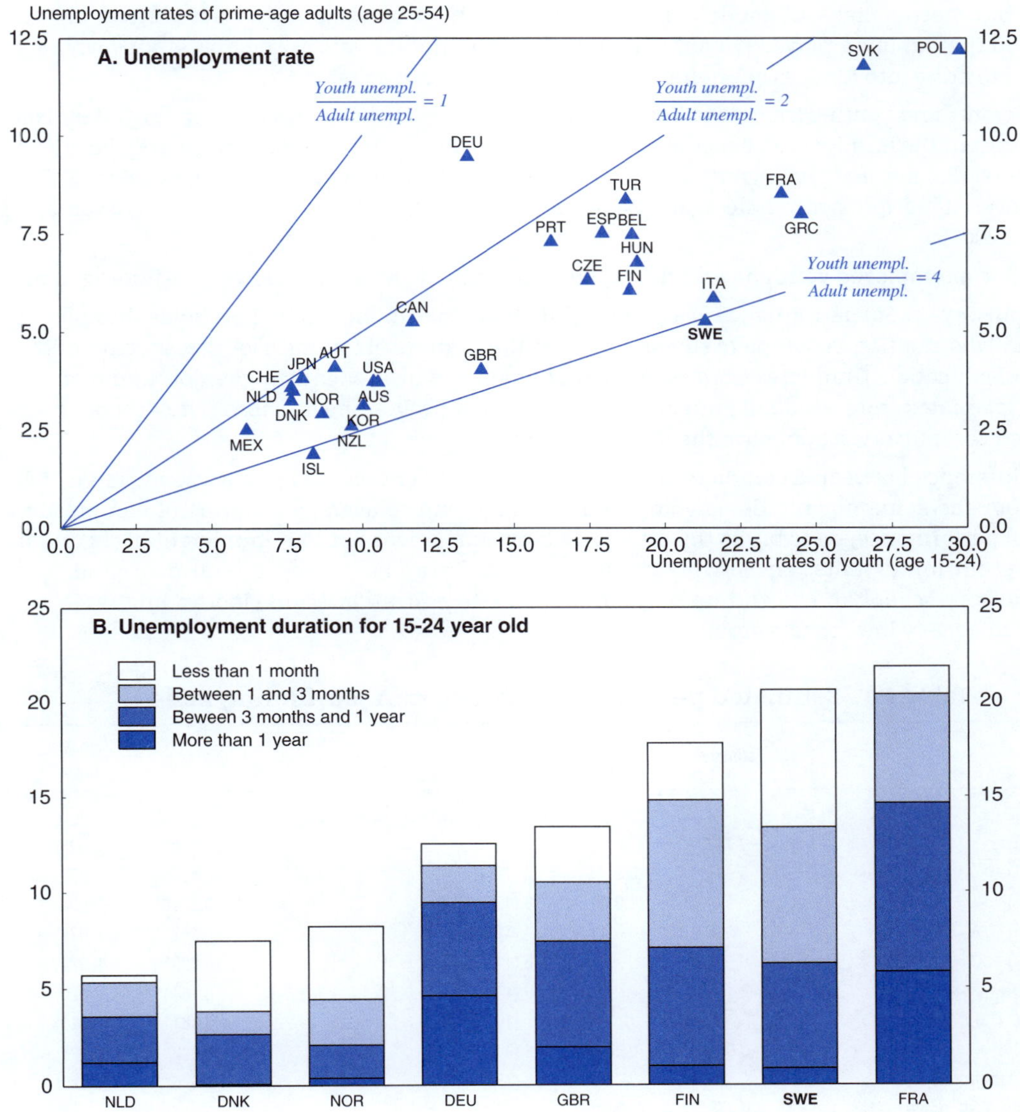

StatLink http://dx.doi.org/10.1787/485377044417

Source: OECD, *LFS database.*

Compulsory education: ensuring a strong start

Giving children a strong foundation in compulsory school is obviously important, because without basic literacy it is hard to manage in virtually any modern workplace or to pursue post-compulsory education. Before turning to secondary education and the school-to-work transition, this section therefore reviews learning outcomes and policies to improve the early stages of education.

Learning outcomes

Swedish learning outcomes are not as good as they used to be. At age 15, student proficiency measured by PISA is above the OECD average for reading but not for

Box 4.2. **Immigrants and school drop-outs are most at risk of long-term unemployment**

An econometric "hazard" model can estimate the effect of various characteristics on the likelihood that an unemployed person will find a job ("job-finding rate"). Thereby, groups who are at risk of drifting into long-term unemployment can be identified (Table 4.1):

- Immigrants and youth born in Sweden with immigrant parents have lower job-finding rates. The more recent the immigration experience, the lower the job-finding rate. This may partly be due to lack of skills, not least as regards proficiency in Swedish. However, there is also evidence that employers tend to discriminate against applicants with foreign-sounding names (Carlsson and Rooth, 2007).
- Very few unemployed youth have children, but those who do have much lower job-finding rates.
- Compulsory school performance is a strong predictor of job-finding rates. This holds throughout the skill distribution. A complete education raises the chances of finding a job, irrespective of the level of education. Graduates from vocational programmes have slightly higher job-finding rates than graduates from academic upper secondary school programmes. Those who do not study beyond compulsory school have the lowest job-finding rates.
- The difference between a complete and an incomplete upper secondary education is large. It is of about the same magnitude as going from the high end to average in terms of compulsory school performance, or as big as the difference between natives without immigrant background and recent immigrants. Those who struggle at school are likely to have both poor grades in compulsory school and to end up with an incomplete education. Thus, job-finding rates are likely to be very low for this group.

Table 4.1. **Estimated percentage differences in job-finding rates**

	Estimate	Standard error		Estimate	Standard error
Age			*Compulsory school grade decile*		
19 (39%)	–0.183***	(0.017)	1 (12%)	–0.518***	(0.026)
20 (24%)	–0.046***	(0.018)	2 (12%)	–0.407***	(0.025)
21 (15%)	0.025	(0.018)	3 (12%)	–0.308***	(0.024)
22 (11%)	0.019	(0.019)	4 (12%)	–0.267***	(0.024)
23 (10%)	(ref)		5 (11%)	–0.229***	(0.024)
Gender			6 (11%)	–0.184***	(0.023)
Female (47%)	(ref)		7 (10%)	–0.161***	(0.024)
Male (53%)	–0.055***	(0.009)	8 (9%)	–0.122***	(0.024)
Immigrant background			9 (7%)	–0.076***	(0.025)
Arrived at age 12 or after (2%)	–0.273***	(0.040)	10 (6%)	(ref)	
Arrived before age 12 (7%)	–0.270***	(0.019)			
Second generation with both parents being immigrants (5%)	–0.131***	(0.021)	*Highest completed education by end of the year*		
Natives (86%)	(ref)		Compulsory (14%)	–0.363***	(0.016)
Family situation			Some vocational upper sec. (10%)	–0.231***	(0.016)
Living with parents (65%)	–0.042***	(0.010)	Complete vocational upper sec. (41%)	(ref)	
No children, not with parents (31%)	(ref)		Some academic upper secondary (4%)	–0.233***	(0.023)
Children and spouse (2%)	–0.160***	(0.032)	Complete academic upper sec. (24%)	–0.026**	(0.012)
Single parent (1%)	–0.277***	(0.047)	Some tertiary (4%)	–0.223***	(0.025)
			Complete tertiary (3%)	0.046	(0.028)

Note: Data are from Public Employment Service registers (Händel) and the Louise database. Results are from a Cox proportional hazard model, N = 77 921. The model is estimated on registered unemployment spells starting in 2005. Jobs are either temporary or regular. Participation in subsidised jobs for 30 days or more is considered finding a job. A random half of those with lost contacts are considered to have found a job. Other exits are censored. Percentages in parentheses indicate the share in the total set of observations. *** (**) indicates significance at the 99% (95%) level.

OECD ECONOMIC SURVEYS: SWEDEN – ISBN 978-92-64-05423-3 – © OECD 2008

mathematics and science (Figure 4.3). Moreover, learning outcomes in 2006 had deteriorated relative to the in-depth assessments of reading in 2000 and mathematics in 2003.[4] In the light of Sweden's ambitions, and as public spending on compulsory education is relatively high, these outcomes are not satisfactory – certainly not when compared to Finland.

In the domestic debate, it is sometimes argued that what really matters is schools' capacity to improve the weakest students' abilities. Indeed, given the features of the Swedish labour market, including high minimum wages, this is vital as the low-skilled are at a high risk of unemployment. But even on this score, Sweden does not rank much better, based on the share of 15-year olds left behind with poor learning outcomes (Figure 4.3): 15% of a cohort only attain proficiency level 1 in reading, *i.e.* they are able to locate explicitly-stated information but struggle to identify information that is not prominent, to deal with competing information and to understand relationships. The share of students at this lowest level of proficiency is three to four times higher than in Finland across all three subject areas – reading, mathematics and science.[5]

Figure 4.3. **Learning outcomes in compulsory education**

Average PISA score, 2006

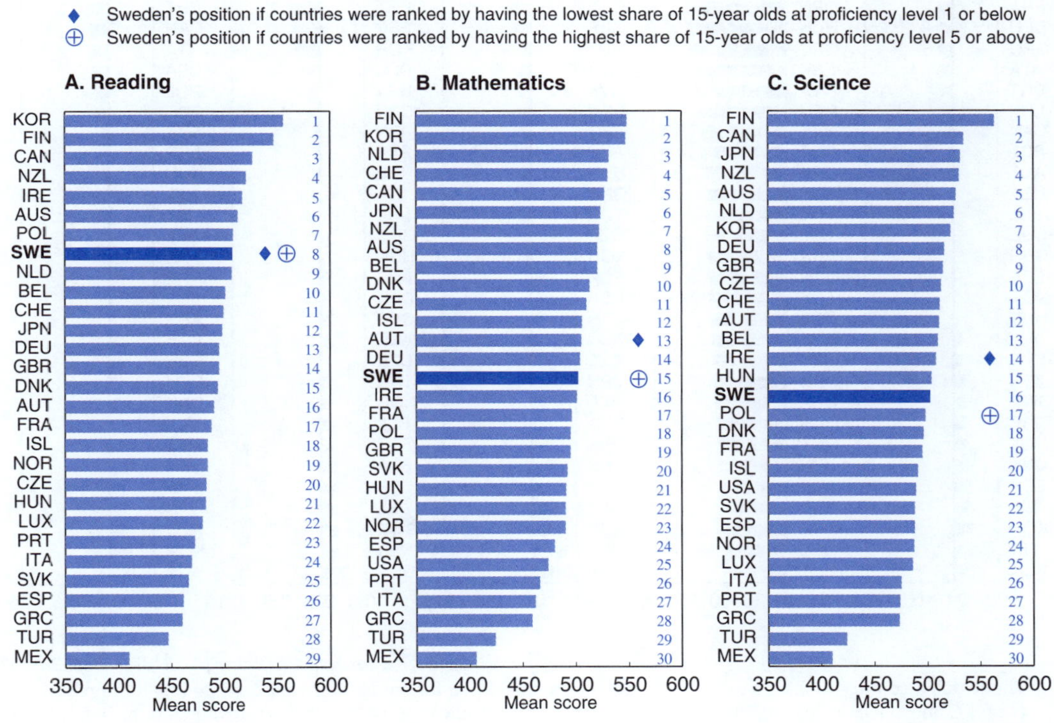

StatLink http://dx.doi.org/10.1787/485408473338

Source: OECD, *PISA Results 2006.*

Science is a weak spot both in terms of proficiency and student interest. Given Sweden's traditionally strong position in engineering and science-related industries, such as electronics and pharmaceuticals, this is of particular concern. For average student proficiency, Sweden ranks in the middle of OECD countries, but what may be most worrying from an employer perspective is that the elite is quite narrow: the share of 15-year olds attaining the highest proficiency levels 5 and 6 reaches 13% in mathematics and merely 8% in science, compared with 24% and 21% respectively in Finland, which has a similar industrial structure. To change this pattern, schools may need to do more, building on childrens' natural curiosity, to nurture the interest to learn more and acquire specific skills and proficiency in science. Sweden is below the OECD average on virtually all measures used in the PISA assessment for student's aspirations and attitudes towards science. Swedish 15-year olds indicate some general interest in learning about science, but less interest when it comes to specific topics, such as acid rain. Only little time is spent on science-related activities outside school. Most remarkably, Swedish youth are among those indicating the least awareness of the science-related aspects of environmental problems and they are rather unconvinced that science promotes economic and social progress (Figure 4.4; OECD, 2007a).[6] This pattern is problematic, as there is clear evidence that early

Figure 4.4. **Aspirations and attitudes towards science at the end of compulsory education**

PISA, 2006

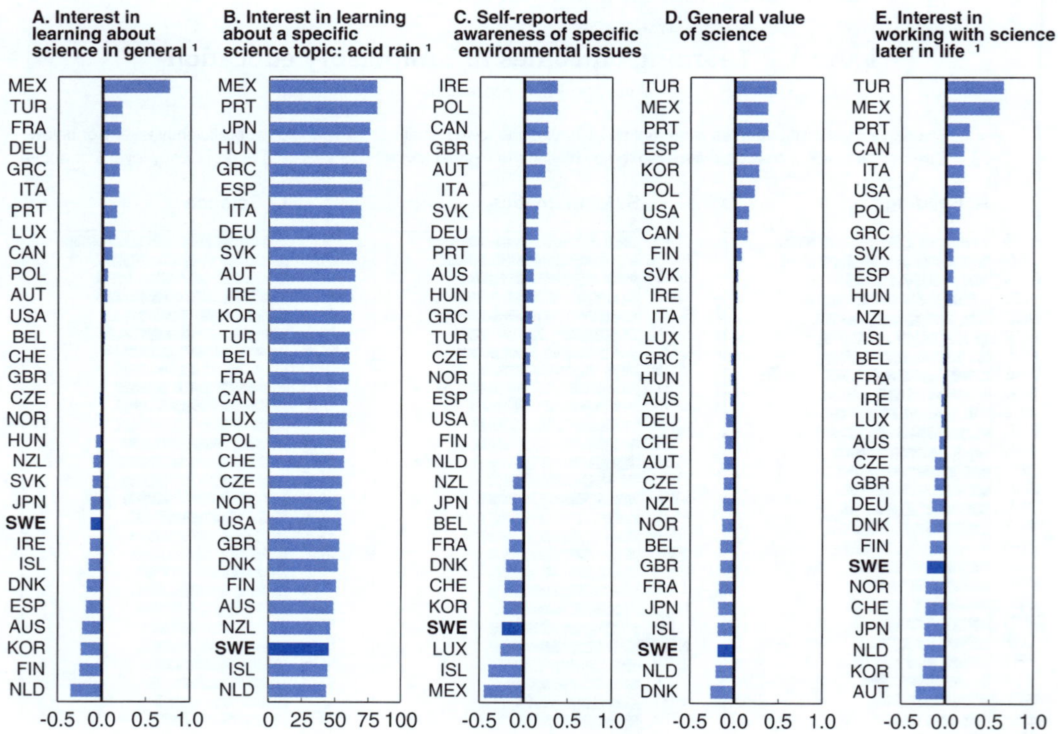

StatLink http://dx.doi.org/10.1787/485435381883

1. The detailed country ranking should be interpreted with caution for panels A, B and E, while it is more reliable for panels C and D (OECD, 2007a). Yet, the indices give a broad indication of Sweden's relative position. Data used in panels:

A. Index for the share of 15-year olds stating high or medium interest in human and plant biology, astronomy, chemistry, physics, geology, the way scientists design experiments and/or the requirement for scientific explanations.

B. Average share of 15-year olds stating high or medium interest in knowing which human activities contribute most to acid rain and learning about technologies that minimise the emission of gases causing acid rain.

C. Index for the share of 15-year olds stating that they are familiar with or know something about the environmental consequences of clearing forests, acid rain, greenhouse gases, nuclear waste and/or use of genetically-modified organisms.

D. Index for the share of 15-year olds stating that science is important for understanding the natural world, and/or that advances in science and technology usually improve people's living conditions, the economy and/or bring social benefits.

E. Index for the share of 15-year olds stating that they would like to have a career involving science, study science after secondary school, work on science projects as an adult and/or spend their life doing advanced science.

Source: OECD, *PISA Results 2006*.

interest in science is a strong predictor of lifelong science learning and/or a career in a science or technology field (OECD, 2006a). Indeed, relatively few Swedish 15-year olds indicate an interest in working with science later in life. The current moderate difficulties for employers to recruit engineering and science graduates might worsen in the future if children's natural capacity and potential to learn science fails to flourish in school.[7]

In the traditional Swedish welfare state, compulsory school plays an important role as an institution building social cohesion. The capacity to engage with people of all backgrounds is also beneficial from an economic perspective, facilitating market flexibility. While variation in learning outcomes is not much smaller than in other countries, it is found within rather than between schools, indicating that there is little segregation between good and less good schools and neighbourhoods (Figure 4.5).

Figure 4.5. **Low between-school variation**

PISA science scale, 2006 [1]

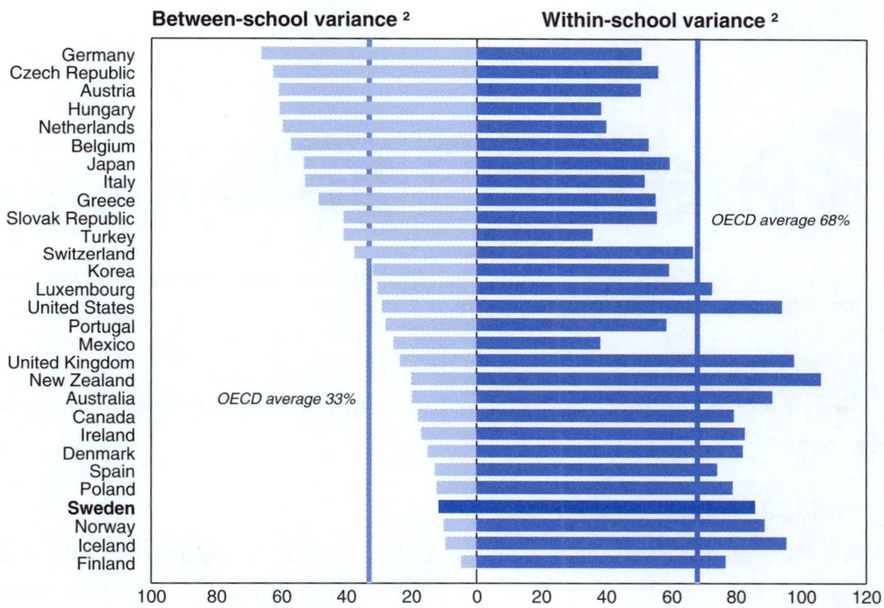

StatLink http://dx.doi.org/10.1787/485468044625

1. For mathematics, measured in 2003, the balance between the two types of variation was similar to that for science shown in the figure, measured in 2006, but for reading, measured in 2000, the share of between-school variance was even smaller.
2. The between-school variance measures PISA scores dispersion between schools within a single country. The within-school variance measures PISA scores dispersion within a representative school in each country.

Source: OECD, *PISA 2006 database*.

The integration of the rapidly-growing immigrant population is particularly important in this context, but the outcomes are difficult to interpret. There is a wide gap between the learning outcomes for immigrants and natives, but that may be hard to avoid given the language barriers. Few immigrant children arrive with prior knowledge of Swedish, which is used as the instruction language in all subjects. The second generation, *i.e.* children born in Sweden from immigrant parents, appear to do much better than the first, the difference being considerably greater than in other OECD countries (Figure 4.6). However, it is hard to know if this reflects a genuine improvement from one generation to the next, or differences in composition, since today's first-generation immigrant families typically

Figure 4.6. **Learning outcomes for immigrant and native students compared**

Average for reading, mathematics and science scales, PISA 2006[1]

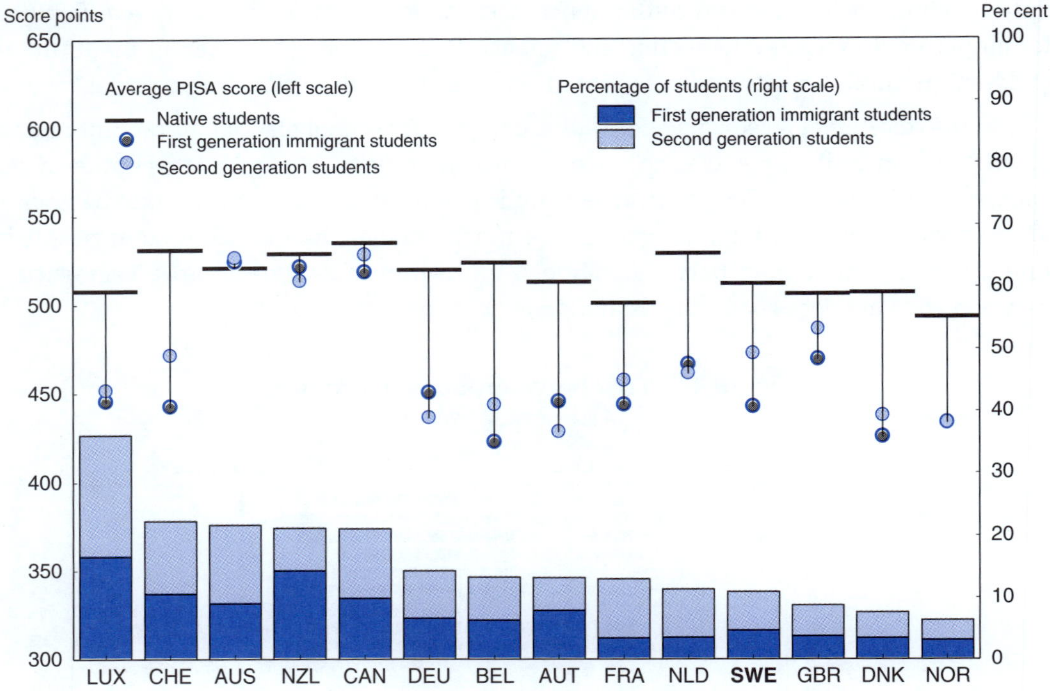

StatLink http://dx.doi.org/10.1787/485474318126

1. Only including countries with at least 3% of students in each category.

Source: OECD, *PISA Results* 2006.

have a less favourable background than the immigrants who arrived in Sweden some decades ago.

Policy initiatives and school efficiency

A number of policy measures have recently been introduced to improve learning processes and monitor outcomes. A new reading-writing-arithmetic initiative was announced in 2008. National tests were introduced some years ago and, from 2009, they will be advanced to start from the third year of compulsory education. National tests are applied again at the fifth year where they now become mandatory also in English. Finally, science tests will be introduced at the ninth year of compulsory education. Moreover, a legislative proposal has been presented with a new scale for marking students to be introduced from the academic year 2011/12.

Swedish schools appear to be at some distance from international best practice in terms of how efficiently they use available resources (Figure 4.7). The use of teachers' time can often be an Achilles heel of efficiency at schools, but a lack of data makes it hard to compare Sweden internationally. Teachers' total statutory working time is above the average for the OECD countries for which there are data. However, total instruction time for students seems to be relatively short, and the student-to-teacher ratio is relatively low (OECD, 2008b). Together, that would indicate that teachers in compulsory school spend less of their time teaching than in other OECD countries. Consequently, there might be scope to employ teachers' capacity more effectively, and reward teachers better when they put in extra teaching effort.

Figure 4.7. **Schools' technical efficiency**[1]

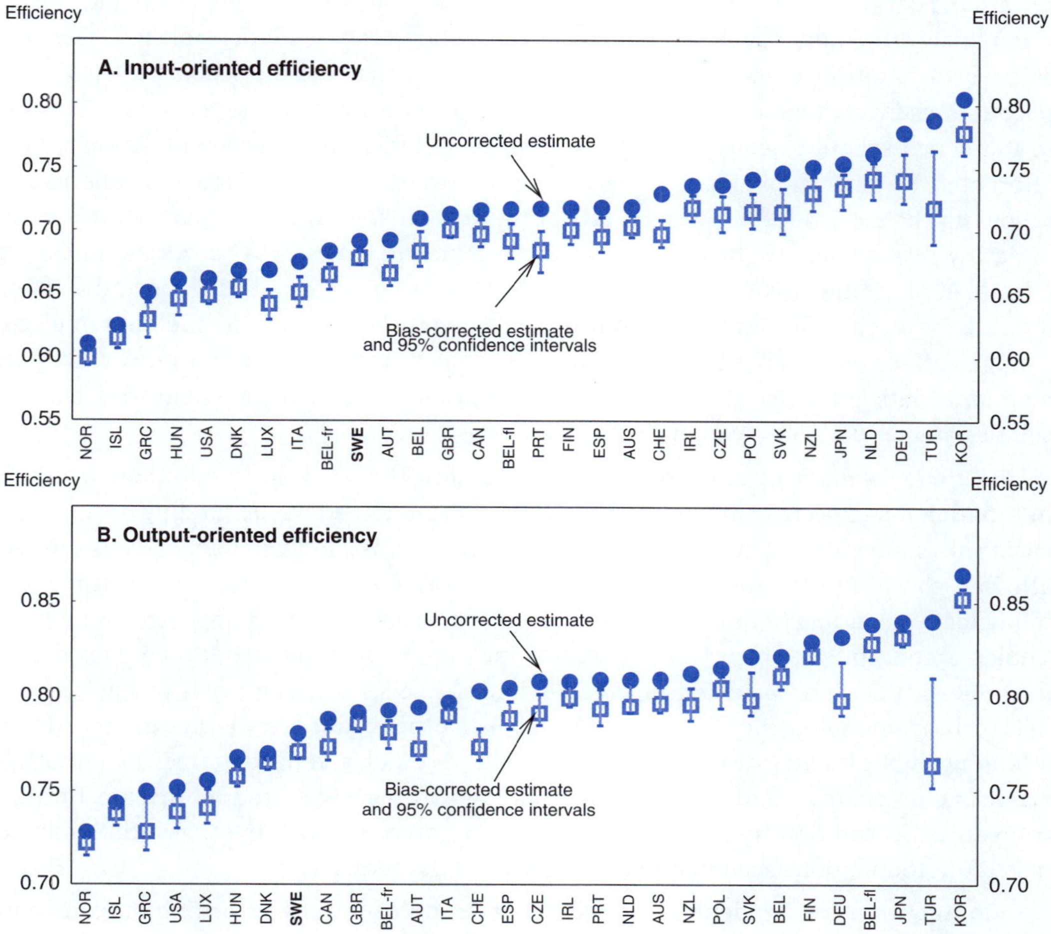

StatLink http://dx.doi.org/10.1787/485522100788

1. Efficiency estimates apply to the median school in each country. The estimates are obtained through data envelopment analysis performed with four inputs (teaching and computing resources, socio-economic status of students. and language background) and one output (average PISA score).

Source: OECD (2008c) and Sutherland *et al.* (2007).

The renewed Swedish policy focus on teacher competence is therefore most welcome. Following the Scottish example, a recent government report has proposed that teachers should go through an accreditation process after graduation (SOU, 2008a). During a probationary year, the new teacher would be introduced to the profession by a mentor. Only if assessed as suitable for the profession, would she or he then be granted accreditation and be able to apply for permanent employment. Additional information about each teacher's profile is to be used by school management to ensure that teachers are competent in the subject areas and functions they handle. To encourage continuing professional development, new advanced professional levels are proposed, accessible via further study or well-documented practical development activities. By contrast, serious neglect would lead to the accreditation being withdrawn. Persons currently working as teachers without a degree would be required to complete a degree. Otherwise they would have to leave the profession when an eight-year transition period expires.

Once the accreditation scheme is well established, greater wage flexibility could reward the best teachers. Some flexibility already exists since 1996 when a fixed pay ladder was replaced by individualised pay and strict working time regulation relaxed. Thereby, salaries are determined in discussions between each teacher and the school principal or in negotiations involving the local teacher trade union. Pay rewards are supposed to be linked to municipal school objectives, even if in practice they are more based on competence, effort etc. The dispersion of teacher earnings is not wide, though, and it actually narrowed following the 1996 reform, perhaps reflecting that individual-pay dispersion has been offset by less dispersion based on age, as the starting salary was raised significantly (Strath, 2004). Still in 2007, the upper quartile of earnings was just 20% above the lower quartile for teachers in compulsory education. When the accreditation scheme is in place, it might offer a basis for stronger rewards to the best teachers and the ones taking on additional duties, classes or longer working hours. Compared with other countries, teacher salaries are not particularly high (OECD, 2008b).[8]

In 1992, Sweden introduced a system of choice that is quite remarkable from an international perspective: independent schools are guaranteed public funding on an equal basis with municipal schools in the same area. By contrast, independent schools are not allowed to charge tuition fees, and they cannot reject students from within the municipality. Funding for public schools responds automatically to changes in attendance. Choice among public schools across municipalities is also allowed. Since choice was introduced, the share enrolled in independent schools has risen rapidly, reaching 9% in 2007/08 (National Agency for Education, 2008). In other countries, the shares of students attending public *versus* private schools is typically very stable, reflecting tradition. Another remarkable factor is that independent schools can be organised as private limited companies, in addition to the forms of teacher or parent co-operatives, associations and non-profit foundations seen in other countries (Lundsgaard, 2003).

Competition from independent schools is found to improve learning outcomes in public schools. Systematic studies find that test scores and final grades in key subjects are better, *ceteris paribus*, in areas where many attend independent schools (Sandström and Bergström, 2005; Ahlin, 2003; Böhlmark and Lindahl, 2007), even if the exact size of the effects is subject to debate (Björklund *et al.*, 2006).[9] The model appears to be a clear success.

To sum up, learning outcomes at age 15 are not as good as they could be, and they should be improved. However, shortcomings in compulsory education alone cannot explain high youth unemployment: Denmark and Norway, for example, display similarly mediocre PISA scores but have much better youth employment outcomes. Therefore, upper secondary and tertiary education as well as labour markets also need attention.

Upper secondary education: preparing better for labour-market entry

Sweden has few problems getting youth to join upper secondary education, but the latter does not fully succeed in making students "job ready". The high incidence of short unemployment spells after upper secondary school might indicate a mismatch between the needs of the workplace and what has been learned at school. A striking example is the media programme, where only a small fraction ends up working in media jobs; the period of unemployment after completing the media programme is a process through which many realise that they have to seek work elsewhere, such as in long-term care for the elderly. These persons might have been better off if, from the outset, they had chosen the programme giving the skills needed in elderly care.

Against this backdrop, an initiative was recently launched to overhaul upper secondary education. A government commission identified two broad problem areas (SOU, 2008b):

- *Programme structure*. The vast range of programmes on offer makes it difficult for students to gain an overview of the alternatives. Consequently, many students (12%) switch programmes during their first year at upper secondary school. Those who receive school leavers (universities, companies and organisations, etc.) find it difficult to assess their capabilities, which may make it more difficult to find a first job.
- *Results, goal fulfilment and efficiency*. Both clear result indicators and an improved evaluation system are needed. For example, there are no data on the extent to which the guaranteed teaching time is satisfied. The Commission has developed a quality measure, namely the share of students achieving basic eligibility for entering higher education in three years; only 62% of all students currently achieve this goal. Streamlining the system towards fewer different alternatives might also lead to lower costs and higher efficiency as, currently, small class sizes increase costs. This is particularly important in a context where student cohorts are set to fall within a few years.

There is also a growing consensus that Swedish upper secondary education could be improved if vocational programmes had closer workplace links. Indeed, this is the main focus of the recommendations in the recent *OECD Policy Review of Vocational Education and Training in Sweden* (OECD, 2008d).[10] International research shows that close co-operation and participation of companies in upper secondary education provide good opportunities for youth to enter the labour market (SOU, 2008b). In principle, 15 weeks of workplace-based training (*Arbetsplatsförlagd utbildning, APU*) are included in all upper secondary vocational programmes. In practice, however, this is not the case everywhere as many schools seek dispensation to allow workplace-based training to take place at school. Against this background, a government commission has recently proposed a revamped three-track upper secondary system, including a new apprenticeship route alongside modernised versions of the traditional academic and vocational routes (Box 4.3). Indeed, workplace learning should be seen as a necessary component of a vocational programme. This is especially important for immigrant and second-generation youth for whom workplace attachment may give not just professional skills but also a wider understanding of relations in a Swedish workplace (Lemaître, 2007).

For the new apprenticeships to function well, workplace activities should involve learning, not just work, and the competencies acquired should be of general value rather than specific to narrowly-defined professions. The experience from countries with long apprenticeships traditions (*e.g.* Austria and Switzerland) is that while youth with apprenticeships find employment more easily, they may later on experience more difficulty if having to change profession than similar persons with school-based vocational training (Ludwig and Pfeiffer, 2005; OECD, 2004a and 2006b). The heart of the problem is that if apprenticeships are too closely linked to existing professions, they may end up providing youth with excessively narrow skills that over time become redundant. Ways to avoid these pitfalls have been identified by the Commission:

- Apprenticeships would be anchored into the structure of the 14 national vocational programmes, sharing the common upper secondary subjects.
- The content of workplace learning would be clearly defined in blocks tied to the programme-specific subjects for the vocational programme in question. Apprentices

Box 4.3. Proposals from the Upper Secondary Reform Commission (*Gymnasieutredningen*)

The curriculum with its approach to knowledge would be preserved in its present form: all study paths in upper secondary schools would continue to prepare students for active participation in society. The reforms would increase the distinction between the academic and vocational tracks in terms of selection, curricular content and routes into tertiary education. Following the report issued in March (SOU, 2008b), preparations are now underway for legislation.

All upper secondary programmes would continue to last three years, with a common basic structure. However, the contents of each of the proposed 14 vocational programmes and five higher-education preparatory programmes would be more targeted than currently, notably by adapting the focus of common upper secondary subjects (Swedish, math, English, etc.) to what is relevant for each particular programme. This should allow vocational programmes to stretch further than today's upper secondary school, leading to a vocational diploma that constitutes a recognised skill qualification and enhances employability.

As a major novelty, the Commission proposes to introduce apprenticeships as an alternative to school-based vocational programmes, leading to the same qualification – a vocational diploma. Upper secondary education would then have three alternative routes:

- *School-based vocational programmes.* A third of the three years would be spent on common upper secondary subjects, individual options and a diploma project, with the remaining two thirds spent on specialisation. There would be 14 national programmes (building and construction; farming and natural resources; electricity and energy; aircraft; vehicle and transport; trade and administrative service; hairdressing and handicraft; hotel and tourism; manufacturing; children and preventive healthcare; restaurant and food; maritime; heating; water and sanitation; health and long-term care). In each of these programmes there would be two to five nationally-defined branches, and schools would have the option to include further specialised in-depth components for up to a third of the three-year programme duration. At least 15 weeks of workplace learning would be compulsory.
- *Apprenticeships.* These so-called upper secondary apprenticeships would be introduced in each of the 14 national programmes. Students would have the same common upper secondary subjects, individual options and diploma project as for school-based vocational programmes, but most or all of the two years' programme-specific learning would happen at a workplace.
- *Higher-education preparatory programmes.* There would be five national programmes (economics and business, arts and humanities, social science and media, natural science, technology), each with three to five nationally-defined branches.

The emphasis on standardised core content would be backed by the introduction of a diploma based on specific objectives for each programme. There would be two types of diploma: a vocational and a higher-education preparatory diploma. A clearly-defined diploma would also help document competencies when going abroad, and assist each industry in adapting its further education and training for possible certification. Students on vocational programmes should have clear options to achieve basic eligibility for higher education within the upper secondary school system, possibly via extended studies.

Finally, a new National Council for Education would be created with representation of those receiving youth once they have completed secondary school, *i.e.* tertiary education institutions and employers, to identify development potentials and satisfy the needs of future industries which currently lack established structures of co-operation. For each of the 14 national programmes, there would also be a Programme Council responsible for content. These councils would involve employers, trade unions, relevant national standard-setting agencies, and they should also make use of students' experiences and views of the programmes. Moreover, local programme councils should be set up for co-operation between local employers and school-governing bodies.

would thereby acquire sufficiently general skills to ensure a capacity to change towards working in other areas, if needed later in life.

- Quality is to be guided and monitored *via* local agreements drawn up between the school governing body and the firms taking apprentices.
- Firms would be obliged to allocate a skilled employee to supervise the apprentice. The supervisor should first have undergone a course arranged by the school governing body.

If these Commission proposals are implemented, the benefits of extensive workplace learning during an apprenticeship are likely to outweigh the potential drawbacks.

The extent of pay received under an apprenticeship is to be decided locally. The school and the participating employers have to agree. Monitoring how this evolves will be important for successful implementation: having firms interested is crucial to be able to offer enough apprenticeship places, and low labour costs are typically essential to secure this interest (Quintini *et al.*, 2007).

With the 2009 Budget, considerable allocations were set aside for an expansion of vocational education. The number of apprenticeship places will be raised from 4 000 in the pilot phase of the academic year 2008/09 to 6 000 in 2009/10. The number of vocational training places in adult education will be increased and vocational higher education will be introduced.

School choice has expanded in upper secondary education

Private independent schools have become an important element in upper secondary education. The same regulations apply for compulsory as for upper secondary schools, but the growth in attendance has been most spectacular for upper secondary: 17% were enrolled in independent upper secondary schools in 2007/08, up from just 3% ten years earlier; for compulsory education the share had reached 9% (National Agency for Education, 2008). At times it is argued that independent schools have grown because they offer music or sport programmes, attracting students with an emphasis on leisure more than learning. Whether this is true in general is hard to ascertain, but there have been specific cases where independent schools did not deliver what they were promising. For potential students to make an informed choice, more transparency is needed about the labour market prospects associated with alternative education routes, such as by publishing data for employment outcomes of recent school leavers (OECD, 2008d). Aside from this, the Swedish model for school choice is a clear success.

The entry of independent schools can reveal valuable information about shortcomings in the established system. For example, it could be questioned whether municipalities are large enough to offer public secondary schools the conditions to thrive. Although about a quarter of all students in public upper secondary education cross municipal borders when going to school, municipalities are often criticised for trying to avoid that youth leave the local community. For the theoretically-oriented programmes, this may not be an issue, but for vocational programmes a larger size may be needed to provide students with modern equipment and build relations with the bigger companies. In Norway, upper secondary schools belong under the counties and in Denmark under the central government, not under the municipalities. In this context, per-student funding, introduced in Denmark in 1991, initiated a process where each public vocational upper secondary school increased its attention to strategic management, often closing courses with too few students to cover costs.[11] It could be interesting to analyse the consequences, in Sweden, of moving the responsibility for upper secondary education to central government, or perhaps the counties, while giving each institution more independence based on per-student funding. It would give public schools more room to merge, re-organise and specialise where that is desirable. Such an analysis could also look at other levels of schooling.

Higher education: shortening delays in study completion

Swedish higher education has a number of strengths. University[12] management has developed significantly over recent decades, with ample representation of external members on university boards, and the implementation of such quality assurance

Figure 4.8. **Wage premia, living costs and internal rates of return**

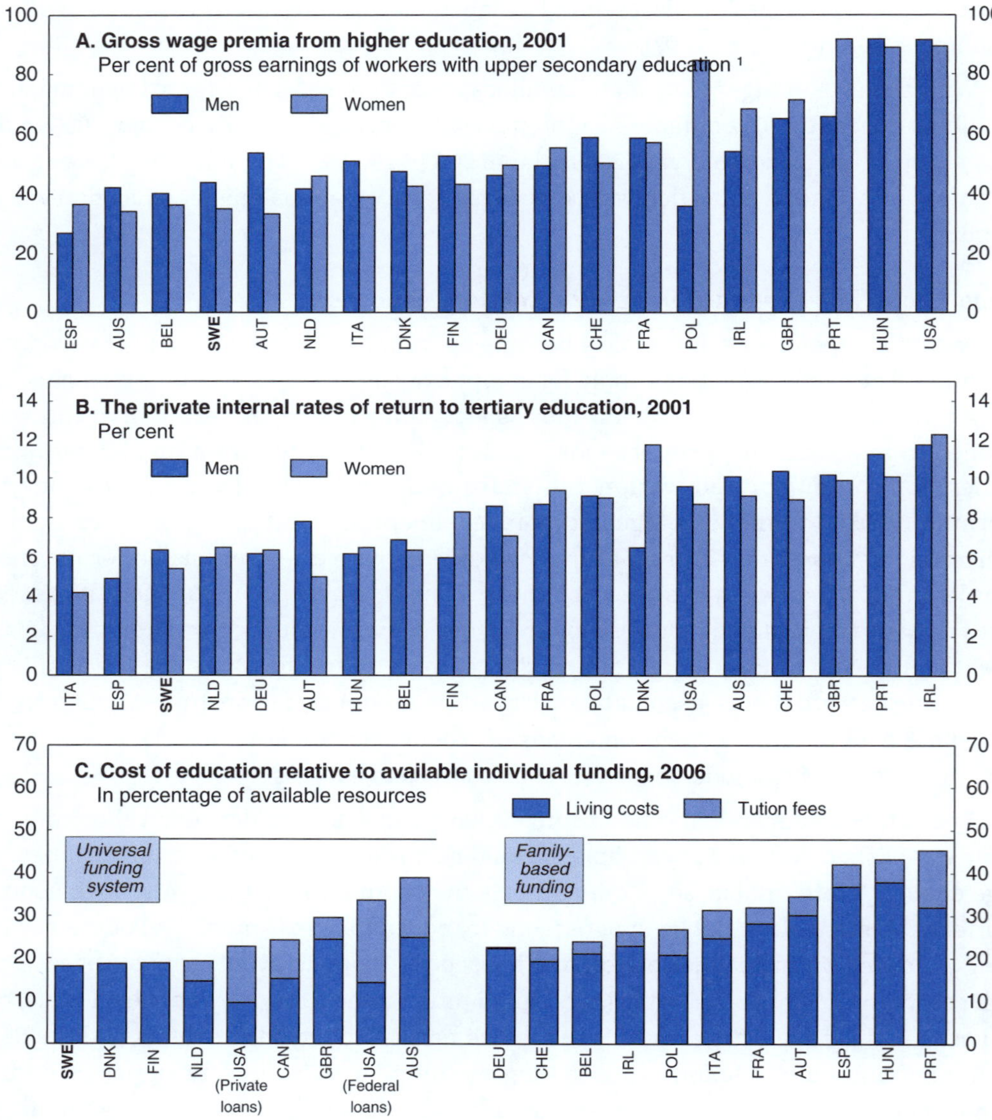

StatLink http://dx.doi.org/10.1787/485526667513

1. The figure shows the how much gross earnings of persons with tertiary education exceed gross earnings of persons with upper secondary education.

Source: OECD (2008c).

methods as regular evaluations. Higher education is easily accessible following strong capacity expansion – a near doubling of the student intake – since the early 1990s, including life-long learning offers.

Yet, there are challenges as well, as identified in the context of the recent *OECD Thematic Review of Tertiary Education* (National Agency for Higher Education, 2006; OECD, 2008e).[13] Specifically, the allocation of core research funding could be based on more transparent criteria, including performance indicators. Knowledge transfer via contacts with business could be deepened to nurture innovation. Retirement of the ageing academic staff will be a challenging transition for some institutions. And the institutions providing higher education could be given more freedom to develop their own strengths. With the 2009 Budget, the allocations for publicly funded research are being raised considerably for the 2009-12 period to reach 1% of GDP. One third of the increase will come *via* a new form of strategic investments in the fields of medicine, technology, climate/environment and finally interdisciplinary, humanity and social sciences. The other two thirds will be channelled *via* the general budgets of higher education institutions, research councils, etc.

A particular challenge relates to the heavy reliance on public funding. Tuition is free and the government offers students grants and loans to cover their living costs. Consequently, prospective students are not troubled by liquidity constraints: the cost of studying, measured relative to available individual funding, is among the lowest in the OECD (Figure 4.8). Meanwhile, wage premia for persons with higher education are low. Private internal rates of return from studying are also relatively low: while boosted by public financial support, they are held down by high and progressive income taxation (Boarini and Strauss, 2007). Two problems require attention: there are incentives for students to start and complete higher education late, and the prohibition of tuition fees constrains the development of the higher education sector as a whole. These two issues are discussed below.

Delays in entering and completing higher education

The median age for entering tertiary education is high in international comparison – a full year higher than in Finland and Norway, and almost three years higher than in the Netherlands, which shares many societal preferences with Nordic countries (Figure 4.9).

Figure 4.9. **Students start and complete tertiary education late**

2006

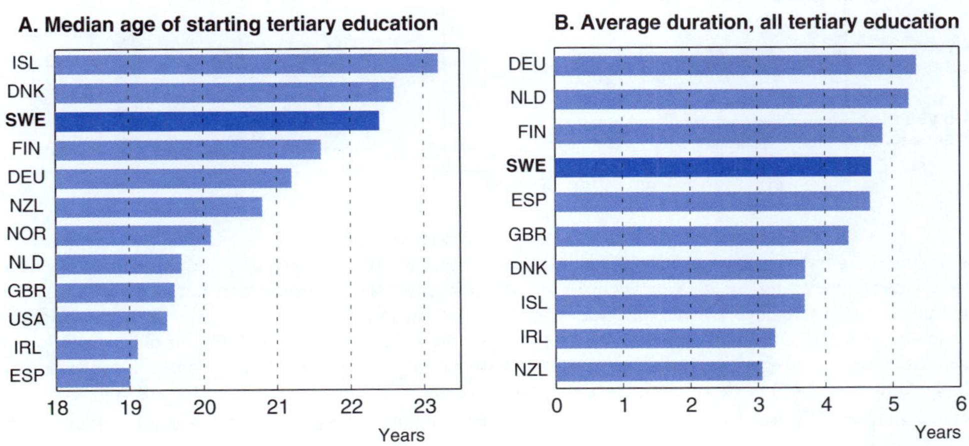

StatLink http://dx.doi.org/10.1787/485532205701

Source: OECD (2008b).

Following recommendations in previous *Surveys*, clear improvements are now being made in the admission criteria: notably, the possibilities to improve grades by repeating secondary school courses in adult education have been reduced (Annex 1.A1). Yet it might be worth reviewing if there are still unintended factors that cause students to defer and delay tertiary education.

The high median starting age would not be a problem if it simply reflected that many participate in life-long learning, thereby boosting higher education entry late in life. However, it is clear that the high median starting age also reflects the large share of youth entering higher education after a fairly long gap following the completion of upper secondary education (Figure 4.10). At age 19 and 20, participation in education drops to 40% and 35%, well below the level in comparable OECD countries. At age 21, the share in education rises – a pattern not seen in any other country, except for Denmark and, to a smaller extent, Norway (Figure 4.11). While many youth appreciate taking a break between secondary and tertiary education – travelling abroad, working in cafés, etc. – this leads to lower income for many years: *ceteris paribus*, two years postponement reduces the present value of lifetime earnings by nearly one half of one year's peak earnings (Holmlund *et al.*, 2008). With high and progressive income taxes, a considerable part of this income loss is carried by the public purse in the form of foregone tax revenue. This creates an adverse incentive for youth to take more gap years than they might have desired, had they themselves retained the full income gain from fewer gap years.

Figure 4.10. **The years between secondary and tertiary education**

2004

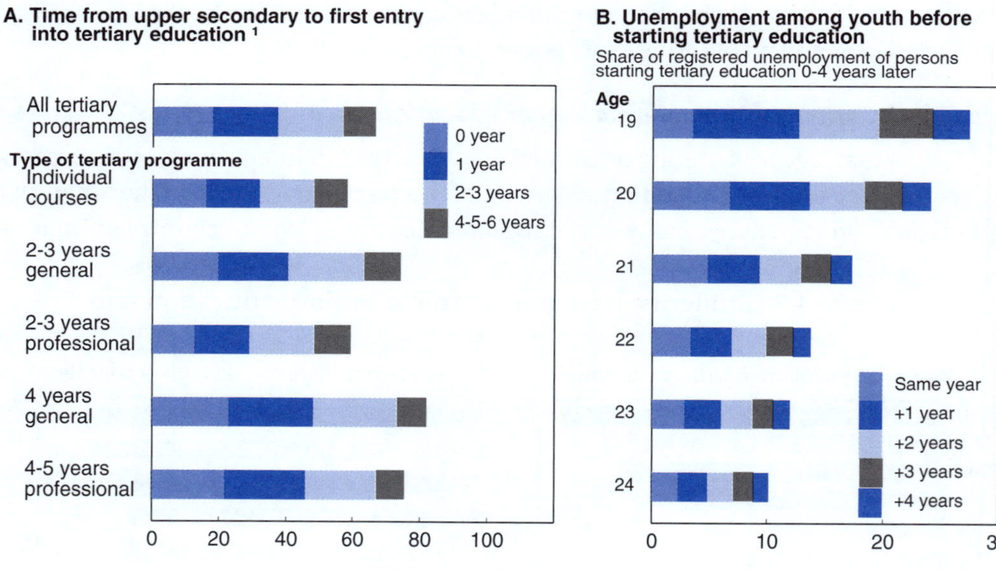

StatLink http://dx.doi.org/10.1787/485556387868

1. Classifications are based on the SUN 2000 classification system (building on ISCED 97). Data include only those either resident in Sweden in 2003 or with a Swedish upper secondary education between 1998 and 2004. Individuals who do not have a Swedish upper secondary education and who had a year of highest achieved education in 2003 before their last year of immigration are dropped. Percentages are fractions of the total and sum to 100. The residual category includes observations with no education from formal upper secondary school (possibly adult education) prior to start of tertiary education – 84 % in this category are 25 years or older.

Source: Own calculations based on population-wide education registers and register-based unemployment (Händel).

Figure 4.11. **Share of youth in education, employment or inactivity by age**

Per cent, 2006

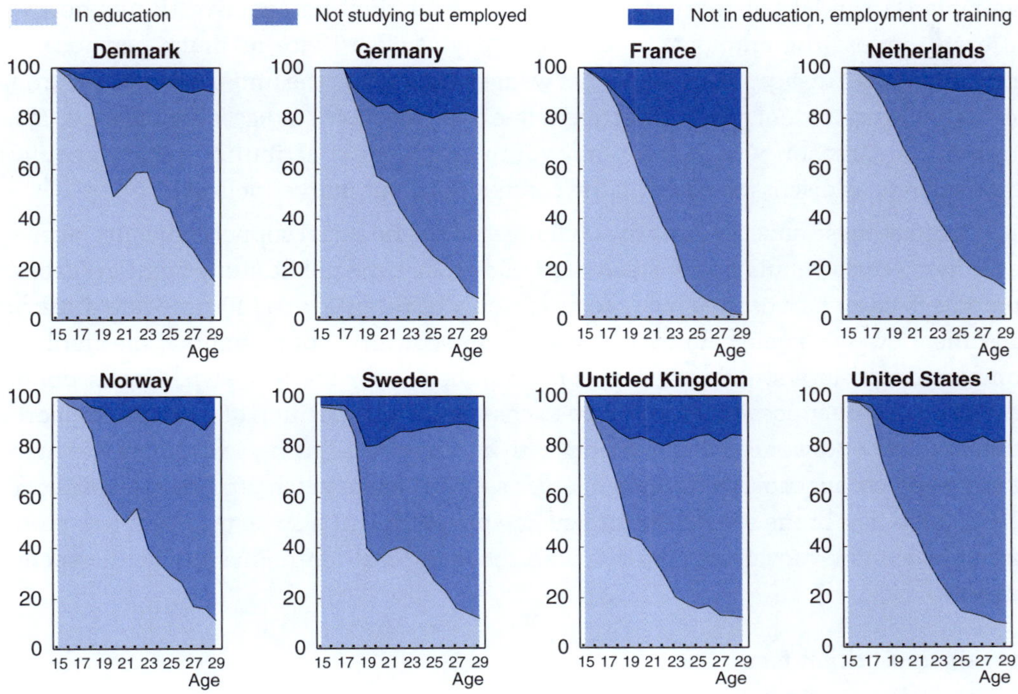

StatLink http://dx.doi.org/10.1787/485567772843

1. Data are for 2005.

Source: OECD Employment Outlook 2008.

A considerable part of youth unemployment consists of persons who have completed an upper secondary course directed at entering higher education, but then wait a few years. Among 19 and 20-year olds, 22-24% of unemployment is experienced by youth who will proceed to tertiary education within three years (Figure 4.10). To avoid that these people take up low-skilled jobs and displace those who lack the capacity needed to study, it would be desirable to encourage less delay before proceeding into higher education.

Sweden's taxes and benefits encourage youth to start and complete studies late – and increasingly so with recent reforms. In a system where marginal tax rates rise with income, there is a general incentive to smooth income over life. Moderate differences in marginal rates are not problematic, but recent reforms have magnified the gap between the marginal tax wedge faced as a graduate, and that faced before and while studying. In particular, the introduction of lower social contributions for youth up to and including 25 raises the opportunity costs of focusing on studies, not work, before age 26.[14] The effect is big enough to warrant attention, because it comes on top of the special excemption of study grants from personal income taxation. While most income benefits (unemployment, sickness and disability benefits, etc.) are taxed as personal income, this is not the case for the public grants available for students to cover part of their living costs. Consequently, it is not uncommon for students to face a zero marginal income tax rate, and with the in-work tax credit, introduced in 2007, this zero marginal rate now extends further up the income scale. With the pending 2009 enlargement of the employer contribution rebate for youth, the initial tax wedge resulting from social contributions and personal income taxation combined is only 27% for students compared to 63% after graduation when many face the state income tax. From a societal perspective it would be beneficial that students sometimes take loans and focus on completing their studies, to make their graduate skills available on the labour market, but from an individual perspective things now look different: unless the employer is willing to pay at least twice as much per hour after graduation, the large gap in marginal tax wedge implies that the initial net hourly earnings are higher from student jobs.[15] Effectively, late completion of studies is encouraged. This is an important reason why the general youth employer contribution rebate should be reconsidered, as discussed below in the context of labour market policies.

To offset these adverse incentives, changes in the financial support students receive to cover living costs should be considered. Already today, the public study grant available for students to cover part of their living costs can only be received at a full-time rate if studying full time. However, some countries go further and convert debt to grants if the studies are completed within a stipulated time, or give a bonus for starting soon after secondary education. Another possibility would be to change the composition of financial support for students further towards loans, possibly with a sliding scale giving a considerable share as grants early on but moving towards a larger share of loans when studies get prolonged.[16] The justification of the special youth housing benefit might also be reconsidered: it offers extra public money for those students who choose a "city-centre lifestyle" with expensive housing.[17]

Introducing tuition fees

Free tuition and generous grants for students' living costs have not achieved their original aim. Traditionally, generous public funding has been motivated by equality of opportunity: a desire to make higher education accessible for students from all family backgrounds alike. More recently, educational subsidies *via* free tuition have been described as the "siamese twin" offsetting the disincentives to human capital formation arising from redistribution *via* high marginal taxes (Bovenberg and Jacobs, 2008).[18] However, the model has not succeeded in significantly reducing differences in the likelihood by which people from different social backgrounds pursue higher education (SOU, 2008c). Indeed, experience from other countries indicates that, so long as ample loans are available to overcome liquidity constraints, moving towards letting students pay part of the tuition costs does not affect the social composition of the student body much (OECD, 2008e).

Moreover, free tuition may be at odds with growing international mobility of graduates. Compared to other countries, Sweden is not receiving that many foreign students, but the number is growing rapidly (Figure 4.12). Persons moving abroad after having studied for free don't contribute to the tax revenues on which the financing of their education relies in Nordic Countries (Welfare Commission, 2006). Previously the magnitude of this problem has, in practice, been small, but that is starting to change: more and more apply from all over the world to benefit from the free tuition, and as universities are obliged to select based on academic criteria, foreign enrolment is rising.[19] Against this background, the Swedish government is planning to introduce tuition charging for students from outside the European Union.[20]

Gradually introducing tuition charging also for Swedish and EU students would give stronger market signals for universities to develop courses in high demand and for students to reflect more on how and what to study. Public funding is allocated based on student numbers, implying some demand signals, and universities have considerable

Figure 4.12. **Foreign students enrolled in tertiary education**

In per cent of all tertiary enrolment[1]

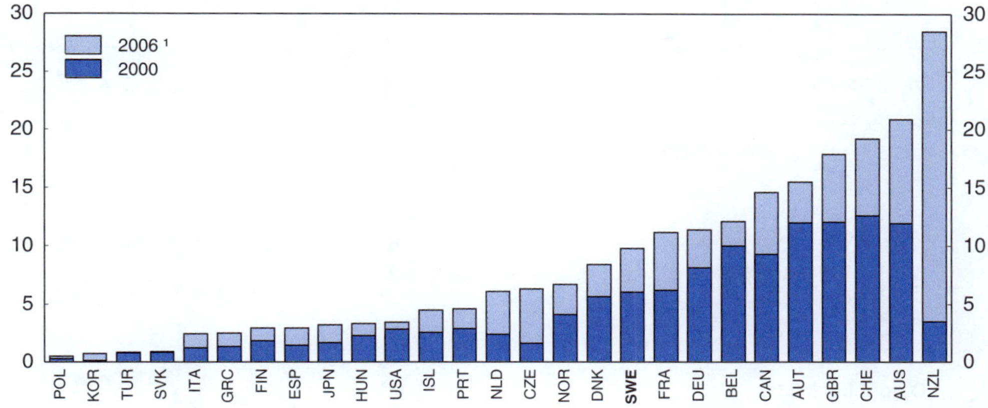

StatLink http://dx.doi.org/10.1787/485572430286

1. 2004 data for the United States and 2005 for Canada.

Source: OECD (2008b).

autonomy in terms of budget allocation, staff matters and other areas of input flexibility (Figure 4.13). Output flexibility is more limited as, in a few fields, a *numerus clausus* is imposed. In general, universities are only allowed to develop courses to be paid for privately, if there is one organisation contracting and paying for the course or programme; universities are not allowed to offer a programme and then charge tuition from students who apply. It would seem natural to give universities more independence and allow them to develop training paid for by tuition fees, with due consideration for the accountability mechanisms that would be a natural counterpart to increased flexibility. As knowledge itself increasingly becomes a tradable service, Swedish universities are unduly disadvantaged as they are largely prevented from developing education offers based on charging (Globalisation Council, 2008).

Financing tuition charges *via* loans with income-contingent repayment can ease access for students from less-advantaged backgrounds as they may be relatively risk averse. Such arrangements exist for tuition costs in countries like Australia, New Zealand and the United Kingdom (OECD, 2005, 2008e and 2008f). However, this would only work in a Swedish context if the high marginal tax wedges are reduced. The reason is that if income-contingency can lead not just to deferral of repayment, but to remission of debt, then it ultimately resembles a marginal tax. In countries with low or intermediate marginal tax wedges, this is not a problem, but in Sweden, where it comes on top of a very high marginal tax wedge, the resulting incentive problems would be large. In fact, Sweden previously had loans for living costs with income-contingent repayment, but these were changed to standard loans for this reason. Introducing loans with income-contingent repayment for tuition charges would therefore only be advisable if marginal income taxes are lowered substantially. This in turn is desirable also for a number of other reasons, as discussed in Chapter 3.

Labour markets: easing the impediments to youth employment

Many of the Swedish labour market's salient features constitute impediments to the entry of youth. In countries with very flexible wage formation, employers can offset the costs of the necessary training in entry jobs for young people by offering lower wages.

Figure 4.13. **Regulation of tertiary education providers**[1]

Increasing flexibility or accountability indicated from 0 to 10, 2005-06; dotted line is average

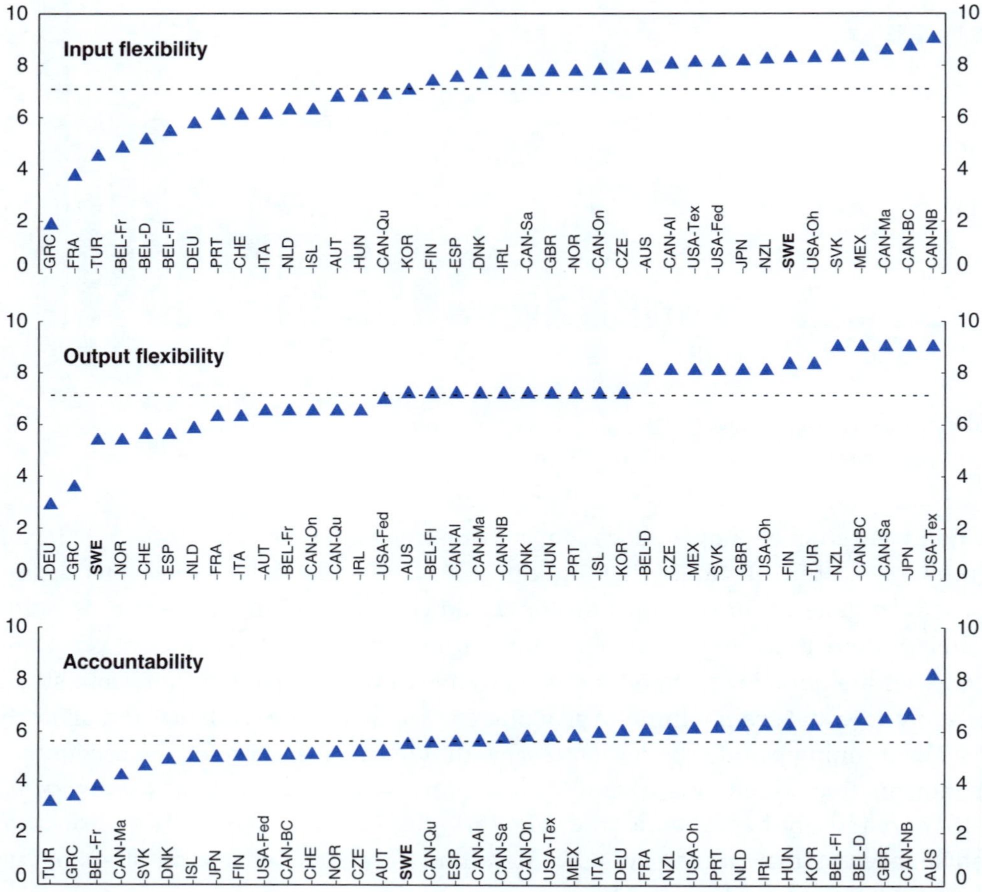

StatLink http://dx.doi.org/10.1787/485601858322

1. Accountability for USA-Fed is indicative as federal funds only account for a small share of total funding of tertiary education institutions. For Belgium, Canada and USA the figure shows selected regions.

Source: Oliveira Martins *et al.* (2007).

Where firing is easy, the risk of hiring young people with unproven skills is relatively small. But in Sweden, the costs and risks may make it unattractive to recruit young people since their wages are pegged to those of older workers and they are hard to lay off from regular contracts if the particular person turns out not to be the right one for the job. Even with the best imaginable education system, Swedish youth unemployment can hardly be brought down to the level of the leading countries without tackling the core rigidities. Minimum wages, employment protection rules, benefits and activation policies are therefore reviewed in turn below.

High minimum wages – can their adverse effects be offset by cuts in employer contributions?

Sweden has no legislated minimum wages, but collective agreements between unions and employers stipulate minimum wages for nearly all workers. These are high by international standards (Skedinger, 2007), following strong increases over the past ten years. Workplaces that are not covered by collective agreement can, in principle, set wages freely, but in practice this seems not to matter much. Unlike in most OECD countries, unions are allowed to take collective action against firms without collective agreements even if the workplace has no union members. Moreover, generous income transfers put a floor under workers' reservation wages.

High minimum wages are likely to inhibit access to employment for youth who are still learning the trade. The effects are mitigated where minimum wages are differentiated depending on experience, *e.g.* increasing after one year of work in the industry, profession or firm. Most agreements also have special arrangements for those younger than 18, either with a lower minimum wage or no contractual minimum wage at all. However, the age limit for eligibility for the adult minimum wage is rarely higher than 20 (Skedinger, 2007).[21] This shapes the earnings dispersion: the ratio between the median and the lowest paid for each age group is higher at age 19 than at age 20 (when the adult minimum wage usually kicks in), whereafter it grows with age (Figure 4.14). Apparently, minimum wages are a real constraint for how flexibly wages can adjust to the productivity of young workers. Quantifying the extent to which this hampers youth employment is difficult given the institutional complexity of Swedish minimum wages. For individual sectors, however, research suggests that minimum wages have had detrimental effects on employment (*e.g.* in hotels and restaurants, see Skedinger, 2006). Other countries, such as the Netherlands, are now making more room for lower starting wages for new graduates/ young workers in collective agreements (OECD, 2008g).

Figure 4.14. **Wage dispersion by age**

Ratio between the median and the lowest decile, base wages, 2005[1]

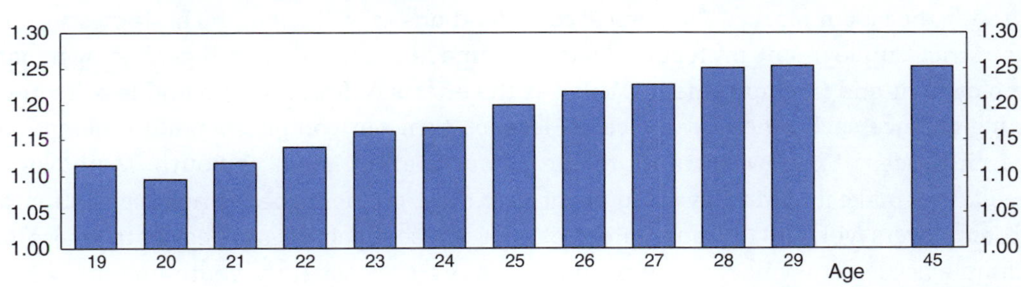

StatLink http://dx.doi.org/10.1787/485616236810

1. Calculated from monthly full-time equivalent base wages ("grundlön") for employees during fall 2005. The exact time of measurement varies across sectors. The calculations are based on the complete population of public-sector employees and a stratified sample of private-sector employees, weighted to correct for stratification and non-responses in the private sector. The sample size is 21 049 workers aged 19 (representing 40 058 individuals), 31 006 workers aged 24 (representing 56 841 individuals) and 57 165 workers aged 45 (representing 85 428 individuals).

Source: Secretariat calculations based on micro data from The Structural Wage Statistics (Strukturlönestatistiken) maintained by the National Mediation Office and Statistics Sweden.

As it has no control over the minimum wage, the government is seeking to boost labour demand via reductions in employer contributions. The first step, introduced in July 2007, reduced gross wage costs for 18-24 year old employees by 8.3% through halving social contributions, except for pensions. A pending proposal would remove an additional quarter of the normal non-pension-related contributions, taking the cumulative reduction in gross wage costs to 12.1% in 2009 (Ministry of Finance, 2008).

Lower employer contributions for youth can mitigate the negative employment effects from high minimum wages, but it may also reduce wage restraint on the union side, leading to further increases in minimum wages. The three-year collective agreements concluded in 2007 imply strong annual pay rises of 6-7% for hotels and restaurants (though half for personnel younger than 20) and 5-6% for inexperienced retail workers (National Mediation Office, 2007).[22] This will attenuate the benefits of the contribution cuts and could spill over to other unemployed marginal groups, such as immigrants, who would become more expensive to employ (they would not benefit from a reduction in contributions).

Another difficulty with across-the-board cuts in contributions is that they are poorly targeted. The payroll tax cut covers all youth, and most of those covered would have found work anyway. The targeted New-Start Job scheme, introduced in 2007, is more promising.[23] For youth, it implies a subsidy lasting for six to 12 months, depending on the length of the jobless spell.[24] Formally, the worker has to apply in order for the employer to get the reduction. However, in contrast to preceding policies, this reduction does not require consent from an employment service case manager. There are no Swedish evaluations of employment subsidies for young workers, but evidence for older unemployed workers suggests that the effects are positive, although there can be substantial displacement effects with subsidies paid to jobs which would have materialised anyway (Calmfors *et al.*, 2004; Forslund *et al.*, 2004). Adding this to the adverse incentive to start and complete studies later discussed above, it would seem worth reconsidering the general contribution rebate for youth in favour of more focused measures.

Relaxing employment protection legislation

Strict employment protection rules are known to be an important obstacle for youth entering the labour market. Theoretical considerations as well as empirical studies suggest that strict employment protection legislation may be neutral with regard to aggregate employment and unemployment insofar as the effects of fewer layoffs and less frequent hiring balance each other out. However, less job turnover complicates and prolongs the search process for new entrants to the labour market, such as youth. Moreover, if regulations make it hard to lay off someone who turns out not to be the right person for the job, employers will tend to restrict hires to those whose capabilities are easier to assess, for example because they have an employment history. Consequently, youth unemployment is higher where employment protection regulations are strict (OECD, 2004b and 2006c; Skedinger, 2008).

The recent extension of the maximum standard duration for temporary contracts allows employers to better "try out" a young person, but also runs the risk of increasing labour market dualism. The so-called general temporary employment contract has now been introduced in legislation, raising the maximum duration of standard temporary contracts from 12 to 24 months.[25] It is now in the process of being implemented in collective agreements. These steps continue the reform approach followed over recent decades. While Swedish regulations for regular employment have remained unchanged, the restrictions on fixed-term contracts and temporary work agencies were eased between the late 1980s and late 1990s.

The downside of this approach is that it may further entrench insider-outsider problems. The incidence of temporary contracts has increased strongly since the early 1990s, in particular for young workers. As a result over half of all youth employment in Sweden is based on temporary contracts, compared with around a quarter in Denmark and Norway, and even less in the United Kingdom (Figure 4.15). It has been suggested that high unemployment rates during the deep economic crisis of the 1990s may have contributed to this development (Holmlund and Storrie, 2002). However, temporary contracts account for a larger share of youth employment now than in the 1990s, indicating that structural changes also play an important role. In particular, today there are more students looking for part-time work and willing to take a temporary contract: enrolment in tertiary education has grown substantially, and reductions in grants to cover living costs may encourage more students to seek work.[26] But in the end, such factors cannot explain why a larger share of employment is on temporary contracts than in otherwise comparable countries: growing duality of employment protection rules seems to be a real problem.

Figure 4.15. **Temporary contracts compared internationally**

Share of temporary contracts among those employed, 2006

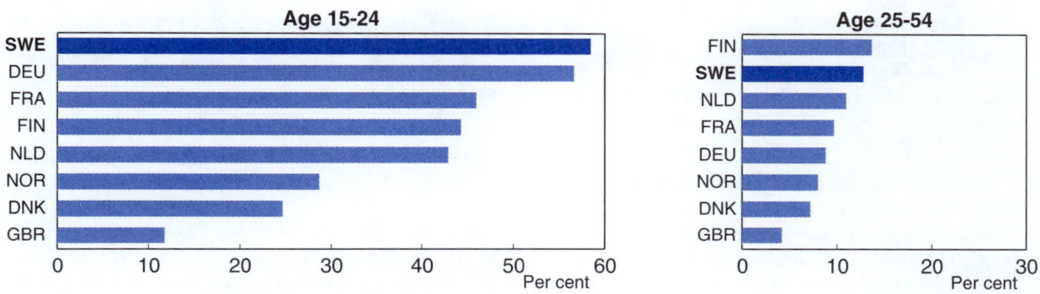

StatLink http://dx.doi.org/10.1787/485618273311

Source: OECD, *LFS database.*

Employers may resort to temporary forms of employment to circumvent strict rules, resulting in people taking a series of temporary contracts, rather than moving to a permanent contract. Indeed, looking at labour market transitions, the most common destination for those leaving unemployment is temporary employment, with only few going directly into regular employment (Figure 4.16). Unemployment is more persistent for prime-age adults than for youth, but when leaving unemployment, youth are less likely to get a permanent contract than prime-age adults. Moreover, youth from less advantaged backgrounds may have more difficulty finding their way in a dual labour market, and they may be more vulnerable to screening by employers who become risk-averse when regulations make it difficult to lay off someone turning out not to be the right person for the job.[27] In the event of an economic downturn, youth and others on temporary contracts may have to bear the brunt of adjustment as they are the least difficult to lay off (OECD, 2004b). Operating within the labour market as it is, individuals are better off taking a temporary job than remaining unemployed,[28] but entry into the labour market for youth in general would be helped substantially by easing the rules for permanent contracts.

The best for youth would be to improve the path to regular employment contracts. To that end, reforms should not deepen the difference between permanent and temporary contracts further; it is anyway hard to think of further marginal changes that could be made. Rather, reforms should address the core of employment protection rules (Box 4.4). In

Figure 4.16. **Transitions in the Swedish labour market**

2007[1]

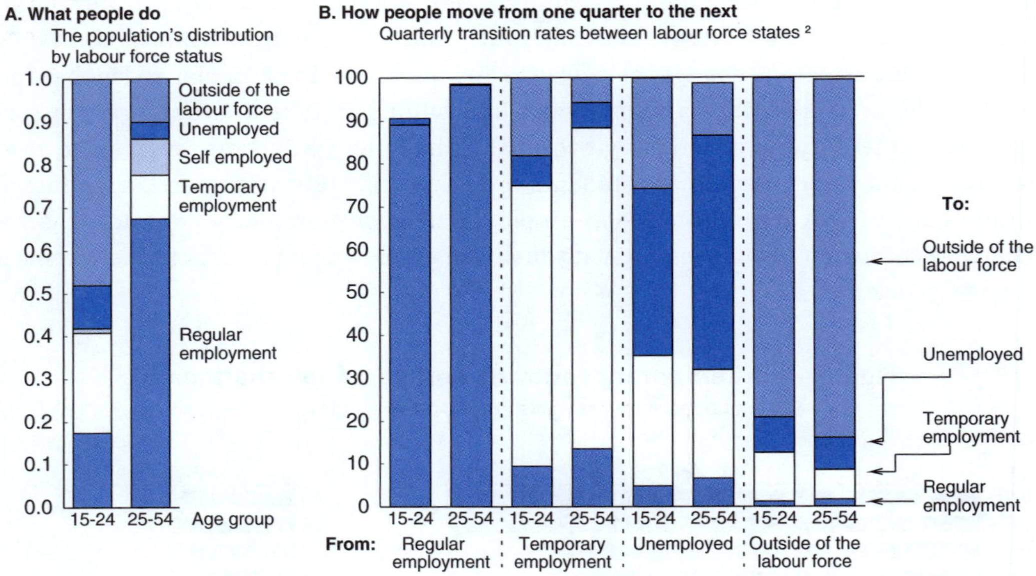

StatLink http://dx.doi.org/10.1787/485625841457

1. Students are included in the Labour Force Survey. It is not possible to exclude students from the decompositions shown in this figure.
2. Yearly averages of quarterly transition rates, calculated using the fraction in each state by starting quarter as weights. Not all transition possibilities are available in the data: self employment is missing as receiving state from all starting states. Transitions from temporary employment to out of the labour force are estimated by assuming no transitions to self employment.

Source: Statistics Sweden and OECD calculations.

particular, the stringency of the criteria for what is a fair dismissal under a regular contract might be reconsidered, with a view to making employers less hesitant to offer youth a regular contract. In order to reduce the gap between temporary and regular contracts, the trial period for regular contracts could also be lengthened.[29] The complexity of these issues would call for a review of the broader implications, including with respect to collective wage bargaining.

Labour market activation and benefits

Active labour policies

Sweden's active labour market policies were reshuffled in 2007, *inter alia* with the introduction of a Job Guarantee for youth: after three months of unemployment, persons below 25 are offered intensified study- and job-coaching; if they don't find a job after another three months, they are oriented to workplace practice, *i.e.* subsidised employment, or training. Half of the participants are expected to be catered for by private contractors. By February 2008, 26% of the registered unemployed youth were participating in a labour market programme of some form, down from 38% in 2006.

The design of the Job Guarantee reflects available research evidence, notably in terms of the emphasis on job-search assistance early in each unemployment spell. The frequent short unemployment spells make youth susceptible to "lock-in effects", *i.e.* reduced job-finding rates due to lower search intensity when enrolled in a labour market programme (Larsson, 2003). In this sense, the Job Guarantee is an improvement relative to its

Box 4.4. **What elements of the strict Swedish employment protection rules may hamper youth entry?**

Regulations giving job security for those who have a permanent contract are relatively elaborate in Sweden. In fact, France is the only high-income country with stricter employment protection legislation. The various aspects of this legislation are here compared to Germany, having similar overall strictness, and Denmark and the United Kingdom, which are generally more liberal (Figure 4.17). Differences are most remarkable for procedural inconveniences and difficulties involved with dismissal of an employee on a regular contract. For example, worker capability or redundancy of the job are adequate and sufficient grounds for individual dismissal in Denmark and the United Kingdom, whereas in Sweden and Germany, a transfer and/or retraining to adapt the person to different work must be attempted prior to dismissal.[1] Moreover the trial period during which the employer can easily terminate a contract must end after six months in Sweden, like in Germany, whereas Denmark and the United Kingdom allow longer trial periods of up to 10½ and 12 months respectively. By contrast, notice periods for individual dismissals are not much longer than elsewhere, and Sweden has no severance pay. For collective dismissals, collective agreements may prolong the notice period, but the other additional requirements are not stricter than elsewhere.

Figure 4.17. **Strictness of employment protection legislation**

Index scale of 0-6, from least to most restrictive, 2003

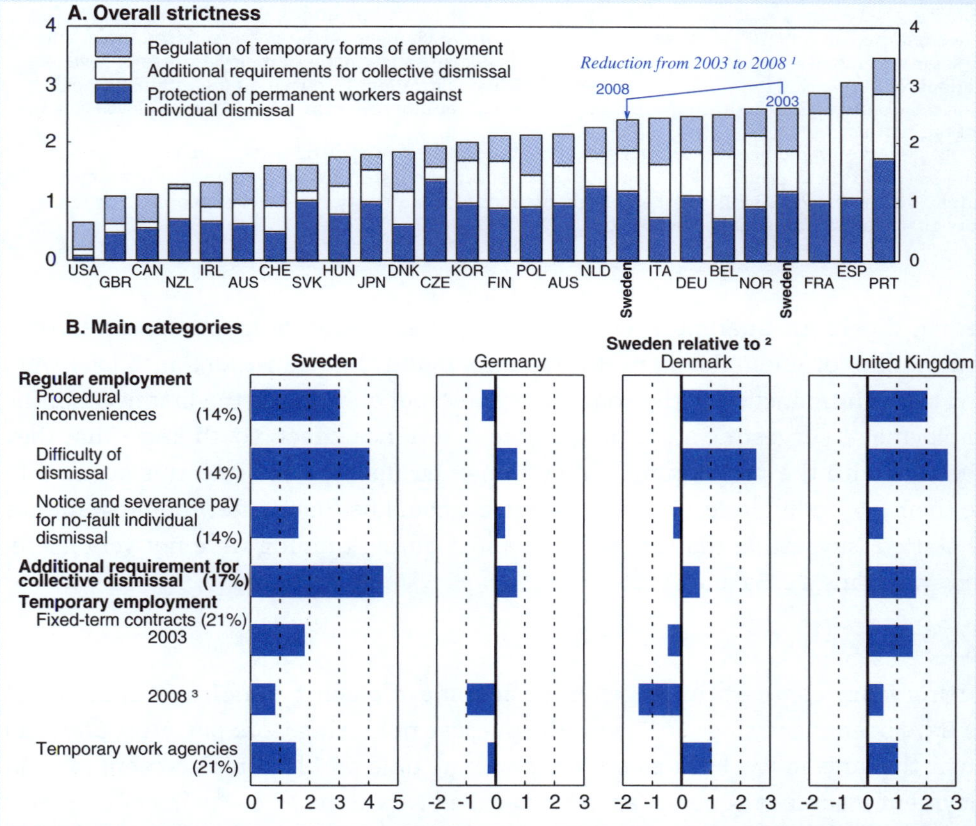

StatLink http://dx.doi.org/10.1787/485726412466

1. The introduction of a "general temporary employment contract" reduced the indicator on fixed-term contracts by 1.0 as there are no more restrictions on the type of work for which temporary employment can be made (0.5 indicator point), and as the maximum duration has gone up from 12 to 24 months (0.5 indicator point). As this has a weight of 21%, it reduces the total indicator by 0.21.
2. The three panels show the indicator value for Sweden minus the indicator value for the comparator country.
3. 2008 data for Sweden compared with 2003 data for Germany, Denmark and United Kingdom.

Source: OECD *Employment Outlook* 2004 and updates based on information from the Swedish authorities.

Box 4.4. What elements of the strict Swedish employment protection rules may hamper youth entry? *(cont.)*

Sweden's last-in-first-out rule for regular employment has been particularly controversial. Introduced in the 1970s, it remains a nationally-legislated rule stipulating that employers lay off staff in reverse order of seniority within each professional segment.[2] In the public sector the employer is defined so narrowly that a teacher or childcare worker will lose their position in the last-in-first-out hierarchy if they shift to work in another municipality, which is very detrimental to labour mobility. The law allows collective agreements between employers and unions to set aside the last-in-first-out rule. Firms undergoing large restructuring therefore often say that the last-in-first-out rule is not a hindrance, as they would anyway have a close dialogue with unions in an effort to facilitate the restructuring. In parts of the labour market, the main effect of the last-in-first-out rule may therefore be to elevate union bargaining power and ensure high union membership, as collective agreements may set the rule aside also for employees that are not union members, at least in principle. For youth, the last-in-first-out rule implies more frequent layoffs, as youth are more likely to have joined the firm recently. However, the rule is more likely to deter employers from hiring a 52- than a 27-year old: the employer might be concerned about how the former would gain seniority and be difficult to lay off when his/her work capacity is declining. Such a concern would not matter for the 27-year old, whose work capacity is likely to grow.

1. According to the Swedish Employment Protection Act, a termination of an employment contract may be deemed unlawful if it had been reasonable to require the employer to provide other work in his or her service for the employee. There is a very well developed case law from the Labour Court concerning this rule. In principle, an employer is not required to "create" work and/or make substantial changes in the organisation to meet this requirement. Nor is the employer required to offer work within the organisation that the employee does not have the right qualifications for. However, if the employee can gain the right qualifications through training within reasonable limits, based on the circumstances in the individual case, the employer must offer the work to the employee before termination of the contract.
2. The rule does not protect outright incompetent workers, though, as these may be dismissed on personal grounds, in which case the last-in-first-out principle does not apply. Moreover, the last-in-first-out rule takes into account education and skills as an employee with longer employment time only has priority over other employees if he or she has satisfactory qualifications for continued work.

predecessor, the Youth Guarantee, where municipal activation programmes set in only after five months of unemployment. Evaluations found that transitions into jobs were increased by the introduction of the Youth Guarantee, but only during the first five months of unemployment, suggesting a pre-programme deterrence effect: youth knew that they would be sent into the programme if they remained unemployed and this seemed to increase their job-finding rates. No positive effects could be found after the programmes actually started, suggesting that the skills acquired during training were not very useful (Forslund and Skans, 2006a and 2006b).[30]

Benefits

Starting from comparatively generous income-replacing benefits, a number of changes have been made since 2007 with the purpose of making work pay. Most affect all age groups: the large in-work tax credit, the declining time profile of replacement rates in unemployment insurance benefits, and the so-called New-Start Jobs waiving of employer contributions for persons coming back to work after prolonged absence. As discussed in the previous *Survey*, these policies can be expected to have a lasting positive effect on the level of employment (OECD, 2007b).

Age-differentiated rules have been introduced for employer contributions, as discussed previously, but only to a small extent for income-replacing benefits. Just two youth-specific benefit changes have been made. First, while the gross replacement rate in

 OECD ECONOMIC SURVEYS: SWEDEN – ISBN 978-92-64-05423-3 – © OECD 2008

unemployment insurance benefits declines from 80% to 70% after 40 weeks for adults, this now happens after only 20 weeks for youth. Second, graduation from secondary or tertiary education no longer gives access to unemployment assistance. This concerns some 10% of the unemployed 19-24 year olds.

In light of the positive experience with differentiating the benefits available for youth and prime-age adults in Denmark, further steps in this direction might be considered. Offering the same benefits across all age groups is likely to cause unemployment and inactivity traps for youth, as they have not yet attained the productivity level of prime-age adults. Moreover, exposing youth to clear economic incentives might appear less problematic from a welfare perspective: youth are less settled and therefore better able to reorient to a new profession or move to another part of the country to take up work. Last, but not least, avoiding benefit dependency among youth is key as they are forming habits that are likely to follow them through adult life. Three issues might warrant attention:

- Unemployment insurance benefits are effectively more generous for youth than for prime-age adults. The formula combines a high gross replacement rate with a ceiling at 75% of average full-time earnings. As youth typically have lower earnings, they are less likely to be facing the ceiling, and they are unlikely to face the high marginal tax rates that prime-age adults may do if they are unemployed only part of the year. Consequently, effective net replacement rates will often be somewhat higher for youth than prime-age adults, even though they might be better able to bear an income reduction as they are less likely to have dependent children. About 5% of the 19-year old registered unemployed receive unemployment insurance benefits, rising to about half of those aged 24. A lower starting replacement rate for youth, say 65%, would give clearer incentives to seek a new job quickly; it would allow the employment service to focus activation efforts on those in genuine need of coaching and training.
- For those who drop out from upper secondary school into inactivity, going back to complete schooling can entail a short-term income loss. This situation arises because from age 19, youth are eligible for the same social assistance as older adults: for a single person, SEK 3 550 per month plus coverage of reasonable expenses for housing, electricity, insurance, etc. On going back to school, the person would, often, no longer be eligible for social assistance, but only for the study grant worth SEK 1 050.[31] The resulting incentive not to return to complete school is problematic not least because persons with incomplete secondary education have a higher risk of unemployment (Box 4.2).[32]
- Withdrawal of social assistance generates a 100% effective marginal tax rate that can discourage taking up temporary or part-time work. How far it extends up the income scale depends on the recipient's housing and family situation. About a third of the registered unemployed aged 19-24 receive social assistance, and this share is likely to grow as an estimated 10% of the registered unemployed 19-24 year olds have lost access to unemployment assistance following the change of rules for school and university graduates.

Social assistance involves complex trade-offs and therefore changes in that area might best be done following a wider review. One could envisage differentiating the level of social assistance for persons below the age of, say, 23 by lowering the standard rates or by introducing a parental means test. The two thirds of the 19-year old social assistance recipients who live with their parents, declining to one third by the age 22, don't need as much public support as an older adult.

Youth entering disability benefits is a highly worrying phenomenon, which has emerged as a major issue in recent years. In 2007, 10% of the persons entering disability benefits were aged 19 to 30, compared with just 4% three years earlier and a stable 2% in the more distant past. One reason for this sudden increase may be that youth attending special schools due to handicaps have gained entitlement to disability benefits; when leaving school, they tend to remain in the system. To break this pattern, consideration should be given to paying handicapped youth in special schools a study grant and removing the automatic entitlement to disability benefits.

Co-ordination between municipalities and central government agencies

Many countries are moving towards integration between the agencies administering benefits and those providing activation, as well as integration between different types of benefits related to unemployment, ill health and social problems. Both Norway and Denmark are following this route, and their experience shows that the way benefit outlays are split between different agencies and levels of government matters a lot for how well activation instruments are used and how many people are granted various benefits. In Sweden, fiscal equalisation compensates municipalities that are likely to have high social spending because of the composition of their population, but costs or gains when actual outlays on social assistance are higher or smaller are fully borne by each municipality. Unemployment insurance benefits are administered by union-organised funds financed by central government subsidies and membership fees. Finally, unemployment assistance, sickness and disability benefits are administered by the public social insurance agency, which is fully financed by central government. These arrangements raise familiar fiscal incentive problems and the fragmentation of service delivery results in users complaining that they are "falling between two stools" as they are sent from one agency to the next without being adequately helped anywhere.

Recent reforms lack clear direction in this respect. The restriction of access to unemployment assistance implies that more youth will come to their municipality for social assistance. However, as the responsibility for youth activation has been shifted to the Job Guarantee scheme run by the central-government Employment Service, municipalities have now lost an important instrument to curb the number of social assistance recipients. A few years ago, the local social security offices were moved from municipalities into a central-government agency. But these offices, which bear the costs of unemployment assistance, sickness and disability benefits, are not linked locally to the Employment Service responsible for activation or municipalities responsible for education. Developing the local coordination between these agencies will be an important challenge.

Conclusions

To tackle high youth unemployment, Sweden needs a broad-based approach touching upon education as well as labour market institutions, taxes and benefits (Box 4.5). A series of education reforms, which virtually all move closer to international best practice, are currently being discussed. These proposals now need to be implemented. The wide-ranging labour market reforms put in place from 2007 to make work pay help, but they could go further for youth by amplifying the incentives to seek work while avoiding encouraging delays in the start and completion of studies.

Box 4.5. **Summary of education and youth employment recommendations**

Compulsory education

- Strengthen compulsory schooling, not least in science, and continue to develop the use of tests to better monitor progressions during school.
- Introduce accreditation of teachers and give more weight to teachers' specific competences when allocating tasks among staff. Once the accreditation scheme is well established, greater wage flexibility could reward the best teachers.

Upper secondary education

- Introduce apprenticeships anchored into the same competence structure as school-based vocational programmes so as to allow hands-on learning while ensuring that apprentices acquire the general skills they will need if later in life they have to reorient professionally. Monitor how pay for apprentices is set locally to ensure ongoing employer interest.
- Increase transparency for potential students about the labour market prospects associated with alternative education choices, *e.g.* by publishing data for employment outcomes of recent school leavers.
- Analyse the possibility of moving the responsibility for upper secondary schools from municipalities to central government, while giving each institution more independence based on per-student funding. This would allow public secondary schools more room to merge, re-organise and specialise, helping vocational programmes in particular. Such an analysis could also look at other levels of schooling.

Higher education

- Base the allocation of core research funding on more transparent criteria and give universities and university colleges (*högskolor*) more freedom to each develop their own strengths.
- Adjust the grants students receive to cover living costs: consider introducing rewards for early entry and on-time completion of studies or changing the composition so that loans become a larger share and grants a smaller share of total financial support when studies get prolonged.
- Consider moving gradually towards a system where not only non-EU students, but also Swedish and EU students are charged for tuition, while extending the government loans available for students to finance tuition costs. If today's high marginal income taxes are reduced, repayment of these loans could be made contingent on graduates' future income.

Labour market institutions, social contributions and benefits

- Reconsider the general reduction in employer contributions for youth in favour of measures that are more narrowly targeted at those with difficulties getting employment.
- Avoid further dualism in employment protection rules. One approach would be to create better in-roads to regular employment, such as by easing the definitions of what is a fair dismissal and lengthening the trial period for regular contracts.
- Focus on job-search coaching in the early phase of youth unemployment spells, as done with the Job Guarantee for Youth, so as to avoid lock-in effects where participation in activation programmes reduces job-search intensity.
- Consider differentiating unemployment benefits by age: lower the initial gross replacement rate in unemployment insurance for persons below 25. Conditions for social assistance might also be reviewed, including for youth living with their parents.
- Pay a study grant, not disability benefits, to handicapped youth in special schools.
- Improve local co-ordination between municipalities, central-government employment services and social insurance offices and unemployment insurance funds.

Notes

1. It is sometimes questioned whether the international definitions are applied in exactly the same way across countries, in particular when it comes to how widely students looking for part-time or holiday employment are included. A simple gauge is to compare the share of full-time students being counted as unemployed and the share of students among all unemployed in the Labour Force Survey. Applying this test to the Sweden-Denmark comparison does not indicate any real problems. The full-time students among the 15-74 year olds were distributed as follows in Sweden, 2006: 158 500 were employed, 88 100 were unemployed, and 535 000 were outside the labour force, meaning that 14.1% of the full-time students not working were counted as unemployed. For Denmark, the same share was 11.4% in 2005 and 11.7% in 2007. Full-time students accounted for a steady 26% of all unemployed (age 15-74) in Sweden, 2005-07, where the economy moved from a slight negative to a slight positive output gap. For Denmark, full-time students accounted for 19% of all unemployed (age 15-66) in 2005, when the economy was close to equilibrium, and 24% in 2007, when there was a clear positive output gap.
2. The short duration of most unemployment spells may partly reflect that the persons concerned enter education or a labour market programme, or simply stop searching. For those registered with the Public Employment Service, it is possible to exclude such cases statistically: for youth, the median duration of unemployment slightly exceeds four months for the spells that end in a job, as against five months for persons in their 40s.
3. Thus NEET treats jobs and education equally on the one side and job search and inactivity equally on the other. It is important to note that participants in all forms of activities, including various labour market programmes, are treated as being active. A consequence is that countries with large volumes of labour market programmes will have lower NEET rates, which may explain part of the more positive picture emerging from these statistics. The position relative to Finland, Norway, the Netherlands and Denmark remain the same as for unemployment: Sweden and Finland appear to be the worst-performing countries in this group.
4. For mathematics, the fall in average PISA score from 2003 to 2006 is statistically significant at the 90% confidence level. For reading, there is a noticeable quantitative fall in the average PISA score from 2000 to 2006, but it is not statistically significant.
5. In Sweden most students with special needs attend ordinary schools, but this should not bias the result as the PISA study generally includes students enrolled in special educational institutions.
6. Given that Swedes are typically known for environment-friendly habits, it may surprise that 15-year olds are not to a larger extent indicating to be aware of the science aspects of important environmental issues. It might reflect a discrepancy between the value attached to environmental protection and the quality of science teaching. Within each country, there is a strong correlation between each student's self-reported awareness of environmental issues and the science score obtained in the PISA test.
7. Employers often point to recruitment difficulties, but as labour is a scarce resource, the key question from an economy-wide perspective is whether labour shortages are more pronounced for certain professional groups than others. A recent study classified 25-54 years olds with tertiary education based on whether they work in the area and at the competence level matching their education (Statistics Sweden, 2007). The traditional longer engineering degree (*civilingenjör*) was among the educational groups having the highest match rate indicating relative scarcity. For natural science graduates and the shorter engineering degree introduced in the early 1990s (*högskoleingenjör*), however, this was not the case.
8. Gross statutory salaries for teachers are, at first glance, among the lowest in the OECD. In 2006, gross salaries for teachers with the minimum training required and 15 years of experience were 88%, 91% and 98% of GDP per capita in primary, lower secondary and upper secondary education, respectively, compared with OECD averages of 122%, 126% and 134% (OECD, 2008b). However, supplements to base salary based on competence may have a larger extent than in most countries. Moreover, employer contributions (24.5% of wage costs) are higher than in most OECD countries (ranging from 0.0% to 29.6%), diminishing gross pay relative to employers' total wage costs.
9. Due to data availability, the studies are all based independent schools in compulsory education. However, there is no particular reason to presume that the effects would not be similar at upper secondary level.
10. The *Learning for Jobs* OECD review is part of a series of country review of vocational education and training prepared by the OECD Education Directorate. Aside from Sweden, reviews are carried out for the United Kingdom, Hungary, Australia, Norway, Mexico, Korea and Switzerland between

late 2007 and late 2008. Together with cross-country analytical work, the country reviews will feed into a final comparative report to be published in early 2009.

11. This development is best documented in an evaluation where school managements was asked about what changes had been initiated by per-student funding (Danish Ministry of Education, 1998).

12. Throughout this *Survey*, the word "university" refers to institutions of higher education in a broad sense. In a Swedish context, it includes universities (universitet) as well as university colleges (högskolor).

13. No country-specific report on Sweden was prepared by the OECD Secretariat as part of this thematic review. However, a seminar was organised on 26 May 2008 discussing *inter alia* the challenges mentioned in the text.

14. Strictly speaking, if wages were completely and uniformly fixed by collective agreements, changes in employer contributions for youth would not affect the hourly earnings of youth. In practice however, youth working on-and-off before and while studying typically take up work in areas with considerable *de facto* wage flexibility, implying that changes in employer contributions would feed through to individual pay. Moreover, as lower contributions makes it more attractive for shops and restaurants etc. to hire youth relative to low-skilled prime-age adults, it will be easier for youth and students to find work, raising the effective earnings net of implicit job-search costs, transport, etc.

15. If the study grant for living costs was liable for income taxation, like most income benefits, the 27% *versus* 63% gap in marginal tax wedge would only apply for earned income up to SEK 13 000, not SEK 45 000. Perhaps the special tax excemption for study grants is less warranted today than it was before the introduction of the in-work tax credit and the employer contribution rebate for youth.

16. The value of the study grants has decreased relative to market wages, from 75% of industrial wages net of taxes to 55% between 1992 and 2005 (LO, 2008). Nevertheless, students are able to attain considerable income: they are allowed to earn SEK 102 500 annually before withdrawal of the study grants starts.

17. This benefit has not been touched in recent reforms: persons aged 18-28 without children are offered compensation for 75% of monthly housing costs in excess of SEK 1 800, followed by 50% of costs in excess of SEK 2 600 up to a ceiling at SEK 3 600. Consequently, the maximum monthly value of the benefit is SEK 1 100. The key question might be whether the grant is warranted at all in its current form: by subsidising a "city-centre lifestyle" it may well prolong study duration. Moreover, the high compensation percentage risks encouraging landlords to raise rents when these are liberalised (Chapter 1).

18. Free tuition and generous grants may attract potential students, but the high marginal tax rates encourage students to emphasise consumption aspects when choosing when and what to study while paying less attention to labour market prospects (Alstadsæter *et al.*, 2008).

19. For example, over half of the students admitted to the new masters programme at Gothenburg Business School come from outside the European Union.

20. A proposal was prepared two years ago (SOU, 2006). In June this year, the government announced its intention to move forward, although more detailed information about how tuition fees for non-EU students would be implemented have not been given yet. EU rules require that students from other EU member states should be treated in the same way as nationals. Consequently, EU students can only be required to pay tuition if Swedish students are.

21. The exception is some white-collar agreements with an age limit of 24 (National Mediation Office, 2007).

22. Already prior to these increases, minimum wages affect many workers in these service sectors: 30% of all employees in areas covered by the hotels-and-restaurants agreement receive the minimum wage; for the retail agreement the share is 20% (NIER, 2007). Youth are heavily affected, as they are overrepresented in these two areas: 29% of employed upper secondary school graduates work in retail trade or hotels and restaurants three years after graduation (Statistics Sweden, 2006). More generally, many young workers find their first lasting jobs in these and other parts of the service sector (Åslund *et al.*, 2007).

23. It should be noted that New-Start Jobs can be combined with the reduction of employers' contributions.

24. The spell can be longer if joblessness was due to sickness.

25. Under 2006 rules, fixed-term contracts could be used without particular time limits under certain circumstances, for example contracts concerning a specified season or specified task, temporary substitute employment, and cases where the employee has attained the age of 67. But aside from these cases, it was possible for an employer to conclude a fixed-term contract with one and the same employee for at most a year within a three-year period (so-called agreed fixed-term employment). An employer was never allowed to have more than five employees with agreed fixed-time employment at the same time.
26. According to Swedish Labour Force Survey estimates, on average 117 000 students aged 15 to 24 worked in 2007, of which 102 000 were enrolled full-time. This means that on average 23% of full-time and part-time students aged 15-24 were employed in a given month during the year. Those who worked did so for on average 14 hours per week. This means that student employment amounts to 43% of all temporary employed youth, or if only counting full-time students, 37%. These numbers only include youth working while studying, and not summer jobs taken in-between studies. The fraction of students on leave among temporary employees during summer is likely to be considerable. Thus, the impact of the supply of students willing to work is likely to have been a major contributor to the growth of temporary contracts.
27. The incidence of temporary employment has been found to be higher for those with lower cognitive ability in countries with stricter employment protection rules (Kahn, 2007).
28. Taking the features of the Swedish labour market as given, the limited available empirical evidence on the consequences of individual behaviour suggests that temporary contracts are beneficial for those taking them up (Larsson *et al.*, 2005).
29. A similar recommendation has been made for Spain (OECD, 2006d).
30. In a longer run, labour market training may have positive effects, and these effects may have improved in recent years (de Luna *et al.*, 2008).
31. There is also an extra assistance of at most SEK 855 for individuals from households with low income. In order to be eligible for social assistance the recipient must search for work; studying is not considered a valid exception. Parents are responsible for children attending compulsory and upper secondary schooling until the age of 21. From the age of 20, individuals attending upper secondary education are eligible for the same financial support as students attending higher education, that is, grants and loans combined to SEK 7 492 per month (4 weeks).
32. In principle, a similar problems arises if dropping out from higher education, but it matters little in practice because the study grant for tertiary education is higher, at SEK 2 572 per month plus loans.

Bibliography

Ahlin, Å. (2003), "Does School Competiton Matter? Effects of a Large-Scale School Choice Reform on Student Performance", Working Paper No. 2003:2, Department of Economics, Uppsala University.

Alstadsæter, A., A.-S. Kolm and B. Larsen (2008), "Money or Joy: The Choice of Educational Type", *European Journal of Political Economy*, Vol. 24.

Åslund, O., R. Erikson, O.N. Skans and A. Sjögren (2006), *Fritt inträde? – Ungdomars och invandrades väg till det första arbetet* (Free Entry? – Youth' and Immigrants' Way to the First Job), SNS Förlag, Stockholm.

Björklund, A., M. Clark, P.-A. Edin, P. Frederiksson and A. Krueger (2006), *The Market Comes to Education in Sweden: An Evaluation of Sweden's Surprising School Reforms*, Russell Sage Foundation Publications.

Boarini, R. and H. Strauss (2007), "The Private Internal Rates of Return to Tertiary Education: New Estimates for 21 OECD countries", OECD *Economics Department Working Paper* No. 591.

Böhlmark, A. and M. Lindahl (2007), "The Impact of School Choice on Pupil Achievement, Segregation and Costs: Swedish Evidence", *IZA Discussion Paper*, No. 2786.

Bovenberg, A. and B. Jacobs (2005), "Redistribution and Education Subsidies are Siamese Twins", *Journal of Public Economics*, Vol. 89, No. 11-12.

Calmfors, L., A. Forslund and M. Hemström (2004), "The Effects of Active Labour Market Policies in Sweden: What Is the Evidence?", in J. Agell, M.J. Keen and A.J. Weichenreider (eds.), *Labor Market Institutions and Public Regulation*, MIT Press, Cambridge, MA.

Carlsson, M. and D. Rooth (2007), "Evidence of Discrimination in the Swedish Labor Market Using Experimental Data", *Labour Economics*, Vol. 14, No. 4.

Confederation of Swedish Enterprise (2008), *Akademi eller verklighet?* (Academy or Reality?), Stockholm.

Danish Ministry of Education (1998), *Rapport om taxameterstyring* (Report on per-student funding), Copenhagen.

de Luna, X., A. Forslund and L. Liljeberg (2008), "Effekter av yrkesinriktad arbetsmarknadsutbildning för deltagare under perioden 2002-04" (Effects of Vocational Training for Participants During 2002-04), *Rapport* 2008:1, IFAU.

Forslund, A., P. Johansson and L. Lindqvist (2004), "Employment Subsidies – A Fast Lane From Unemployment to Work?", Working Paper No. 2004:18, IFAU.

Forslund, A. and O. Skans (2006a), "Swedish Youth Labour Market Policies Revisited", *Vierteljahrshefte zur Wirtschaftsforschung*, Vol. 75, No. 3.

Forslund, A. and O. Skans (2006b), "(Hur) hjälps ungdomar av arbetsmarknadspolitiska program för unga?" (How are Youth Helped by Labour Market Programmes for Youth?), *Rapport* 2006:5, IFAU.

Globalisation Council (2008), *Globaliseringen och den högre utbildningen*, Stockholm.

Holmlund, B. and D. Storrie (2002), "Temporary Work in Turbulent Times: Swedish Experiences", *Economic Journal*, Vol. 112, No. 480.

Holmlund, B., Liu Q. and O. Skans (2008), "Mind the Gap? Estimating the Effects of Postponing Higher Education", forthcoming in *Oxford Economic Papers*.

Kahn, L. (2007), "The Impact of Employment Protection Mandates on Demographic Temporary Employment Patterns: International Microeconomic Evidence", *Economic Journal*, Vol. 117, No. 521.

Larsson, L. (2003), "Evaluation of Swedish Youth Programs", *Journal of Human Resources*, Vol. 38, No. 4.

Lemaître, G. (2007), "The Integration of Immigrants into the Labour Market: the Case of Sweden", OECD Social, Employment and Migration Working Paper No. 48.

LO (2008), *Etableringen på arbetsmarknaden – hur klass, kön och etnicitet styr ungdomars villkor* (Establishing on the Labour Market – How Class, Gender and Ethnicity Determines Youth's Conditions), Landsorganisationen i Sverige, Stockholm.

Ludwig, V. and F. Pfeiffer (2005), "Abschreibungsraten allgemeiner und beruflicher Ausbildungsinhalte", (Depreciation Rates for General and Vocational Curricula), ZEW Discussion Paper No. 05-36.

Lundsgaard, J. (2003), "Competition and Efficiency in Publicly Funded Services"*OECD Economic Studies*, No. 35.

Ministry of Finance (2008), *Kraftfullare nedsättning av socialavgifter för unga* (Stronger reduction in social contribution for youth), *Promemoria*, 15 May, Stockholm.

National Agency for Education (2008), *Barn, elever och personal* (Children, Students and Personnel), Report No. 315, Stockholm.

National Agency for Higher Education (2006), *OECD Thematic Review of Tertiary Education – Country Background Report for Sweden*, Stockholm.

National Mediation Office (2007), *Avtalsrörelsen och lönebildningen 2007* (Collective Agreements and Wage Formation 2007), Stockholm.

NIER (2007), *Lönebildningsrapporten 2007* (Wage Formation Report 2007), National Institute for Economic Research, Stockholm.

OECD (2004a), *OECD Economic Surveys: Germany*, Paris.

OECD (2004b), "Employment Protection Regulation and Labour Market Performance", *OECD Employment Outlook*, Paris.

OECD (2005), *OECD Economic Surveys: United Kingdom*, Paris.

OECD (2006a), *Assessing Scientific, Reading and Mathematical Literacy: A Framework for PISA 2006*, Paris.

OECD (2006b), *OECD Economic Surveys: Germany*, Paris.

OECD (2006c), *Boosting Jobs and Incomes – Policy Lessons from Reassessing the OECD Jobs Strategy*, Paris.

OECD (2006d), *Jobs for Youth: Spain*, Paris.

OECD (2007a), *PISA 2006 – Science Competencies for Tomorrow's World*, Paris.

OECD (2007b), *OECD Economic Surveys: Sweden*, Paris.

OECD (2008a), "Off to a Good Start? Youth Labour Market Transitions in OECD Countries", *OECD Employment Outlook*, Paris.

OECD (2008b), *Education at a Glance*, Paris.

OECD (2008c), *Going for Growth*, Paris.

OECD (2008d), *Learning for Jobs: The OECD Policy Review of Vocational Education and Training in Sweden*, Paris.

OECD (2008e), *Tertiary Education for the Knowledge Society*, Paris.

OECD (2008f), *OECD Economic Surveys: Australia*, Paris.

OECD (2008g), *Jobs for Youth: The Netherlands*, Paris.

OECD (2008h), *OECD Economic Surveys: Norway*, Paris.

Oliveira Martins, J. *et al.* (2007), "The Policy Determinants of Investment in Tertiary Education", OECD *Economics Department Working Paper* No. 576.

Quintini, G., J. Martin and S. Martin (2007), "The Changing Nature of the School to Work Transition Process in OECD countries", IZA Discussion Paper No. 2582, Bonn.

Quintini, G. and S. Martin (2006), "Starting Well or Losing their Way?: The Position of Youth in the Labour Market in OECD Countries", OECD Social Employment and Migration Working Paper No. 39.

SACO (2008), *Kundskapens läge 2008* (The State of Knowledge 2008), Stockholm.

Sandström, M. and F. Bergström (2005), "School Vouchers in Practice: Competition Will Not Hurt You", Journal of Public Economics, Vol. 89, No. 2-3.

Skans, O. (2004), "Scarring Effects of the First Labour Market Experience", Working Paper No. 2004:14, IFAU.

Skedinger, P. (2006), "Minimum Wages and Employment in Swedish Hotels and Restaurants", *Labour Economics*, Vol. 13, No. 2.

Skedinger, P. (2007), "The Design and Effects of Collectively Agreed Minimum Wages. Evidence from Sweden", IFN Working Paper No. 700.

Skedinger, P. (2008), *Effekter av Anställningsskydd* (Effects of Employment Protection), SNS Förlag, Stockholm.

SOU (2006), *Studieavgifter i högskolan* (Tuition Fees in Higher Education), Swedish Government Official Reports, No. 2006:7.

SOU (2008a), *Legitimation och skärpta behörighetsregler* (Registration and Stricter Qualifying Rules), Swedish Government Official Reports, No. 2008:52.

SOU (2008b), *Framtidsvägen – en reformerad gymnasieskola* (The Future Path – A Reformed Secondary School), Swedish Government Official Reports, No. 2008:27.

SOU (2008c), *Välja fritt och välja rätt* (Choosing Freely and Making the Right Choices), Swedish Government Official Reports, No. 2008:69.

Statistics Sweden (2006), "Inträdet på arbetsmarknaden" (Entry into the Labour Market), UF 86 SM 0601, Stockholm.

Statistics Sweden (2007), "Sambandet mellan utbildning och yrke – En studie om högskoleutbildningar" (The Link between Education and Profession), *Befolkning and Välfärd*, No. 1, Stockholm.

Strath, A. (2004), *Teacher Policy Reforms in Sweden: The Case of Individualised Pay*, Paper submitted by the Swedish Ministry of Education and Science to the International Institute for Educational Planning under UNESCO.

Welfare Commission (2006), *Fremtidens velfærd – vores valg* (The Future Welfare – Our Choice), Final report of the Danish Welfare Commission, Copenhagen.

ISBN 978-92-64-05423-3
OECD Economic Surveys: Sweden
© OECD 2008

Chapter 5

Privatisation: The next phase

For many years, public ownership has been relatively widespread in Sweden – even in sectors where, typically, private companies operate on market conditions. Recently, privatisation has become a policy priority. Empirical evidence suggests that privatisation leads to improved firm performance and higher productivity growth. However, the benefits are contingent on enhancing the degree of competition – privatisation in itself is not enough. This chapter reviews these links and considers what steps to take next. Recent financial market turmoil may require some deals to be postponed, but that aside, privatisation should continue. After completing the current first wave of sales, the way to proceed would be a combination of further privatisation and market liberalisation together with consideration of other methods for providing government support where a market failure or social objective remains.

The Swedish State owns 52 companies (39 wholly and 13 partly), employing some 180 000 staff. The portfolio of state-owned enterprises (SOEs) is estimated to be worth around one-quarter of the market capitalisation of the Stockholm stock exchange. Also, state ownership is spread broadly across the economy. Accordingly, Sweden has a higher-than-average proportion of sectors where the State has an equity stake in at least one firm (Figure 5.1). Local governments also have extensive ownership of enterprises.[1] Previous OECD *Economic Surveys*, successive issues of *Going for Growth* and the 2007 *OECD Review of Regulatory Reform – Sweden* have all called for reduced public sector involvement in competitive markets.

Figure 5.1. **The Swedish State owns enterprises in a wide range of sectors**[1]

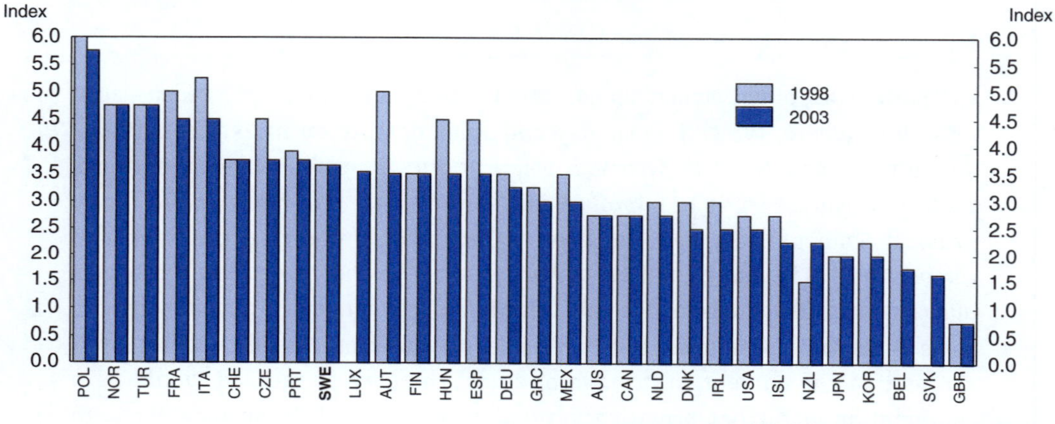

StatLink http://dx.doi.org/10.1787/485730035064

1. The indicator measures the pervasiveness of State ownership across business sectors as the proportion of sectors in which the State has an equity stake in at least one firm. A higher index value implies State ownership in more sectors.

Source: OECD, *Product Market Regulation database.*

The government announced in December 2006 that it would undertake the sale of six wholly or partly owned SOEs as part of a larger divestment programme. The programme is estimated to deliver proceeds of around SEK 50 billion (€ 5.3 billion) per year between 2007 and 2011, although this estimate is uncertain and depends on market conditions. Priorities for privatisation in the first round were: shareholdings in the financial sector (Nordea, the region's largest bank; OMX, owner of several Nordic and Baltic stock exchanges; and SBAB, a mortgage lender); TeliaSonera, a major telecommunications operator in the Nordic region; Vasakronan, a commercial real estate company; and V&S Group (the producer of Absolut Vodka). In 2007, approval was granted to divest all or part of Arbetslivsresurs, a company providing employee rehabilitation services. The government also has the authority to sell Imego, a research firm focusing on microelectronics (Swedish Government, 2008a).

In May 2007, the State sold 8% of the shares in TeliaSonera bringing its ownership down from 45.3% to 37.3% of the total shares in the company. In February 2008, it sold its

6.6% interest in OMX to Borse Dubai, who then sold the shares to NASDAQ, thereby creating the NASDAQ OMX Group. In March 2008, the State's 100% interest in V&S Group was sold to Pernod Ricard S.A. In April 2008, plans were announced for a merger between Posten and Post Danmark. The Swedish state will hold 49.8% of the voting rights in the new venture with the remaining shares held by the Danish state, a private company and the employees of both Posten and Post Danmark.[2] In July 2008, the government sold Vasakronan to AP Fastigheter.[3] In 2008, Sweden has thereby become one of the main sources of privatisation activity in Europe (Figure 5.2) in a context, however, where turmoil in international financial markets has damped the momentum of such operations (Megginson, 2008).

Figure 5.2. **Privatisation proceeds in OECD Europe**[1]

$USD billion

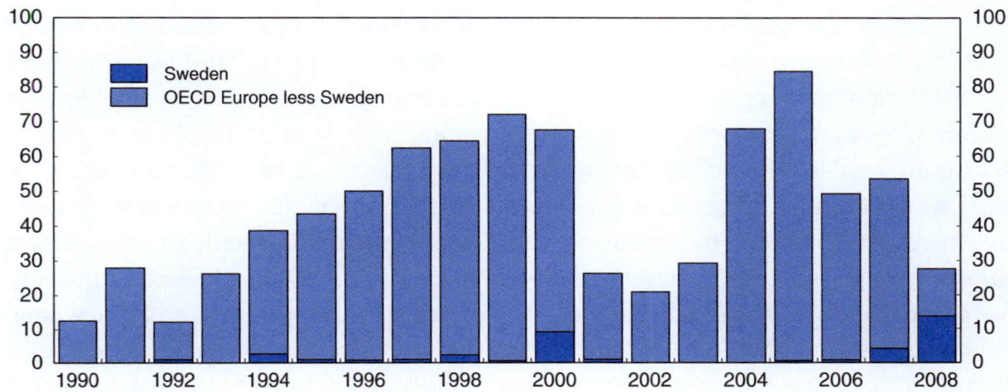

StatLink http://dx.doi.org/10.1787/485740804128

1. Includes data up to 30 June 2008.

Source: Privatisation Barometer online database.

Why privatise?

The basic case for privatisation is to promote productivity and innovation. Government ownership makes it difficult to define the goals of the firm since governments often have objectives other than wealth maximisation. SOE managers do not face the same incentives to maximise profits or minimise costs since they do not reap the benefits of such actions. Even when the SOE is given a clear profit-maximising objective, it is unlikely to face the same market discipline as a private firm, since the government will typically be reluctant to let the SOE fail. A strong governance framework for SOEs may not be sufficient in the absence of a credible shut-down threat (Megginson, 2005). Publicly-owned enterprises may face problems with rent-seeking and political influence. Privatisation may lead to increased entrepreneurial activity and product or service innovation. To the extent that government ownership limits firms managers' ability to implement strategic change, privatisation may lead to more planning and development of market and industry analysis; greater discretion to refine firm goals and structures; and greater incentives to undertake new activities, develop new products or adopt new technologies to enhance shareholder value (Antoncic and Hisrich, 2003; Zahra *et al.*, 2000).

The risk of regulatory failure in network industries is reduced when direct control is replaced by arms' length regulation. However, particularly in network industries, productivity gains following privatisation rely on the creation of sufficient market pressures in the potentially competitive segments of the industry, as well as regulation of access to the non-competitive segments. In general, privatisation has the greatest positive impact when the role for government in minimising a market failure is smallest (Megginson and Netter, 2001; Nicoletti and Scarpetta, 2003).

There is some debate about whether privatisation is necessary to achieve maximum efficiency gains, or whether introducing competition and deregulation are sufficient (Box 5.1). Some studies have identified a positive impact on firm performance from improved incentive arrangements and compensation for both managers and employees, while others find that such incentives are ineffective because the government is unable to implement them (Megginson and Netter, 2001). Government involvement may deter potential competitors from entering, as they may judge that regulations favour publicly-owned incumbents. Privatisation, by contrast, shows commitment to a level playing field.

In practice, the main motivations underpinning privatisation in OECD countries have been: improving the efficiency of publicly-owned enterprises and general market liberalisation; alleviating the restriction on expansion that may stem from government ownership (budget processes may constrain capital injections and SOEs may therefore resort more to debt financing); technological changes (*e.g.* in telecommunications and electricity generation) that reduce or eliminate existing monopoly power; development of domestic capital markets (by increasing share ownership and deepening domestic equity markets through public offerings); a change in political or ideological views of the role of government; and fiscal pressures and the use of privatisation proceeds to reduce debt or fund budget deficits (OECD, 2003). The Swedish privatisation programme has been driven primarily by a desire to improve efficiency and remove restrictions on expansion (Swedish Government, 2007) and to reduce the potential conflict between the government's roles as owner and regulator in some markets. The impact of technological change on the ability to maintain a monopoly is likely to be an increasing issue going forward.

Fiscal objectives should not be a motivation for privatisation in Sweden. Using privatisation proceeds to reduce net debt leaves the government's fiscal position broadly unchanged, apart from the possibility of higher tax revenues or lower subsidy costs due to improvement in corporate efficiency and performance of the former SOE. Using privatisation proceeds to finance increased spending is likely to worsen the fiscal position. Furthermore, the fact that many of the Swedish SOEs earn returns above the government's cost of borrowing is not an argument for retaining them, since this excess return is compensation for higher risk associated with the returns on equity. Despite the current strong fiscal position (Chapter 2), Swedish gross government debt is still more than 40% of GDP and asset sale proceeds should be used to reduce this debt. If there was a desire to hold equity as a financial investment strategy, it would be important to clearly link this to the fiscal policy framework. The focus of analysis on SOEs should then be whether the current portfolio of equities represents an appropriate balance of risk and return and whether the governance framework is appropriate if the investment is purely financially motivated.

How to proceed with the privatisation programme

The government has made strenuous efforts over a number of years to provide a sound governance structure for SOE activities based on the corporate regulation framework applying to private sector companies (Box 5.2). This framework increases the transparency

Box 5.1. **Evidence on the benefits of privatisation**

Many studies have attempted to test whether the theoretical predictions about the benefits of privatisation are realised in practice. There is overwhelming (although not unanimous) support for the view that privatisation significantly increases profitability, real output and efficiency, and reduces leverage in privatised companies (implying that their initial capital structure was sub-optimal). However, it is more difficult to discern from empirical studies whether all the benefits arise from privatisation or whether they are mainly due to the market liberalisation and deregulation that often accompanies it.

The increase in efficiency is particularly notable when the firm operates in a competitive environment. Profitability increases more and productivity less in regulated or less competitive sectors. Some studies report that the benefits of privatisation flowed to the shareholders in the form of increased profits but that consumers did not share in these gains due to insufficient competition. Sectors where privatised companies were required to make up significant investments in infrastructure saw price rises rather than falls following privatisation (OECD, 2003).

Empirical evidence supports two distinct effects of privatisation – an anticipation effect, where the firm's performance improves ahead of privatisation (possibly due to reforms aimed at making the firm more attractive for sale) and a follow-through effect, whereby firm performance continues to improve after the sale. The gains from privatisation are often attributed to better incentives and, to a lesser extent, lower employment costs. There is evidence that privatisation can affect competitors' pricing and market value. Privatisation is also associated with a reduction in leverage of the privatised firm (Megginson and Netter, 2001), consistent with the idea that government ownership might restrict access to equity capital and force greater reliance on borrowing.

Many studies report that privatisation is associated with reduced employment in the privatised firm, possibly because firms slated for privatisation are overstaffed. While employment may fall, some studies report increased salaries and better terms for the remaining employees, accompanied by decreased job security and longer working hours (OECD, 2003; Megginson and Netter, 2001). However, these studies likely do not capture the full dynamic effects of increased competition on growth and employment in the longer term.

A range of studies have taken a more macroeconomic approach looking at the link between competition and economy-wide performance. Lower barriers to trade and competition in less regulated countries seems to have increased the level and rate of growth of productivity by stimulating business investment and promoting innovation and technological catch-up. Importantly, countries with less restrictive regulatory environments tend to invest more in ICT capital, a significant contributor to productivity growth in recent decades (Nicoletti and Scarpetta, 2005; Conway *et al.*, 2006). Privatisation has been found to be positively related to productivity growth but, as with firm and industry-level studies, the gains depend on adequate promotion of competition in the markets in which the newly-privatised firms operate (Nicoletti and Scarpetta, 2003). Both deregulation and privatisation are found to lead to greater aggregate investment (Alesina *et al.*, 2005).*

* From a theoretical perspective, it is unclear whether privatisation should lead to higher or lower investment. On the one hand, agency problems and political mandates affecting public-sector managers might suggest that publicly-owned companies may over-accumulate capital. Privatisation might thus result in lower investment. On the other hand, increased competition might reduce mark-ups and the penalty associated with expansion in a non-competitive market. This suggests that privatisation should increase investment.

Box 5.2. **Corporate governance of state-owned enterprises in Sweden**

The Swedish government is an active manager of SOEs, with the overarching objective being the creation of value and, in some cases, to contribute to special societal interests. The Minister for Enterprise and Energy has been delegated responsibility under the Constitution for matters relating to the operation of SOEs, except where authorisation for sale has been approved by Parliament, in which case the Minister for Local Government and Financial Markets is responsible for the sales process. The Ministry of Enterprise, Energy and Communications is mainly responsible for administering the government's ownership policy, although other ministries are responsible in relation to companies particularly relevant to their portfolio interests (for example, issues related to Apoteket's pharmacies are handled by the Ministry of Health and Social Affairs).

The government's ownership policy for SOEs requires that they comply with the Swedish Code for Corporate Governance, which applies to private companies, unless there are sound reasons for departure in which case these must be reported (Swedish Government, 2006). SOEs are subject to the same corporate law as private companies and in some circumstances to specific legislation relating to the activities of the individual enterprise (*e.g.* the Postal Services Act in relation to Posten). Members of the Riksdag have the right to attend annual general meetings of companies where the state owns more than 50% of the shares and which have more than 50 employees. Large SOEs are expected to hold a public event related to the annual general meeting to allow the general public to ask questions of the board. Board nominations are undertaken by the Ministry of Enterprise, Energy and Communications based on competence, with a target of at least 40% participation by each gender. Boards are expected to have between six and eight members. Boards are required to establish strategies for handling environmental considerations, social issues, human rights, gender equality, diversity and ethics. In contrast to the Code for Corporate Governance applying to private companies, an SOE's chief executive officer is generally not a member of the board of the SOEs. Remuneration of staff can include performance incentives (except for CEOs) which should not exceed four months' salary. Capital contributions to SOEs are governed by EU rules on state aid and additional legislation has been adopted to ensure transparent reporting of such grants. Guidelines for external reporting complement general rules for company reporting applying to private companies, requiring SOEs to report on environmental issues, financial and operational risks, equal opportunity policies, dividend policy and a description of the work of the board.

Financial targets vary from company to company according to their purpose. In general, the higher the risk in the company, the higher the minimum profitability target; the higher the operating risk, the higher the proportion of equity required; and the lower the growth of the company, the higher the dividend share. Companies are classified as those operating under market conditions and those operating with special societal interests. Companies operating under market conditions should be subject to the same financial constraints as other participants in the market. The state sets targets to ensure that capital structure and return on capital objectives do not unduly affect competition. Companies operating with special societal interests can face goal conflict between optimising financial targets and promoting their social objectives. Financial targets are therefore set to take social interests into account to facilitate target achievement and ensure that the company is operating as efficiently as possible within its constraints. Part of the dividends from SOEs has been earmarked for used as capital contributions to other SOEs (Swedish Government, 2008b).

and accountability of SOEs, so reduces the likelihood of significant inefficiency relative to competing private firms. The argument for privatisation therefore relies more on those factors which affect SOEs performance despite the strong governance framework – the fact that the government is unlikely to let them fail and that their flexibility is constrained by objectives and rules that are not applied to private firms.

One key element of the corporate governance framework for SOEs is the distinct treatment of companies deemed to be operating under market conditions *versus* those with specific social objectives. However, even some of the companies defined as operating under market conditions are not completely open to competition or receive some grant funding (Table 5.1). The first phase of the government's privatisation programme involved selling those large companies that clearly operate in competitive markets. Anticipating the completion of the sales of the companies which the Riksdag has already approved, the next phase should proceed in two steps.

First, the remaining firms that operate in competitive markets, where minimal changes in regulation or operation would be required to move the company into private hands, should be considered for privatisation.[4] Second, consideration should be given to the regulatory arrangements and scope for increased competition in relation to companies that are not currently operating in a competitive market. Improving competition in these markets could boost productivity and help prepare for future privatisation if that is deemed appropriate.

In the case of companies whose main aim is to promote a particular social objective, alternative ways to deliver these objectives could be considered, with the aim of increasing competition and enhancing consumer welfare. These include competitive tendering of grant funding; partial privatisation, possibly through divesture or contracting out of parts of the SOE where alternative providers already exist; and liberalisation of monopoly restrictions.

The following sections selectively review some of the industries in which government currently has substantial presence.

Transport

Several of the companies owned by the Swedish State in the transport sector are in rail. The structure of railway markets in OECD countries varies widely because of the different roles played by rail in different countries (domestic, international, passenger, freight, etc.) and because of the degree of competition from other modes of transport (cars, trucks, buses, air). In general, OECD country experience points to the need for unbundling vertically-integrated railway companies and the importance of non-discriminatory access to rolling stock for the development of competition. Contracting out railway passenger services could increase competition but this must be done in a way that does not discriminate against new entrants (Høj *et al.*, 2007).

The introduction of competition in the rail sector in Sweden has had positive effects in terms of innovation, streamlining of activities and lower costs. The process started with vertical separation, with the railway infrastructure being retained by the State through the National Rail Administration and operations vested with SJ for passenger traffic and Green Cargo for freight. In passenger traffic, the government directly contracts for the provision of services on routes that are not considered profitable. However, for other routes SJ holds a monopoly position. In fact, SJ itself decides which routes are profitable, and therefore

Table 5.1. **Sweden central government-owned enterprises**

		Listed/Market conditions/ Special societal interests	Govt share %	Competition/ Grant financing	Net turnover + other income, SEK million, 2007
Transport					
SAS AB	Airline	Listed	21.4		52 251
Posten AB	National postal service	Market conditions	100	Partial grant financing	30 132
SJ AB	Rail	Market conditions	100	Partial competition	8 267
Green Cargo AB	Rail operator specialising in environmental friendly modes	Market conditions	100		6 157
Botniabanan	Commissioned by the Swedish government to build the Bothnia Line, a railway running from Nyland, north of Kramfors, via Örnsköldsvik, to Umeå	Special societal interests	91		2 258
AB Svensk Bilprovning[1]	Motor vehicle inspection	Special societal interests	52	Statutory monopoly	1 533
SVEDAB	Owns 50% of The Øresundsbro Konsortiet which operates the fixed link between Malmö and Copenhagen and the Swedish land based approaches to the Øresund bridge	Special societal interests	100		858
SwedCarrier AB	Rail	Market conditions	100	Partial competition	696
Rymdbolaget (Swedish Space Corporation)	Designs, launches, tests and operates space and aerospace systems	Market conditions	100		561
A-Banan projekt AB	Stockholm-Arlanda rail link	Special societal interests	100		62
SweRoad AB	Provides consultancy services within road and transport sector to clients outside Sweden	Market conditions	100		54
Zenit Shipping AB	Liquidating formerly nationalised ships	Being wound up	100		
Finance					
Nordea Bank AB	*Bank*	*Listed*	*19.9*		*71 836*
SBAB	*Mortgage originator*	*Market conditions*	*100*		*1 177*
Svensk Exportkredit AB	Export and infrastructure finance	Market conditions	100		833
Venantius AB	Manages loans to tenant-owner associations and property companies	Market conditions	100		180
Svenska Skeppshypoteks Kassan (Swedish Ships Mortgage Bank)	Provides loans for shipping companies to purchase ships	Market conditions	100		331
Swedfund International AB	Offers risk capital in the form of share capital, loans, guarantees and part-financing of leasing agreements for investment in Africa, Asia, Latin America and Eastern Europe (non-EU members)	Special societal interests	100		212
Bostadsgaranti AB	Provides warranties and guarantees for building construction	Special societal interests	50		33
Forvaltingsaktiebolaget Stattum	Holding company	Market conditions	100		0
Property					
Akademiska Hus AB	Higher education facilities	Market conditions	100	Partial competition	4 786
Specialfastigheter Sverige AB	Special purpose buildings	Market conditions	100	Partial competition	1 209
Vasallen AB	Converts former defence force properties into commercial developments	Market conditions	100		220
Kasernen Fastighets AB	Accommodation for armed forces personnel	Market conditions	100		20
A/O Dom Shvetsii	Owns property in St Petersburg currently rented by the Swedish Consulate General and the Swedish Trade Council	Market conditions	36		18
Statens Bostadsomvandling AB	Regenerating vacant municipal housing stock	Special societal interests	100		13
Research and development					
ALMI Företagspartner	Financing and business development	Special societal interests	100	Partial grant financing	796
SP Sveriges Tekniska Forskningsinstitut AB	Research and consulting in technical evaluation and metrology	Special societal interests	100	Partial grant financing	769
IRECO Holding AB	Support for industrial research institutes	Special societal interests	100	Partial grant financing	345
Imego AB	*Nano and micro technology*	*Market conditions*	*100*	*Partial grant financing*	*56*

Table 5.1. **Sweden central government-owned enterprises** *(cont.)*

		Listed/Market conditions/ Special societal interests	Govt share %	Competition/ Grant financing	Net turnover + other income, SEK million, 2007
Innovationsbron AB	Helps identify research and development related ideas with commercial potential and contribute to commercialization	Special societal interests	83.7		50
Business services					
Lernia AB	Temporary employment, training, rehabilitation services	Market conditions	100		2 280
Arbetslivsresurs AR AB	*Employee rehabilitation*	*Market conditions*	*100*		*197*
Swedesurvey AB	National land management systems	Market conditions	100		109
Svenska Miljöstyrningsrådet AB[2]	Encouraging sustainable development by supporting the environmental initiatives of business and the public sector	Special societal interests	85	Sole operator, partial grant financing	12
Norrland Center AB	Regional policy focus on Norrland region	Special societal interests	33.3		5
Retail					
Apoteket AB	Pharmaceuticals	Special societal interests	100	Statutory monopoly	39 505
AB Svenska Spel	Gaming	Special societal interests	100	Partial monopoly	21 716
Systembolaget AB	Alcohol	Special societal interests	100	Statutory monopoly	20 581
Communications					
TeliaSonera AB	*Fixed and mobile telephony, internet and data communications*	*Listed*	*37.3*		*96 965*
Teracom AB	Radio and television	Market conditions	100	Partial monopoly	3 312
SOS Alarm Sverige AB	Emergency services call centre	Special societal interests	50	Partial competition	731
Tourism					
VisitSweden AB	Tourism promotion activities	Special societal interests	50	Partial grant financing	155
Göta kanalbolag AB	Owner and operator of the Göta Canal	Special societal interests	100	Partial grant financing	54
Leisure					
Kungliga Operan AB	Owner of the Royal Opera	Special societal interests	100	Partial grant financing	448
Kungliga Dramatiska Teatern AB	Owner of the Royal Dramatic Theatre	Special societal interests	100	Partial grant financing	244
Other					
Vattenfall AB – Energy	Electricity and heat	Market conditions	100		145 421
LKAB – Mining and manufacturing	Iron ore	Market conditions	100		16 584
Samhall AB	Employs people with disabilities in a range of roles	Special societal interests	100	Partial grant financing	7 432
Sveaskog AB – Forestry	Forestry and timber manufacturing	Market conditions	100		7 373
Voksenåsen AS	Swedish/Norwegian cultural exchange	Special societal interests	100	Sole operator, partial grant financing	55
SIS Miljömärkning	Promotion of environmental labelling of products	Special societal interests	10	Partial grant financing	34

Note: Italics means already approved for sale.

1. Co-owned by the Swedish government, organisations of the Swedish motor industry, motor associations and motor insurance companies.
2. Owned jointly by the Swedish government, the Confederation of Swedish Enterprises and the Swedish Association of Local Authorities and Regions.

Source: Swedish government (2008a) and various company websites.

which ones it should have a monopoly over, and is not under any obligations regarding service standards. SJ's monopoly position should be phased out (OECD, 2005a). At the very least, or in the meantime, an independent authority should decide on the routes that SJ should have a monopoly over.

The rail freight market has been exposed to more competition than the passenger market, but Green Cargo still retains a dominant position in the market. If market dominance is deemed too strong to consider privatisation, separating TGOJ Trafik, a subsidiary of Green Cargo, from its parent company would foster additional competition (OECD, 2005a).

Financial services

The State owns a number of finance companies that operate in specific segments of the market. Authority has been provided to sell Nordea and SBAB, the mortgage originator. Nordea, in its current form, emerged from Nordbanken, which was nationalised during the financial crisis of the early 1990s. As the current financial crisis has evolved, the Swedish handling of the previous crisis has gained renown. This included separating the nationalised financial institutions' "good" assets from their "bad" assets and establishing adequately capitalised asset management companies to rejuvenate or liquidate the bad assets (Ergungor, 2007). This experience suggests that, as the current financial crisis passes, privatisation will in due course re-emerge as an important policy issue in many countries.

The Swedish Ships Mortgage Bank, which competes directly with domestic banks and international financiers, is a subsequent candidate for corporatisation and privatisation. Consideration could be given to increasing the flexibility the company has in determining loan conditions in order to better tailor products to the market,[5] although this may increase the risk ultimately borne by the State if the company remains in government hands.

Properties and building maintenance

The Swedish State owns a number of companies that effectively perform the same function – to own and lease buildings.[6] The rationale for government ownership appears to be that these buildings are special-purpose buildings and are used to provide public services: university buildings, prisons, police facilities, state special schools, etc. To the extent that buildings are fit for purpose, the tenants have a clear interest in renting the premises for the long term. Hence the risk that properties will be vacant is low. On the other hand, should a tenant move out it might be difficult to find another one. Specialfastigheter, an SOE which owns and manages special purpose buildings, itself acknowledges the increase in competition in the market for specialist buildings and intends to respond by strengthening its expertise in project management for refurbishment, extension and new building. The trend among tenants to concentrate their activities on larger units also means that the risk of vacancies in properties is increasing, leading to a greater focus on the capacity to improve and dispose of properties (Specialfastigheter, 2007).

An alternative model is to have private sector interests take ownership of the buildings and/or the companies that own them. This would have little impact on the tenant, as they would continue to rent the property from an external provider. The risk with selling the properties is that the private owner may charge rents higher than the market price since they know that it would be very difficult or costly for the (public sector) tenant to find replacement accommodation. This suggests the need for strong negotiation and contract management skills on the part of the renters.

Research and development and venture capital

Research and development is important for innovation and economic growth and government support is justified on the grounds that there is likely to be under-investment due to positive spill-overs, non-appropriability and uncertainty. Even if the returns to R&D can be captured through intellectual property protection, subsidies or tax incentives, it may be difficult or costly for firms to access external capital due to asymmetric information. This can be addressed through government funding for start-ups or the development of venture capital markets (Hall, 2002).

In addition to providing substantial R&D funding directly through universities, the Swedish government also owns a number of enterprises that either offer capital and assistance to other R&D companies or directly conduct research. The government already has the authority to sell Imego and consideration could be given to whether the research efforts of SP Sveriges Tekniska Forskningsinstitut could be privately provided.

In the area of venture capital, previous OECD reports have suggested consolidating and simplifying public equity funding and targeting it more towards pump-priming of private funding in start-ups (Baygan, 2003). Other government initiatives to promote access to finance on the part of small businesses, such as deferral of capital gains tax on closely-held companies and the abolition of the wealth tax should, over time, reduce the need for SOE involvement in financing small businesses.

Retail

Pharmaceuticals retailing

The Swedish pharmacy monopoly, Apoteket, is unique among OECD countries and was designed to safeguard the future supply of pharmaceuticals, ensure safe and efficient distribution and keep prices down.[7] Pharmaceutical prices paid by the government to manufacturers are on average among the highest in Europe, whereas the average consumer price faced by the public is lower than the European average. Retail and wholesale margins are low partly because distribution costs in Sweden are relatively low, despite lack of competition at the retail level.

Deregulation in the market for prescription drugs alone would not necessarily result in cost savings to retail purchasers, since reimbursement prices paid by the government are set in law. Any prescription-drug price discounts achieved from manufacturers or wholesalers through competition would be captured by retailers. Deregulation could be combined with making the reimbursement price a maximum rather than a fixed price. Also, there are a relatively small number of pharmacies in proportion to the population and hours of operation are limited, so consumer welfare would be increased by widening opening hours and introducing competitive tendering for subsidies to sales agents in remote or regional areas. Further consumer savings and improved access in remote areas would be achieved by allowing retail competition for non-prescription drugs, for which safety concerns are minimal (Moise and Docteur, 2007; OECD, 2005b). The Swedish Competition Authority has recommended ending Apoteket's monopoly combined with other measures such as prohibiting the ownership of pharmacies by manufacturers of medicines and making Apoteket's computerised system for prescription transfers available to all pharmacies (Swedish Competition Authority, 2007).

A government report in early 2008 recommended a number of the changes outlined above, including limiting Apoteket's market share by selling some pharmacies, separating the database and information infrastructure from Apoteket and retaining these in state control but with a competitively-neutral access regime, and allowing for reductions in prices of pharmaceuticals that do not have patent cover and face generic competition (SOU, 2008). A bill has been introduced to the Riksdag covering the separation of information systems and Apoteket was restructured in early 2008 pending a future process of divesting pharmacies. The Swedish government has also introduced measures in the 2009 Budget to increase choice in health care provision. One of the main goals of this measure is to promote private entrepreneurship within the health-care sector with the aim of raising productivity within the sector in the long run.

Alcohol retailing

In alcohol retailing, technological change and pressures from EU integration are making the existing monopoly arrangement harder to maintain. The SOE Systembolaget has the legal monopoly to sell alcohol directly to consumers, the aim of the monopoly being to reduce harm caused by alcohol consumption and to limit total consumption of alcohol. Access to alcohol is limited by regulating the establishment of outlets and opening hours, and through selling rules. However, Systembolaget's share of total consumption, measured in pure alcohol, was only 48% in 2005. The other main sources of supply were imports by travellers (22%), smuggling and home-produced alcohol (13%), and restaurant sales (10%) (OECD, 2006). There are anecdotal reports of increasing efforts to bypass the state monopoly.[8]

Consumer welfare would be improved by liberalising opening hours and licensing of other selected vendors, in anticipation of full privatisation. Health policy objectives might be better dealt with through education on the harmful effects of excessive alcohol consumption, particularly for youth since their tastes are still being formed, or increasing excise taxes on alcohol (Sassi and Hurst, 2008).

Gambling

Gambling is another case where technological change and globalisation may drive alternatives to the current ownership arrangement. The market regulation of gambling and lotteries does not prescribe a strict monopoly, but gives exclusive rights to several groups, including the State and the horse-racing community. The largest market actor is Svenska Spel, an SOE controlling 56% of commercial gambling in Sweden. The gambling market is growing rapidly, not least through internet-based betting, roulette and poker offered by foreign suppliers. Svenska Spel has responded to increased competition from foreign gambling enterprises, and in 2005 the government authorised it to organise poker games on the Internet. Moreover, the monopoly may not be compatible with EU law, which precludes legislation preventing competition from foreign actors (OECD, 2006).

Conclusions

Focusing state ownership on segments of the economy where it has a clear rationale will likely lead to better provision of public services and promote efficiency. The ongoing sale of large companies is an important step and should continue – although financial market turmoil may require some transactions to be postponed so as to secure the right price. Looking ahead, further privatisations should be considered alongside other measures to increase competition (Box 5.3).

Box 5.3. **Summary of privatisation recommendations**

- Firms that already operate in competitive markets with no monopoly power or grant funding should be privatised. There are examples in the transport, property, finance and forestry sectors.
- Consideration should be given to reducing monopoly power, such as in the rail and retail sectors, along with appropriate regulatory changes to safeguard consumer welfare. Once markets are opened to competition, partial or complete privatisation of today's state-owned companies should be considered.
- With regard to firms that are entrusted with particular societal interests, consideration should be given to whether there are forms of policy intervention other than public ownership that might achieve the same goals. For example, the need for government ownership of venture capital funds and R&D companies would seem to be limited.

Notes

1. Data from Statistics Sweden suggest that the overall number of publicly-owned companies exceeds 2 100, of which some 500 are owned by the central government, some 1 500 by municipalities and about 100 by county councils. In relation to the central government, the discrepancy between these figures and the 52 companies mentioned in the text mainly relates to the fact that the central government reports company groupings rather than individual legal entities. About half of the municipal public companies operate in the real estate, renting and business activities sector, likely reflecting the structure of the rental housing market in Sweden (reviewed in the 2007 *Survey*). 60% of county-council-owned companies operate in the transport, storage and communications sector (Statistics Sweden, 2008).
2. The shareholders' agreement is to provide for mechanisms to broaden the shareholder base by seeking a future listing on OMX stock exchange (Swedish Government, 2008b).
3. As part of the deal, Sweden's National Property Board and the SOE Specialfastigheter AB acquired some properties deemed to be of national interest from Vasakronan.
4. The companies which are classified as operating under market conditions and have no grant funding, and therefore might be considered as the next candidates for privatisation, include Green Cargo, the Swedish Space Corporation, SweRoad, Svenska Exportkredit, Venantius, Swedish Ships Mortgage Bank, Kasernen Fastighets, A/O Dom Shvetsii, Lernia, SwedSurvey and Sveaskog (Table 5.1). The government has stated that it does not intend to sell LKAB (mining) and Vattenfall (electricity generation) even though they operate in competitive markets. In the case of LKAB, this is due to the need to move a substantial part of the mining town of Kiruna in order to expand an iron ore mine. Vattenfall will not be privatised because of concerns of market dominance in the electricity industry.
5. The Bank's operations are governed by the Swedish Ships' Mortgage Bank Act. The Act specifies that the Bank can only finance Swedish shipping companies or foreign shipping companies with a significant Swedish interest; the loan term must be no more than 15 years and the loan must be paid off in full when the ship reaches the age of 20 years (unless there are special circumstances); and there are limits on the proportion of the ship's value that can be lent.
6. In May 2008, Vasallen announced that its task of developing and divesting facilities and buildings belonging to Försvarsmakten (the defence force) is reaching its end within the next two years. Hence, the Vasallen board is now is now investigating the possibility of winding up the business.
7. A core element of Swedish pharmaceuticals policy is ensuring that prices for drugs are the same in all parts of the country. Apoteket also sells non-prescription drugs over the Internet and by telephone. Prices for subsidised pharmaceutical products are set by the Pharmaceutical Benefits Board. Most but not all prescription drugs are subsidised. Prices for other drugs are decided by Apoteket.
8. For example, "Entrepreneurs crack Swedish 'System' in effort to allow free flow of alcohol", *Financial Times*, 4 August 2008.

Bibliography

Alesina, A., S. Ardagna, G. Nicoletti, and F. Schiantarelli (2005), "Regulation and Investment", *Journal of the European Economic Association*, Vol. 3, No. 4.

Antoncic, B. and R. Hisrich (2003), "Privatisation, Corporate Entrepreneurship and Performance: Testing a Normative Model", *Journal of Developmental Entrepreneurship*, December.

Baygan, G. (2003), "Venture Capital Policies in Sweden", OECD Science, Technology and Industry Working Paper, No. 2003/11.

Conway, P., D. de Rosa, G. Nicoletti, and F. Steiner (2006), "Regulation, Competition and Productivity Convergence", OECD *Economics Department Working Paper*, No. 509.

Ergungor, O.E. (2007), "On the Resolution of Financial Crises: The Swedish Experience", Federal Reserve Bank of Cleveland Policy Discussion Paper No. 21, June.

Hall, B. (2002), "The Financing of Research and Development", *NBER Working Paper*, No. 8773.

Høj, J., M. Jimenez, M. Maher, G. Nicoletti, and M. Wise (2007), "Product Market Competition in the OECD Countries: Taking Stock and Moving Forward", OECD *Economics DepartmentWorking Paper*, No. 575.

Megginson, W. and J. Netter (2001), "From State to Market: A Survey of Empirical Studies on Privatisation", *Journal of Economic Literature*, Vol. 39, No. 2.

Megginson, W. (2005), *The Financial Economics of Privatization*, Oxford University Press, Oxford.

Megginson, W. ed. (2008), "The PB Interim Report June 2008", The Privatisation Barometer.

Moise, P. and E. Docteur (2007), "Pharmaceutical Pricing and Reimbursement Policies in Sweden", OECD Health Working Paper, No. 28.

Nicoletti, G., and S. Scarpetta (2003), "Regulation, Productivity and Growth: OECD Evidence", *Economic Policy*, April.

Nicoletti, G., and S. Scarpetta (2005), "Regulation and Economic Performance: Product Market Reforms and Productivity in the OECD", OECD *Economics Department Working Paper*, No. 240.

OECD (2003), *Privatising State-Owned Enterprises: An Overview of Policies and Practices in OECD Countries*, Paris.

OECD (2005a), "Structural Reform in the Rail Industry", Policy Roundtables, Paris.

OECD (2005b), *OECD Economic Surveys: Sweden*, Paris.

OECD (2006), *Sweden – The Role of Competition Policy in Regulatory Reform*, Paris.

OECD (2007), *Sweden: Achieving Results for Sustained Growth*, OECD Reviews of Regulatory Reform, Paris.

Sassi, F. and J. Hurst (2008), "The Prevention of Lifestyle-Related Chronic Diseases: An Economic Framework", OECD Health Working Paper, No. 32.

SOU (2008), *Omreglering av apoteksmarknaden* (Re-regulation of the retail market for pharmaceuticals), Swedish Government Official Reports, No. 2008:4.

Specialfastigheter (2007), *Annual Report 2007*, Stockholm.

Statistics Sweden (2008), *Public Finances in Sweden 2008*, Stockholm.

Swedish Competition Authority (2007), "Avveckla apoteksmonopolet med konsumentnyttan i fokus!" (Phase out the pharmaceutical retail monopoly with a consumer focus!), Stockholm.

Swedish Government (2006), *State Ownership Policy 2006*, Stockholm.

Swedish Government (2007), "Sale of Certain State-Owned Companies", Government Bill 2006/07:57, Stockholm.

Swedish Government (2008a), *Annual Report on State Owned Companies 2007*, Stockholm.

Swedish Government (2008b), "Samgående mellan Posten AB och Post Danmark A/S" (Merger of Posten AB and Post Denmark A/S), Government Bill 2007/08:143, Stockholm.

Zahra, S., R. Ireland, I. Gutierrez, and M. Hitt (2000), "Privatisation and Entrepreneurial Transformation: Emerging Issues and a Future Research Agenda", *The Academy of Management Review*, Vol. 25, No. 3.

OECD PUBLISHING, 2, rue André-Pascal, 75775 PARIS CEDEX 16
PRINTED IN FRANCE
(10 2008 20 1 P) ISBN 978-92-64-05423-3 – No. 56465 2008